BRAIN GAMES™

SUDOKU

LARGE PRINT

Publications International, Ltd.

Puzzle Constructors: Conceptis Puzzles Ltd., Howard Tomlinson

Illustrators: Elizabeth Gerber, Robin Humer, Jen Torche

Brain Games is a trademark of Publications International, Ltd.

Louis Weber, CEO
Publications International, Ltd.
7373 North Cicero Avenue
Lincolnwood, Illinois 60712

Permission is never granted for commercial purposes.

ISBN-13: 978-1-4508-2714-0
ISBN-10: 1-4508-2714-4

Manufactured in U.S.A.

8 7 6 5 4 3 2 1

Easy on the Eyes, Not on the Brain

Join the sudoku puzzle craze without straining your eyes with *Brain Games*™: *Large Print Sudoku*! Including sudoku in the mix of puzzles you do each day will add fresh challenges to your mental workout and help keep your brain cognitively fit, flexible, and young—all while giving your eyes the rest they need. Many gerontologists and physicians recommend working puzzles as one way to keep your mind sharp. Puzzles demand focused attention, help increase mental flexibility, and require the use of problem-solving skills, all of which are important cognitive functions. We can think of puzzles as mini brain workouts. And don't let all the numbers scare you off: There's no math involved in these brain exercises—only logic.

This book is loaded with more than 160 sudoku puzzles of varying difficulty, beginning with easier puzzles in the first level, moving on to medium, and then finally to the most challenging ones that will really build your mental muscle. Each puzzle takes up an entire page so you can strain your brain—not your eyes—as you work each one. If you've never worked a sudoku puzzle before, you may want to start with a few easier puzzles before working your way up to

the more challenging levels. Once you've learned the ropes, skip around the book and try your hand at the tougher ones. You will be a sudoku pro before you know it!

With all this in mind, now is a great time to start solving! A sudoku puzzle is basically a 9 by 9 grid of squares; the challenge is to place the numbers 1 through 9 once in each horizontal row, vertical column, and 3 by 3 box of squares (indicated by heavy outline). The puzzles have some numbers filled in— you work out the rest. And don't forget that you'll never have to guess, as all the puzzles can be solved by logic.

Getting Started

First, look at the numbers already placed in the grid; by using a process of elimination, you should be able to fill in some of the empty squares. Study the rows, columns, and boxes, especially those that have the most numbers already in place. Find situations where only a single number can fit into a single square. For instance, in the puzzle example shown (see next page), the number 4 is missing from the top right box. To place this missing 4 correctly in one of the box's empty squares, start by examining the rows and columns that

	1	5			6	9	3	
	3			8		5	4	
4		3		6	2		7	
				2		7	6	
6		8		5			1	
1	4	7						
2		4	9		1			5
	1		4		8			
9	8	7			3	4		

intersect with this box. If you check the third row from the top, you'll see that a 4 already appears over in the top left box. Because each number can appear only once in any row (or column, or box), you know you can't put the missing 4 between the 2 and the 7 in the top right box.

Now take a look at the columns. If you examine the third column from the right, you'll see a 4 way down in the bottom row of the puzzle; you can therefore eliminate the empty square between the 2 and the 6 as a place for the missing 4 in the top right box. The only spot now left for the 4 is the empty square between the 3 and the 7 in the rightmost column. (Remember, discovering where numbers *cannot* be placed will help you discover where they *can* be placed.)

Congratulations—you've just placed your first number!

Pencil in Possibilities

If, after using the aforementioned method, you still have empty squares, try using pencil marks. In each empty square, pencil in every number that could go in that square; make the numbers very small. Before writing in these tiny numbers, check the rest of that square's row, column, and box to rule out any numbers that already appear.

Start by working on rows, columns, and boxes with the most numbers already correctly positioned—you may be able to fill in a few of the remaining squares quickly. If you find a number that appears only once in the pencil marks for any row, column, or box, you know that number must be in that square. Be sure to erase that number from the pencil marks in the other squares of that row, column, or box.

As you can see, much of sudoku solving is a process of elimination. As you work more sudoku puzzles, you'll discover your own techniques for solving them. For more advanced methods, go to www.conceptispuzzles.com, and click on "Sudoku" and then "Sudoku techniques."

Now that you have the basic information, it's time to grab your pencil and start giving your brain a good, healthy workout and your eyes a rest— the sudoku way!

I

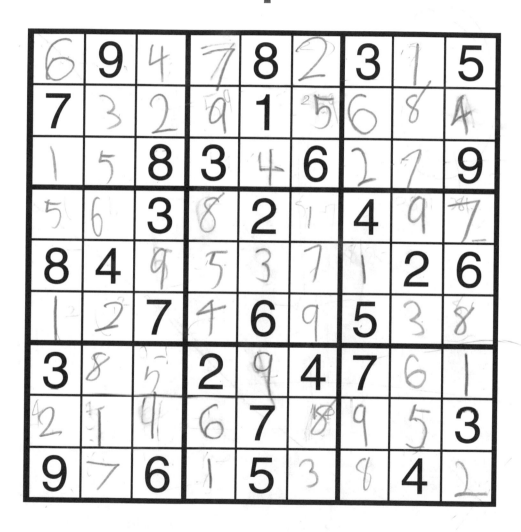

Answer on page 166.

2

3		4				7		1
	1		7		9		8	
			8		3			
	4	1		2		9	6	
	7			8			3	
	2	3		5		1	7	
			2		5			
	9		4		6		2	
7		2				3		4

Answer on page 166.

3

	1	2					6	
4				8	6			9
		6		1	2	4		3
	6	8	1		3			
	7	9				1	5	
			8		5	7	3	
1		7	6	5		3		
9			3	2				7
	8					5	2	

Answer on page 166.

4

	4	1		6				5
2	8		5				1	9
		5	1		8			4
				3	9	5		
5		4				8		1
		2	8	1				
1			2		7	4		
4	5				1		9	3
8				4		1	5	

Answer on page 166.

5

	5		7			9	4	
9		8	5	4	1	2	3	
		1	3	2				6
						6		
		9	2		5	4		
		2						
1				7	8	3		
	3	7	6	9	2	1		8
	2	6			3		9	

Answer on page 166.

6

		3	1				9	
7	1	4	6			2		8
	9	6	8	7	5			
		8		2	9			1
4			7	6		8		
			2	5	6	1	4	
9		1			4	7	6	2
	4				7	5		

Answer on page 166.

7

8	1							4
3		9	2			6		8
	7			8				
	9	6	5		8	1	4	3
			4		7			
4	8	5	1		6	7	9	
				6			1	
2		1			3	5		9
9							3	6

Answer on page 167.

8

					9	4		7
2	7			5				
	9	4			7			5
6			8			9	2	1
		8				3		
4	1	3			2			8
7			5			8	9	
				8			7	3
5		9	3					

Answer on page 167.

9

	7	2		9	4			6
							7	
		3		1				2
6				5		3	9	
	2		4	3	9		6	
	5	9		6				8
8				7		9		
	3							
5			6	2		7	8	

Answer on page 167.

10

9	8			2				5
3	4							
		2	5	8			3	1
	1				3			
6		9		5		8		4
			2				6	
1	9			7	2	3		
							1	2
4				3			9	8

Answer on page 167.

11

	6		3		9			2
		3	4			7		
	2	1						
2	3		9		7			5
	1			3			9	
5			1		2		6	4
						4	3	
		6			5	9		
1			6		3		7	

Answer on page 167.

12

			4					6
9		1		3	6			2
					9	5		7
		3		6			4	8
	6			1			7	
1	9			2		3		
4		2	6					
6			2	9		8		4
8				1				

Answer on page 167.

16

13

3		8	1		2			9
		7					8	
	6	4			8	2	1	
4	1							
			4	2	6			
							2	3
	4	9	5			1	3	
	7					5		
2			8		1	7		4

Answer on page 168.

14

				1		2	3	7
				8				4
		3			5	8		1
	9			3		4		
	1	8		4		9	7	
		4		2			8	
3		1	2			6		
9				6				
5	7	6		9				

Answer on page 168.

15

			7	8				4
		2	6				9	
			1			7	3	
								6
1		5		2		8		3
4								
	5	1			4			
	4				6	5		
7				9	5			

Answer on page 168.

16

	5			3		4	2	
		8		4				
4	9		5					
			1		2			9
		5				3		
1			8		3			
					7		6	3
				8		5		
	6	9		2			1	

Answer on page 168.

17

			3	2	1			4
	2	1		5	9			
								9
	4		1					6
	3						8	
6					7		4	
1								
			7	1		2	9	
8			4	9	2			

Answer on page 168.

18

		1						6
					4		5	
6	4		9	3		7		
			5			3		
	5		3		7		6	
		8			9			
		5		4	3		8	1
	3		8					
1						9		

Answer on page 168.

19

	6		1			4		
7					8	9		
		3						2
	5	8	3					6
			6		1			
9					5	7	3	
1						6		
		2	4					9
		5			6		2	

Answer on page 169.

20

4					2			9
	7	3		6			8	
				7			5	
6			1		3			
	5	8				1	9	
			4		8			3
	4			8				
	9			1		5	4	
8			6					1

Answer on page 169.

21

			7	3			6	
7						2		
	8	3	1		5	7		
		1				9		4
6								5
3		8				6		
		5	9		8	1	3	
		9						7
	6			7	4			

Answer on page 169.

22

	4				3		1	
7				2				9
8		3	7			6		5
2						5		
	3						2	
		9						6
4		5			8	1		3
3				9				7
	8		6				9	

Answer on page 169.

23

		1			3		5	
		2	8	7				1
9								4
4		7				9		
	3			2			7	
		9				6		5
1								3
3				6	5	2		
	5		9			4		

Answer on page 169.

24

	9	2					1	
8		3		4			5	6
4	6			5		8		
			5	6				
	7						9	
				2	9			
		1		3			8	5
9	8			7		3		4
	2					7	6	

Answer on page 169.

25

		7		4	5	8		
	6	4		9		1	5	
7			5		2			
6		8				2		
			6		9			3
	5	1		3		6	8	
		3	4	5		9		

Answer on page 170.

26

		3		9		8		
			1		2			
5		2				7		3
	9						1	
4			7	8	9			5
	2						7	
3		7				5		9
			3		8			
		4		7		6		

Answer on page 170.

27

					7	8		
	1	4					5	
			6		5	9		
	6			1	9			5
9	8						2	4
5			2	8			1	
		9	3		8			
	3					4	6	
		6	4					

Answer on page 170.

28

		8		5	3		9	
	1		2				5	6
4			9					
	4	6						3
5								7
8						4	1	
					4			2
9	6				1		7	
	2		8	6		5		

Answer on page 170.

29

	9	7		6		2	1	
5				2				3
		3	8			7		
						5		
7	8						4	6
		1						
		2			4	9		
4				1				8
	6	8		7		1	5	

Answer on page 170.

30

	7						6	
	4			6			3	
6			1		5			9
9		8		4		3		5
				8				
5		2		3		8		1
7			8		4			3
	5			2			1	
	9						8	

Answer on page 170.

31

9	7					5		1
	2		8		1		9	
			9					6
	1	3	6			2		
				3				
		2			8	9	7	
5					9			
	3		4		7		6	
6		1					4	9

Answer on page 171.

32

	9	5	2		7			
	2				8		9	3
					9			8
5	3	1						2
9						5	1	7
1			8					
6	5		1				3	
			4		5	8	2	

Answer on page 171.

33

	9		1		6		8	
2	1						4	9
		3		4		2		
9			7		3			8
		6		1		4		
3			2		4			5
		8		7		5		
6	7						2	3
	2		4		8		1	

Answer on page 171.

34

			3		1	5		
		3	9	7		6		
8	9				6		7	
6		2	8		7		4	5
	8						1	
1	7		5		2	8		6
	4		1				6	9
		6		8	9	2		
		5	6		4			

Answer on page 171.

35

		7	9		3	2		
	1	6	2		5	3	4	
				6				
1	5		7		2		9	6
		8				4		
6	4		8		9		7	1
				2				
	7	9	3		6	1	2	
		1	5		4	7		

Answer on page 171.

36

		7		4	1		9	
6	1				9	8	5	
	2	9			5	1		6
1	3	6						
4			7		3			1
						6	3	5
5		3	2			7	6	
	7	1	9				8	4
	6		4	3		5		

Answer on page 171.

37

				6		1	9	7
			9	3				4
	9	8	1		2	6		
5		2			6			9
1	3						5	8
8			7			3		6
		5	4		9	8	6	
3				1	5			
9	6	4		2				

Answer on page 172.

38

	9		2	3	4			
				7		3		5
	8		5					
4						5		1
2	6						7	8
8		5						4
				1		8		
1		4		2				
			9	4	3		6	

Answer on page 172.

39

			2		7			
			9		4			
4	5						1	7
3	7			6			2	5
			1		5			
6	2			3			8	4
8	6						4	3
			8		6			
			3		2			

Answer on page 172.

40

			1		2			
		6					1	
	9				6		8	
7		2						4
			8		5			
4						5		1
	3		2				7	
		8				9		
			4		7			

Answer on page 172.

41

	7		2			1		
					4			2
9		8	3			6		
	9					8		5
				6				
6		2					9	
		1			5	3		6
5			7					
		4			8		1	

Answer on page 172.

42

7		1				8	2	
		5						6
8				1	2			
					8	1		
4				2				3
		9	4					
			1	8				5
	3					7		
	5	2				3		6

Answer on page 172.

43

	4			3			5	
7		6			9			3
				8			2	
	5							
2		8		4		9		6
							7	
	7			5				
6			8			3		4
	3			9			1	

Answer on page 173.

44

	7		5					
		3				4		1
	6	9				8	2	
				7				9
			3	8	4			
2				5				
	3	2				1	6	
1		4				7		
					9		8	

Answer on page 173.

45

					7			4
		6		5	4		2	
2		3			8			
7			8					
	3						1	
					3			2
			5			3		8
	9		1	7		5		
6			3					

Answer on page 173.

46

	6						1	
1			2			7		3
			6		9		8	
	7	5				9		
				5				
		2				5	4	
	8		1		6			
5		3			2			8
	9						2	

Answer on page 173.

47

		2			6	5		
		9				7		
5	7			9			4	8
6			7		2			
		3				8		
			8		9			6
1	3			2			7	5
		8				1		
		4	5			9		

Answer on page 173.

48

		3	4		9		5	
						7		8
7					8		6	
8			5			2		6
9		2			7			1
	6		7					3
4		9						
	2		3		1	4		

Answer on page 173.

49

			2		5			
		2		4		8		
1			3		8			2
5		4				6		9
	3						2	
6		9				1		3
2			1		3			5
		3		6		7		
			8		9			

Answer on page 174.

50

2	6			8			9	7
	3						4	
8		9				5		3
			7		4			
	9						3	
			6		8			
6		2				9		1
	4						6	
3	5			2			7	8

Answer on page 174.

51

5	4				8			7
			5		3	6		9
	2							
2	8						9	
				5				
	7						2	8
							6	
1		6	9		7			
8			4				3	5

Answer on page 174.

52

	6	4			5		7	9
8			7					
9			2				1	
	9					1		3
		7		5		4		
2		1					8	
	4			3				
				2				7
3	8		4			5	6	

Answer on page 174.

53

			6		5			
6				9				7
		5				1		
1			5		8			9
	2						4	
8			7		6			2
		6				3		
9				3				8
			8		9			

Answer on page 174.

54

6		1		3				4
		3	9		8			
				2			5	3
	4						3	
5		7				1		2
	8						6	
8	7			1				
			4		2	8		
9				6		2		5

Answer on page 174.

55

7					9		1	
	5	1				8	3	
			1					
				3		5	8	
5		2				3		7
	8	3		1				
					2			
	2	8				6	4	
	7		9	8				5

Answer on page 175.

56

	2		3	4	5			
								7
8	5	9	6					
3		4	5					
	6						8	
					2	7		6
					8	4	1	2
9								
			2	5	1		9	

Answer on page 175.

57

1		3				8		2
		8		5				
7			9				3	
2			4			5		1
			6		7			
8		9			5			7
	7				9			5
				7		1		
9		2				4		6

Answer on page 175.

58

	4			7				
					3		6	5
	7		6			4		2
								8
	5	1	8		2	9	3	
9								
8		5			1		9	
2	1		5					
				6			2	

Answer on page 175.

59

	6		9					
4							3	9
2				4	5	6		
	2							3
		8		6		4		
9							8	
		5	8	3				7
6	3							8
					4		9	

Answer on page 175.

60

	8	3		7				
			4					
2					8		3	5
7	1			5		6		
		5				2		
		6		1			7	4
9	4		1					2
					5			
				2		1	6	

Answer on page 175.

61

2			8			6		
7		1			2	8		
	8	9			5			
	7			3	6			
			5	9			8	
			6			2	5	
		5	2			7		8
		8			3			6

Answer on page 176.

62

		5	6		2			1
	1				7		3	
						4		9
		9		6				2
	2			1			6	
4				8		3		
2		4						
	7		3				5	
6			1		4	2		

Answer on page 176.

63

		4		6		9	8	
	5				2			
			3		4			5
		9			8			
	3	1		4		8	6	
			1			4		
4			5		6			
			8				7	
	9	8		2		1		

Answer on page 176.

64

		5	6					
3	1	6	4					
				9	7			1
	9	4					1	
			1	8	5			
	3					7	5	
4			7	5				
					4	8	2	7
					2	9		

Answer on page 176.

65

			4		3		7	
6			8			4		
		8					5	1
			3			1		
	2	9				5	3	
		5			8			
3	7					9		
		4			2			8
	8		1		7			

Answer on page 176.

66

8	1				6		9	
	9		3			1		
			1					8
2	6	1		5				
				4		9	7	6
4					9			
		5			2		6	
	8		6				2	9

Answer on page 176.

67

9		4	7					
		6		3			7	1
	8				2			
6		3		4				
4								5
				1		6		3
			5				2	
2	3			8		7		
					3	1		8

Answer on page 177.

68

	9			6	3			
3		7		5				
6		8			2		7	
					1	4		9
			7					
1		6	8					
	3		1			9		2
				9		8		3
			5	3			6	

Answer on page 177.

69

	8						2	
		6			9	4		
		1	2	5				8
	5			3				9
8								4
1				7			6	
7				9	8	6		
		3	7			9		
	6						1	

Answer on page 177.

70

		7	5				4	
							9	6
			9	4		2		3
5				9				
			3	5	6			
				1				4
4		1		7	5			
3	8							
	2				1	8		

Answer on page 177.

71

9	3			2				8
	8				7			5
		7	5				4	
3	2	6						7
5						4	6	1
	6				1	7		
2			9				1	
7				8			5	2

Answer on page 177.

72

	2			7	4		9	
		9	2					
5	3		6					
			3			5	2	
	7						4	
	9	2			8			
					2		7	1
					3	4		
	8		9	5			3	

Answer on page 177.

73

	9	5		8				2
		7			3	6	8	
						3	9	
			5	1			3	8
5	1		4	3				
	5	4						
	7	2	3			9		
8				2		7	6	

Answer on page 178.

74

						7	2	
		3						
2	9		8	5			4	
5				4	6		3	
3			2		5			4
	6		1	8				2
	3			6	8		9	1
						5		
	1	6						

Answer on page 178.

75

		3					7	9
	8		4		2			
	7				5	1		
2			5		6			
	1			3			5	
			1		8			6
		4	2				9	
			7		4		1	
3	5					4		

Answer on page 178.

76

	1	3						9
2	6					7		
	5				8			
4	2		3	1				
				2				
				5	6		8	3
			6				1	
		7					3	5
3						8	7	

Answer on page 178.

77

	5		2					1
		6				2		7
			8	6				9
		7	1					
5				9				3
					6	1		
9				8	3			
1		8				4		
7					4		5	

Answer on page 178.

78

4	3			8				
8			1		9			3
	7				5			
	1	6						
9		2		4		5		6
						8	3	
			5				2	
1			6		4			8
				7			6	1

Answer on page 178.

79

7			6				8	
						3		
8						9	2	7
	1		7			6		9
		3		9		5		
9		5			4		3	
5	8	7						3
		9						
	4				7			8

Answer on page 179.

80

9		7			8			
			6					2
	8			3			7	
6		2	8	4				
	1			7			6	
				9	6	5		4
	9			8			2	
8					2			
			3			8		6

Answer on page 179.

81

		8		3	1	2		
					9		3	7
			5			1		6
	2	1				9	5	
	8	5				6	4	
5		9			7			
8	6		3					
		7	8	1		5		

Answer on page 179.

82

				8	4		6	
4	1						2	8
9			5			1		3
	5	7			1			
			9			2	7	
5		2			3			7
7	3						8	4
	4		6	9				

Answer on page 179.

83

			8				4	
2		3						1
9				5	3		8	
			3		7			8
1		5				7		2
8			9		5			
	9		1	7				4
3						1		5
	1				6			

Answer on page 179.

84

2								
	5						7	3
3	6	4	9			1		
9	2				7			
8		5				3		6
			2				1	9
		2			9	4	3	1
5	3						9	
								8

Answer on page 179.

85

	3					9	2	
1					7		6	
		5	4				8	
5		1		9		8		
			8		6			
		9		5		3		2
	1				9	6		
	5		2					9
	7	8					3	

Answer on page 180.

86

1							4	
8					1	9		7
4		9		2		8		
	9		1				5	
	8			9		2		
	7		4			8		3
5		8	9					4
	2							5

Answer on page 180.

87

		4		7		5		3
7								
	5		3	4				
2		6		3		7		
	4			5			9	
		3		1		2		6
				8	5		3	
								2
8		5		2		6		

Answer on page 180.

88

		6	1					9
5							3	
1			6		2			
	2	8						
4		5		8		9		3
						5	1	
			3		9			2
	4							1
2					4	8		

Answer on page 180.

89

4	6		2					3
						9	5	
7		2				6		
				6	2		1	
			8		9			
	9		5	7				
		3				4		1
	8	7						
9					3		2	7

Answer on page 180.

90

	2		4	9		8	3	
			3	1	8		6	
						5		
							2	9
			9	5	7			
8	7							
		7						
	6		5	4	3			
	3	1		8	2		4	

Answer on page 180.

91

	3				8	5		
2	7			6	9			
		9					6	
7		3	2					
	4						8	
					3	6		9
	5					8		
			8	1			4	6
		4	7				3	

Answer on page 181.

92

	9		4	7	8			
	8						6	
	5							4
		5		2				3
4			9		3			6
2				8		5		
5							1	
	4						9	
			5	4	6		2	

Answer on page 181.

93

3					7		1	
	4		5	2				
7		9	4					
1		2						
		7	9		6	8		
						3		7
					9	2		6
			7	4			3	
	6		2					4

Answer on page 181.

94

	6							
		7		9				
4		3			6	2	1	
	5				3	8		7
			1		7			
9		8	4				6	
	1	9	3			4		2
				4		6		
							7	

Answer on page 181.

95

		1			3		5	
		3			8			
			7	2		8		
8		2	4					7
9	3						6	2
4					2	9		1
		8		7	9			
			3			7		
	5		1			3		

Answer on page 181.

96

4			5				9	
		7	8	3		6		
2	1							
	5					9		1
	6			7			4	
3		9					2	
							3	2
		5		9	1	4		
	2				5			9

Answer on page 181.

97

	6		7			2	9	
				3			5	
								7
	2			1	5	9		
	9	5				6	7	
		4	3	7			1	
8								
	4			9				
	7	9			2		6	

Answer on page 182.

98

				9	3		6	
		6	4			1		9
					7			4
				9	6			3
5								8
2		9	5					
7			6					
8		1			5	2		
	2		3	4				

Answer on page 182.

99

1	5							
	4		2	3		1		
	8				4			
			7			4	5	
			8	1	3			
	2	8			5			
			5				4	
		6		8	2		3	
							1	6

Answer on page 182.

100

		8				3		
	4						5	
7		6		1		9		4
2			3		7			5
9								3
5			6		4			9
4		9		2		6		8
	3						4	
		7				5		

Answer on page 182.

101

	6			4			9	
		8	2					5
5					3	1		
		4			9			2
			1		6			
8			4			5		
		6	9					4
4					8	2		
	9			2			5	

Answer on page 182.

102

							7	2
			2		4			1
				9	3	5		
4		5	7			9		
			3		8			
		2			9	6		5
		1	4	8				
2			5		6			
7	6							

Answer on page 182.

103

						3	5	6
	3				7		4	
	5			9	6			
5					8	1		
4								3
		1	4					8
			6	2			8	
	8		5				6	
7	9	6						

Answer on page 183.

104

		2						
	1	7			5			
	6				7			1
7				6	3			
8		1		2		9		5
			1	5				4
9			8				4	
			6			7	1	
						8		

Answer on page 183.

105

	5							
1	8		3					2
	4				8			3
			2	7		9	5	
				3				
	2	6		5	4			
9			1				4	
2					3		7	8
							2	

Answer on page 183.

106

		5					1	8
					3	2		
	1		2		4			
5	9				7	3		
				8				
		7	5				4	9
			4		5		7	
		4	3					
3	2					1		

Answer on page 183.

107

9				4	2	6		
	7					8		
6	2				8	3		
4	3				7		6	
	6		2				9	4
		3	4				8	7
		6					3	
		2	9	5				6

Answer on page 183.

108

		6					8	
		4		1	5	2		
	8			7		1		
					7	9		4
			9		2			
3		2	1					
		8		3			5	
		1	5	4		7		
	7					8		

Answer on page 183.

109

6		9						
		7	9	2			1	
				6	3			
		6	3				4	
4				1				9
	3				6	5		
			5	4				
	5			9	2	1		
						7		2

Answer on page 184.

110

				7			4	
		2					5	
7			6			3		
3			2			4		
	2	1		8		6	7	
		6			9			8
		5			3			9
	9					2		
	7			1				

Answer on page 184.

III

3			4					8
			7		5			
		9		2		7		
	9						6	2
		6				5		
1	4						8	
		5		4		3		
			2		8			
4					9			7

Answer on page 184.

112

	1			6			8	
7			8		1			4
					2			
	5			1		7	2	
6								1
	2	3		8			5	
			4					
9			1		5			2
	8			2			1	

Answer on page 184.

113

		7		8	4		1	
		1						4
9	2		5					
		2			3			7
7								3
8			9			1		
					8		3	1
6						9		
	3		2	9		8		

Answer on page 184.

114

		1						
4							7	2
			3	2	9		4	
	6				2	3		
8				7				4
		3	6				5	
	8		1	3	7			
1	7							5
						4		

Answer on page 184.

115

	6	2		1	5			
		3	8			6	7	
					6			
4	5						8	
	9						5	2
			6					
	4	7			1	9		
			7	5		8	1	

Answer on page 185.

116

					7		8	6
		9		5		2		7
3		2	6					
6		7				9		2
					5	3		1
8		6		2		5		
4	3		8					

Answer on page 185.

117

				3		1		
1						7	2	
8				4	1			
	7					5		
3			9		8			2
		6					8	
			8	6		9		3
	2	3						4
		5		9				

Answer on page 185.

118

	4	2					3	
	5			9				
1				8	7			
	6		5					
7	1			4			5	3
					3		7	
			8	5				6
				1			9	
	7					5	8	

Answer on page 185.

119

	7		2				4	1
					7	9		
2					4		3	
		5	4					8
			8		9			
9					5	6		
	4		9					3
		3	6					
7	9				3		6	

Answer on page 185.

120

			1					5
		1					8	
	2			7				9
7	1			6			4	3
6	4			9			1	7
9				3			7	
	5					4		
8					5			

Answer on page 185.

121

			7			9	4	5
		4		3				8
	6			1				7
3								
	5	8				7	6	
								1
1				6			2	
6				5		3		
5	9	3			8			

Answer on page 186.

122

				9		1		3
7			4			6		
			5			8		
		3						7
5			6	2	9			4
6						9		
		9			5			
		4			1			9
8		1		7				

Answer on page 186.

123

6	5		2					
7			8				5	
					7		9	8
	6	2						
9				3				7
						1	2	
2	4		7					
	9				4			1
					5		7	9

Answer on page 186.

124

	5					8		
			4		7		6	
1			3					7
6							9	
7		8				4		2
	1							3
8					1			9
	4		6		9			
		1					2	

Answer on page 186.

125

	8				7		6	
		2	9	1		4		
4			8		5		7	
	9						2	
	2		3		1			8
		3		7	6	1		
	4		5				9	

Answer on page 186.

126

	4						8	1
					5	4	2	7
3				2				
					7			8
		6		5		2		
1			2					
				7				2
8	9	1	4					
4	2						9	

Answer on page 186.

127

	3		5		6		8	
		2				6		
				7				
9			7		5			2
		5				1		
7			2		4			9
				2				
		6				7		
	8		4		9		3	

Answer on page 187.

128

	9			2			3	
4	2			8	7		6	9
	5							
2	3			9			8	4
								5
8	6		9	4			2	1
	7			3			9	

Answer on page 187.

129

					8	5	3	
			4			6		7
3	2						8	9
	3			4				
		6	5		2	7		
				8			9	
9	1						5	2
6		3			5			
	7	5	1					

Answer on page 187.

130

	4				1	5		
		8		6	2			
					4		9	2
	1		6					5
5				1				4
2					3		1	
1	9		8					
			9	4		7		
		6	1				3	

Answer on page 187.

131

		3			5	7	9	
					3	5		6
8		5			9		2	
			3					
9				7				1
					2			
	9		2			3		4
4		1	8					
	3	6	5			1		

Answer on page 187.

132

4		5			6			
1					8		3	
		6		3				
2	4					1	9	
3				9				4
	6	9					5	8
				1		5		
	9		5					3
			2			7		9

Answer on page 187.

133

	3				6	7		4
					9		5	6
				4		1		9
				8	2			
		4				3		
			7	3				
5		6		1				
9	4		6					
2		3	5				1	

Answer on page 188.

134

8			6		7			
								4
4	9					7	1	6
7						5		
			5	6	2			
		6						9
5	7	8					2	3
9								
			4		3			7

Answer on page 188.

135

2			7	9				
	3					8	9	5
		9						
			9					7
	8		3	6	4		1	
9					5			
						1		
5	1	3					4	
				1	8			2

Answer on page 188.

136

	2		1			4		
9		3	8					
	4				9			2
8	6					1		
				5				
		7					5	6
1			9				6	
					4	3		9
		4			6		7	

Answer on page 188.

137

			9			2		
	7	9				3		4
	1				6			7
3			4					
			8	9	2			
					7			1
1			6				2	
2		3				4	5	
		4			8			

Answer on page 188.

138

	1							
			1		9		7	8
4	5		2	3				
		2						
	8		6	4	5		1	
						3		
				7	2		9	1
9	6		4		1			
							5	

Answer on page 188.

139

	4	6						
5		1	9				4	
7		3						8
			4					
8			6	7	3			9
					2			
1						4		3
	3				8	5		7
						6	1	

Answer on page 189.

140

						1		9
					1		6	
2		6		4	5			
4	2						9	6
		1				5		
5	3						8	1
			7	8		2		4
	9		2					
1		2						

Answer on page 189.

141

		4						
			4	2	6	9		
7					8			6
	7	2						
	9	8	6		2	1	7	
						8	6	
1			5					3
		5	3	7	1			
						7		

Answer on page 189.

142

	5						3	9
3		1						
				1		7		
					8	6		1
	9		6	5	4		2	
2		5	3					
		9		8				
						2		4
6	1						8	

Answer on page 189.

143

7		4	1			3		6
	2				9		8	
							2	
1				8				
3			2		6			7
			4					3
	6							
	5		6				7	
9		3			4	5		8

Answer on page 189.

144

					1		9	
8						5		
4			9	7				2
			3				6	
		1	5		7	3		
	2				6			
3				6	2			7
		4						1
	8		4					

Answer on page 189.

145

			4		3	9		
6					7		1	
		8		9			4	
2	3		7					
9								7
					8		9	3
	2			7		4		
	7		9					8
		5	8		2			

Answer on page 190.

146

		3	7		5	4		
			9		3			
9								2
8	9						4	6
6	1						5	8
1								4
			6		9			
		8	5		2	7		

Answer on page 190.

147

			4				5	
	2	3	8					7
	6				3			
2	3				6	5		
		9	5				8	1
			3				9	
5					4	3	1	
	4			9				

Answer on page 190.

148

			7		3			
		1	4		2	7		
	8						9	
9	2						5	8
				6				
1	7						3	4
	3						1	
		2	1		7	3		
			8		5			

Answer on page 190.

149

		3	1			7		
	6			5			8	
2					6			1
		8						2
	3						6	
6						8		
9			6					7
	5			8			4	
		6			2	3		

Answer on page 190.

150

		4	8		7	6		
	1			4			7	
					1			
2		1		9				8
	4						2	
6				3		5		9
			6					
	7			2			5	
		8	5		4	3		

Answer on page 190.

151

4			3	7			8	
		7					9	1
9	6							
				2	5			
		8	4		6	5		
			8	9				
							5	7
8	2					6		
	7			5	3			8

Answer on page 191.

152

		7	3					1
	5						4	2
					9			
		5			7		6	
3		1	9		5	2		7
	2		1			5		
			8					
2	1						7	
8					3	9		

Answer on page 191.

153

	3		4	5		2		
2		6	3				8	
6		3		2		7		1
4		8		1		5		2
	9				1	8		3
		1		3	9		7	

Answer on page 191.

154

			1				6	3
				4		8		
						4	2	9
5			3				1	
		8		7		9		
	3				5			2
2	4	5						
		1		9				
3	9				2			

Answer on page 191.

155

			9	4				
	9		5		3		8	
		5				3		
	6						7	2
7				2				1
3	1						6	
		4				1		
	8		6		4		5	
				1	8			

Answer on page 191.

156

				2	5			6
					3	9	1	4
3								
5	2			3				
	9			1			3	
				8			7	5
								8
9	7	5	3					
8			9	6				

Answer on page 191.

157

1	8		3					4
	4		7				2	
					1	6		
	2					7		
		9		6		2		
		6					5	
		1	8					
	3				2		6	
4					9		1	3

Answer on page 192.

158

	7	4		5				6
1						8		
			7		3			9
	6		9				1	
4								5
	3				2		7	
7			3		8			
		3						1
2				7		4	5	

Answer on page 192.

159

3		8	2					
		6	9	1		5		
	1					6		
1							9	
	8		7		5		2	
	7							6
		7					5	
		5		4	1	2		
					9	3		4

Answer on page 192.

160

				3		5		
	8				2		6	
1		2			4	7		
	5	1						
7								9
						3	4	
		5	8			1		2
	6		1				7	
		4		2				

Answer on page 192.

161

						4	5	
			6					7
2			5	4				1
		8			6			2
7	6						8	9
3			9			1		
5				7	9			3
9					1			
	3	6						

Answer on page 192.

ANSWERS

1

6	9	4	7	8	2	3	1	5
7	3	2	9	1	5	6	8	4
1	5	8	3	4	6	2	7	9
5	6	3	8	2	1	4	9	7
8	4	9	5	3	7	1	2	6
2	1	7	4	6	9	5	3	8
3	8	5	2	9	4	7	6	1
4	2	1	6	7	8	9	5	3
9	7	6	1	5	3	8	4	2

4

9	4	1	3	6	2	7	8	5
2	8	3	5	7	4	6	1	9
7	6	5	1	9	8	3	2	4
6	1	8	4	3	9	5	7	2
5	9	4	7	2	6	8	3	1
3	7	2	8	1	5	9	4	6
1	3	9	2	5	7	4	6	8
4	5	7	6	8	1	2	9	3
8	2	6	9	4	3	1	5	7

2

3	8	4	5	6	2	7	9	1
2	1	6	7	4	9	5	8	3
9	5	7	8	1	3	2	4	6
8	4	1	3	2	7	9	6	5
5	7	9	6	8	1	4	3	2
6	2	3	9	5	4	1	7	8
4	3	8	2	7	5	6	1	9
1	9	5	4	3	6	8	2	7
7	6	2	1	9	8	3	5	4

5

2	5	3	7	8	6	9	4	1
9	6	8	5	4	1	2	3	7
7	4	1	3	2	9	5	8	6
5	1	4	8	3	7	6	2	9
6	8	9	2	1	5	4	7	3
3	7	2	9	6	4	8	1	5
1	9	5	4	7	8	3	6	2
4	3	7	6	9	2	1	5	8
8	2	6	1	5	3	7	9	4

3

7	1	2	4	3	9	8	6	5
4	3	5	7	8	6	2	1	9
8	9	6	5	1	2	4	7	3
5	6	8	1	7	3	9	4	2
3	7	9	2	6	4	1	5	8
2	4	1	8	9	5	7	3	6
1	2	7	6	5	8	3	9	4
9	5	4	3	2	1	6	8	7
6	8	3	9	4	7	5	2	1

6

5	8	3	1	4	2	6	9	7
7	1	4	6	9	3	2	5	8
2	9	6	8	7	5	3	1	4
3	6	8	5	2	9	4	7	1
1	7	5	4	3	8	9	2	6
4	2	9	7	6	1	8	3	5
8	3	7	2	5	6	1	4	9
9	5	1	3	8	4	7	6	2
6	4	2	9	1	7	5	8	3

7

8	1	2	6	7	9	3	5	4
3	5	9	2	1	4	6	7	8
6	7	4	3	8	5	9	2	1
7	9	6	5	2	8	1	4	3
1	2	3	4	9	7	8	6	5
4	8	5	1	3	6	7	9	2
5	3	8	9	6	2	4	1	7
2	6	1	7	4	3	5	8	9
9	4	7	8	5	1	2	3	6

10

9	8	1	3	2	7	6	4	5
3	4	5	9	1	6	2	8	7
7	6	2	5	8	4	9	3	1
2	1	4	8	6	3	5	7	9
6	3	9	7	5	1	8	2	4
8	5	7	2	4	9	1	6	3
1	9	8	4	7	2	3	5	6
5	7	3	6	9	8	4	1	2
4	2	6	1	3	5	7	9	8

8

8	6	5	2	3	9	4	1	7
2	7	1	4	5	8	6	3	9
3	9	4	1	6	7	2	8	5
6	5	7	8	4	3	9	2	1
9	2	8	7	1	5	3	4	6
4	1	3	6	9	2	7	5	8
7	3	6	5	2	1	8	9	4
1	4	2	9	8	6	5	7	3
5	8	9	3	7	4	1	6	2

11

4	6	7	3	1	9	8	5	2
8	5	3	4	2	6	7	1	9
9	2	1	7	5	8	6	4	3
2	3	4	9	6	7	1	8	5
6	1	8	5	3	4	2	9	7
5	7	9	1	8	2	3	6	4
7	8	5	2	9	1	4	3	6
3	4	6	8	7	5	9	2	1
1	9	2	6	4	3	5	7	8

9

1	7	2	5	9	4	8	3	6
4	6	5	2	8	3	1	7	9
9	8	3	7	1	6	4	5	2
6	4	1	8	5	2	3	9	7
7	2	8	4	3	9	5	6	1
3	5	9	1	6	7	2	4	8
8	1	6	3	7	5	9	2	4
2	3	7	9	4	8	6	1	5
5	9	4	6	2	1	7	8	3

12

3	8	5	4	7	2	9	1	6
9	7	1	5	3	6	4	8	2
2	4	6	1	8	9	5	3	7
7	2	3	9	6	5	1	4	8
5	6	8	3	1	4	2	7	9
1	9	4	8	2	7	3	6	5
4	3	2	6	5	8	7	9	1
6	1	7	2	9	3	8	5	4
8	5	9	7	4	1	6	2	3

Answers

13

3	5	8	1	7	2	6	4	9
1	2	7	6	4	9	3	8	5
9	6	4	3	5	8	2	1	7
4	1	2	7	8	3	9	5	6
5	9	3	4	2	6	8	7	1
7	8	6	9	1	5	4	2	3
8	4	9	5	6	7	1	3	2
6	7	1	2	3	4	5	9	8
2	3	5	8	9	1	7	6	4

16

7	5	1	6	3	9	4	2	8
6	3	8	2	4	1	9	7	5
4	9	2	5	7	8	1	3	6
8	7	3	1	5	2	6	4	9
9	2	5	7	6	4	3	8	1
1	4	6	8	9	3	7	5	2
5	8	4	9	1	7	2	6	3
2	1	7	3	8	6	5	9	4
3	6	9	4	2	5	8	1	7

14

8	5	9	6	1	4	2	3	7
1	6	7	3	8	2	5	9	4
4	2	3	9	7	5	8	6	1
7	9	5	8	3	1	4	2	6
2	1	8	5	4	6	9	7	3
6	3	4	7	2	9	1	8	5
3	8	1	2	5	7	6	4	9
9	4	2	1	6	3	7	5	8
5	7	6	4	9	8	3	1	2

17

9	7	6	3	2	1	8	5	4
4	2	1	8	5	9	3	6	7
5	8	3	6	7	4	1	2	9
2	4	9	1	8	5	7	3	6
7	3	5	2	4	6	9	8	1
6	1	8	9	3	7	5	4	2
1	9	2	5	6	3	4	7	8
3	6	4	7	1	8	2	9	5
8	5	7	4	9	2	6	1	3

15

5	1	3	7	8	9	6	2	4
8	7	2	6	4	3	1	9	5
6	9	4	1	5	2	7	3	8
2	8	7	4	3	1	9	5	6
1	6	5	9	2	7	8	4	3
4	3	9	5	6	8	2	1	7
9	5	1	8	7	4	3	6	2
3	4	8	2	1	6	5	7	9
7	2	6	3	9	5	4	8	1

18

5	9	1	2	7	8	4	3	6
8	7	3	1	6	4	2	5	9
6	4	2	9	3	5	7	1	8
7	1	4	5	8	6	3	9	2
2	5	9	3	1	7	8	6	4
3	6	8	4	2	9	1	7	5
9	2	5	7	4	3	6	8	1
4	3	6	8	9	1	5	2	7
1	8	7	6	5	2	9	4	3

19

8	6	9	1	3	2	4	5	7
7	2	1	5	4	8	9	6	3
5	4	3	9	6	7	8	1	2
2	5	8	3	7	4	1	9	6
3	7	4	6	9	1	2	8	5
9	1	6	8	2	5	7	3	4
1	3	7	2	5	9	6	4	8
6	8	2	4	1	3	5	7	9
4	9	5	7	8	6	3	2	1

22

9	4	6	8	5	3	7	1	2
7	5	1	4	2	6	3	8	9
8	2	3	7	1	9	6	4	5
2	7	4	9	6	1	5	3	8
6	3	8	5	4	7	9	2	1
5	1	9	3	8	2	4	7	6
4	9	5	2	7	8	1	6	3
3	6	2	1	9	4	8	5	7
1	8	7	6	3	5	2	9	4

20

4	6	5	8	3	2	7	1	9
9	7	3	5	6	1	4	8	2
1	8	2	9	7	4	3	5	6
6	2	4	1	9	3	8	7	5
3	5	8	7	2	6	1	9	4
7	1	9	4	5	8	2	6	3
5	4	1	2	8	9	6	3	7
2	9	6	3	1	7	5	4	8
8	3	7	6	4	5	9	2	1

23

7	4	1	2	9	3	8	5	6
5	6	2	8	7	4	3	9	1
9	8	3	6	5	1	7	2	4
4	1	7	5	8	6	9	3	2
6	3	5	4	2	9	1	7	8
8	2	9	3	1	7	6	4	5
1	9	8	7	4	2	5	6	3
3	7	4	1	6	5	2	8	9
2	5	6	9	3	8	4	1	7

21

9	5	4	7	3	2	8	6	1
7	1	6	8	4	9	2	5	3
2	8	3	1	6	5	7	4	9
5	2	1	6	8	3	9	7	4
6	4	7	2	9	1	3	8	5
3	9	8	4	5	7	6	1	2
4	7	5	9	2	8	1	3	6
8	3	9	5	1	6	4	2	7
1	6	2	3	7	4	5	9	8

24

5	9	2	3	8	6	4	1	7
8	1	3	9	4	7	2	5	6
4	6	7	2	5	1	8	3	9
2	3	9	5	6	4	1	7	8
6	7	4	8	1	3	5	9	2
1	5	8	7	2	9	6	4	3
7	4	1	6	3	2	9	8	5
9	8	6	1	7	5	3	2	4
3	2	5	4	9	8	7	6	1

Answers

25

3	9	7	1	4	5	8	2	6
1	2	5	7	6	8	3	4	9
8	6	4	2	9	3	1	5	7
7	3	9	5	1	2	4	6	8
6	1	8	3	7	4	2	9	5
5	4	2	6	8	9	7	1	3
4	5	1	9	3	7	6	8	2
9	7	6	8	2	1	5	3	4
2	8	3	4	5	6	9	7	1

28

6	7	8	1	5	3	2	9	4
3	1	9	2	4	8	7	5	6
4	5	2	9	7	6	8	3	1
2	4	6	7	1	5	9	8	3
5	3	1	4	8	9	6	2	7
8	9	7	6	3	2	4	1	5
7	8	5	3	9	4	1	6	2
9	6	4	5	2	1	3	7	8
1	2	3	8	6	7	5	4	9

26

6	4	3	5	9	7	8	2	1
9	7	8	1	3	2	4	5	6
5	1	2	8	4	6	7	9	3
7	9	6	2	5	4	3	1	8
4	3	1	7	8	9	2	6	5
8	2	5	6	1	3	9	7	4
3	6	7	4	2	1	5	8	9
2	5	9	3	6	8	1	4	7
1	8	4	9	7	5	6	3	2

29

8	9	7	4	6	3	2	1	5
5	1	6	9	2	7	4	8	3
2	4	3	8	5	1	7	6	9
6	2	4	7	3	8	5	9	1
7	8	5	1	9	2	3	4	6
9	3	1	5	4	6	8	7	2
1	5	2	6	8	4	9	3	7
4	7	9	3	1	5	6	2	8
3	6	8	2	7	9	1	5	4

27

3	9	5	1	2	7	8	4	6
6	1	4	8	9	3	2	5	7
7	2	8	6	4	5	9	3	1
4	6	2	7	1	9	3	8	5
9	8	1	5	3	6	7	2	4
5	7	3	2	8	4	6	1	9
1	4	9	3	6	8	5	7	2
2	3	7	9	5	1	4	6	8
8	5	6	4	7	2	1	9	3

30

2	7	5	4	9	3	1	6	8
1	4	9	2	6	8	5	3	7
6	8	3	1	7	5	4	2	9
9	1	8	6	4	2	3	7	5
4	3	7	5	8	1	6	9	2
5	6	2	9	3	7	8	4	1
7	2	6	8	1	4	9	5	3
8	5	4	3	2	9	7	1	6
3	9	1	7	5	6	2	8	4

31

9	7	8	2	4	6	5	3	1
3	2	6	8	5	1	4	9	7
1	5	4	9	7	3	8	2	6
7	1	3	6	9	4	2	5	8
8	9	5	7	3	2	6	1	4
4	6	2	5	1	8	9	7	3
5	4	7	1	6	9	3	8	2
2	3	9	4	8	7	1	6	5
6	8	1	3	2	5	7	4	9

34

2	6	7	3	4	1	5	9	8
4	5	3	9	7	8	6	2	1
8	9	1	2	5	6	4	7	3
6	3	2	8	1	7	9	4	5
5	8	9	4	6	3	7	1	2
1	7	4	5	9	2	8	3	6
7	4	8	1	2	5	3	6	9
3	1	6	7	8	9	2	5	4
9	2	5	6	3	4	1	8	7

32

8	9	5	2	3	7	1	4	6
4	2	6	5	1	8	7	9	3
7	1	3	6	4	9	2	5	8
5	3	1	7	8	4	9	6	2
2	6	7	9	5	1	3	8	4
9	8	4	3	2	6	5	1	7
1	4	2	8	9	3	6	7	5
6	5	8	1	7	2	4	3	9
3	7	9	4	6	5	8	2	1

35

4	8	7	9	1	3	2	6	5
9	1	6	2	7	5	3	4	8
3	2	5	4	6	8	9	1	7
1	5	3	7	4	2	8	9	6
7	9	8	6	5	1	4	3	2
6	4	2	8	3	9	5	7	1
8	3	4	1	2	7	6	5	9
5	7	9	3	8	6	1	2	4
2	6	1	5	9	4	7	8	3

33

4	9	5	1	2	6	3	8	7
2	1	7	3	8	5	6	4	9
8	6	3	9	4	7	2	5	1
9	4	2	7	5	3	1	6	8
7	5	6	8	1	9	4	3	2
3	8	1	2	6	4	9	7	5
1	3	8	6	7	2	5	9	4
6	7	4	5	9	1	8	2	3
5	2	9	4	3	8	7	1	6

36

8	5	7	6	4	1	2	9	3
6	1	4	3	2	9	8	5	7
3	2	9	8	7	5	1	4	6
1	3	6	5	9	2	4	7	8
4	8	5	7	6	3	9	2	1
7	9	2	1	8	4	6	3	5
5	4	3	2	1	8	7	6	9
2	7	1	9	5	6	3	8	4
9	6	8	4	3	7	5	1	2

37

4	2	3	5	6	8	1	9	7
6	5	1	9	3	7	2	8	4
7	9	8	1	4	2	6	3	5
5	7	2	3	8	6	4	1	9
1	3	6	2	9	4	7	5	8
8	4	9	7	5	1	3	2	6
2	1	5	4	7	9	8	6	3
3	8	7	6	1	5	9	4	2
9	6	4	8	2	3	5	7	1

40

8	4	7	1	5	2	3	9	6
3	2	6	9	8	4	1	5	7
5	9	1	3	7	6	4	8	2
7	5	2	6	1	9	8	3	4
6	1	3	8	4	5	7	2	9
4	8	9	7	2	3	5	6	1
1	3	4	2	9	8	6	7	5
2	7	8	5	6	1	9	4	3
9	6	5	4	3	7	2	1	8

38

5	9	7	2	3	4	8	1	6
6	4	2	1	7	8	3	9	5
3	8	1	5	6	9	2	4	7
4	7	9	6	8	2	5	3	1
2	6	3	4	1	5	9	7	8
8	1	5	3	9	7	6	2	4
9	2	6	7	5	1	4	8	3
1	3	4	8	2	6	7	5	9
7	5	8	9	4	3	1	6	2

41

4	7	5	2	9	6	1	3	8
3	1	6	8	7	4	9	5	2
9	2	8	3	5	1	6	4	7
1	9	7	4	3	2	8	6	5
8	4	3	5	6	9	7	2	1
6	5	2	1	8	7	4	9	3
2	8	1	9	4	5	3	7	6
5	6	9	7	1	3	2	8	4
7	3	4	6	2	8	5	1	9

39

1	8	6	2	5	7	4	3	9
2	3	7	9	1	4	6	5	8
4	5	9	6	8	3	2	1	7
3	7	1	4	6	8	9	2	5
9	4	8	1	2	5	3	7	6
6	2	5	7	3	9	1	8	4
8	6	2	5	9	1	7	4	3
7	1	3	8	4	6	5	9	2
5	9	4	3	7	2	8	6	1

42

7	6	1	3	4	5	8	2	9
3	2	5	8	7	9	4	6	1
8	9	4	6	1	2	5	3	7
5	7	3	9	6	8	1	4	2
4	8	6	5	2	1	9	7	3
2	1	9	4	3	7	6	5	8
6	4	7	1	8	3	2	9	5
9	3	8	2	5	6	7	1	4
1	5	2	7	9	4	3	8	6

43

1	4	2	6	3	7	8	5	9
7	8	6	5	2	9	1	4	3
5	9	3	1	8	4	6	2	7
3	5	7	9	6	2	4	8	1
2	1	8	7	4	5	9	3	6
4	6	9	3	1	8	5	7	2
9	7	1	4	5	3	2	6	8
6	2	5	8	7	1	3	9	4
8	3	4	2	9	6	7	1	5

46

4	6	8	3	7	5	2	1	9
1	5	9	2	8	4	7	6	3
3	2	7	6	1	9	4	8	5
8	7	5	4	2	1	9	3	6
6	4	1	9	5	3	8	7	2
9	3	2	8	6	7	5	4	1
2	8	4	1	9	6	3	5	7
5	1	3	7	4	2	6	9	8
7	9	6	5	3	8	1	2	4

44

4	7	1	5	2	8	9	3	6
8	2	3	7	9	6	4	5	1
5	6	9	4	1	3	8	2	7
3	1	8	6	7	2	5	4	9
7	9	5	3	8	4	6	1	2
2	4	6	9	5	1	3	7	8
9	3	2	8	4	7	1	6	5
1	8	4	2	6	5	7	9	3
6	5	7	1	3	9	2	8	4

47

8	4	2	1	7	6	5	3	9
3	6	9	4	8	5	7	2	1
5	7	1	2	9	3	6	4	8
6	8	5	7	1	2	3	9	4
2	9	3	6	5	4	8	1	7
4	1	7	8	3	9	2	5	6
1	3	6	9	2	8	4	7	5
9	5	8	3	4	7	1	6	2
7	2	4	5	6	1	9	8	3

45

9	1	5	2	3	7	6	8	4
8	7	6	9	5	4	1	2	3
2	4	3	6	1	8	9	5	7
7	6	9	8	2	1	4	3	5
4	3	2	7	6	5	8	1	9
5	8	1	4	9	3	7	6	2
1	2	7	5	4	6	3	9	8
3	9	8	1	7	2	5	4	6
6	5	4	3	8	9	2	7	1

48

6	8	3	4	7	9	1	5	2
2	9	4	1	5	6	7	3	8
7	1	5	2	3	8	9	6	4
8	7	1	5	4	3	2	9	6
3	4	6	9	1	2	8	7	5
9	5	2	6	8	7	3	4	1
1	6	8	7	9	4	5	2	3
4	3	9	8	2	5	6	1	7
5	2	7	3	6	1	4	8	9

Answers

49

8	4	6	2	1	5	3	9	7
3	9	2	6	4	7	8	5	1
1	7	5	3	9	8	4	6	2
5	2	4	7	3	1	6	8	9
7	3	1	9	8	6	5	2	4
6	8	9	5	2	4	1	7	3
2	6	8	1	7	3	9	4	5
9	5	3	4	6	2	7	1	8
4	1	7	8	5	9	2	3	6

52

1	6	4	3	8	5	2	7	9
8	2	5	7	9	1	6	3	4
9	7	3	2	4	6	8	1	5
4	9	8	6	2	7	1	5	3
6	3	7	1	5	8	4	9	2
2	5	1	9	3	4	7	8	6
7	4	6	5	1	3	9	2	8
5	1	9	8	6	2	3	4	7
3	8	2	4	7	9	5	6	1

50

2	6	4	5	8	3	1	9	7
1	3	5	2	7	9	8	4	6
8	7	9	4	6	1	5	2	3
5	1	6	7	3	4	2	8	9
7	9	8	1	5	2	6	3	4
4	2	3	6	9	8	7	1	5
6	8	2	3	4	7	9	5	1
9	4	7	8	1	5	3	6	2
3	5	1	9	2	6	4	7	8

53

2	1	3	6	7	5	9	8	4
6	4	8	3	9	1	2	5	7
7	9	5	4	8	2	1	6	3
1	6	4	5	2	8	7	3	9
5	2	7	9	1	3	8	4	6
8	3	9	7	4	6	5	1	2
4	8	6	2	5	7	3	9	1
9	5	2	1	3	4	6	7	8
3	7	1	8	6	9	4	2	5

51

5	4	3	6	9	8	2	1	7
7	1	8	5	2	3	6	4	9
6	2	9	7	4	1	8	5	3
2	8	5	3	7	4	1	9	6
9	6	1	8	5	2	3	7	4
3	7	4	1	6	9	5	2	8
4	3	7	2	8	5	9	6	1
1	5	6	9	3	7	4	8	2
8	9	2	4	1	6	7	3	5

54

6	2	1	7	3	5	9	8	4
7	5	3	9	4	8	6	2	1
4	9	8	1	2	6	7	5	3
1	4	6	2	9	7	5	3	8
5	3	7	6	8	4	1	9	2
2	8	9	3	5	1	4	6	7
8	7	2	5	1	9	3	4	6
3	6	5	4	7	2	8	1	9
9	1	4	8	6	3	2	7	5

55

7	3	4	8	5	9	2	1	6
2	5	1	6	4	7	8	3	9
8	6	9	1	2	3	7	5	4
4	9	7	2	3	6	5	8	1
5	1	2	4	9	8	3	6	7
6	8	3	7	1	5	4	9	2
1	4	5	3	6	2	9	7	8
9	2	8	5	7	1	6	4	3
3	7	6	9	8	4	1	2	5

58

6	4	8	2	7	5	3	1	9
1	2	9	4	8	3	7	6	5
5	7	3	6	1	9	4	8	2
3	6	2	9	5	7	1	4	8
7	5	1	8	4	2	9	3	6
9	8	4	1	3	6	2	5	7
8	3	5	7	2	1	6	9	4
2	1	6	5	9	4	8	7	3
4	9	7	3	6	8	5	2	1

56

7	2	1	3	4	5	8	6	9
6	4	3	1	8	9	2	5	7
8	5	9	6	2	7	1	3	4
3	8	4	5	7	6	9	2	1
2	6	7	9	1	4	3	8	5
1	9	5	8	3	2	7	4	6
5	3	6	7	9	8	4	1	2
9	1	2	4	6	3	5	7	8
4	7	8	2	5	1	6	9	3

59

5	6	3	9	7	1	8	2	4
4	1	7	6	8	2	5	3	9
2	8	9	3	4	5	6	7	1
7	2	1	4	5	8	9	6	3
3	5	8	7	6	9	4	1	2
9	4	6	1	2	3	7	8	5
1	9	5	8	3	6	2	4	7
6	3	4	2	9	7	1	5	8
8	7	2	5	1	4	3	9	6

57

1	9	3	7	4	6	8	5	2
6	4	8	3	5	2	7	1	9
7	2	5	9	8	1	6	3	4
2	3	7	4	9	8	5	6	1
5	1	4	6	2	7	9	8	3
8	6	9	1	3	5	2	4	7
4	7	1	8	6	9	3	2	5
3	5	6	2	7	4	1	9	8
9	8	2	5	1	3	4	7	6

60

4	8	3	5	7	1	9	2	6
6	5	9	4	3	2	7	8	1
2	7	1	9	6	8	4	3	5
7	1	4	2	5	3	6	9	8
8	9	5	6	4	7	2	1	3
3	2	6	8	1	9	5	7	4
9	4	7	1	8	6	3	5	2
1	6	2	3	9	5	8	4	7
5	3	8	7	2	4	1	6	9

Answers

61

2	5	3	8	4	1	6	7	9
7	4	1	9	6	2	8	3	5
6	8	9	3	7	5	1	2	4
8	7	2	4	3	6	5	9	1
5	9	4	1	2	8	3	6	7
1	3	6	5	9	7	4	8	2
9	1	7	6	8	4	2	5	3
3	6	5	2	1	9	7	4	8
4	2	8	7	5	3	9	1	6

64

9	7	5	6	3	1	2	8	4
3	1	6	4	2	8	5	7	9
2	4	8	5	9	7	3	6	1
5	9	4	2	7	3	6	1	8
6	2	7	1	8	5	4	9	3
8	3	1	9	4	6	7	5	2
4	8	2	7	5	9	1	3	6
1	5	9	3	6	4	8	2	7
7	6	3	8	1	2	9	4	5

62

9	4	5	6	3	2	7	8	1
8	1	2	9	4	7	5	3	6
7	3	6	8	5	1	4	2	9
5	8	9	7	6	3	1	4	2
3	2	7	4	1	9	8	6	5
4	6	1	2	8	5	3	9	7
2	9	4	5	7	8	6	1	3
1	7	8	3	2	6	9	5	4
6	5	3	1	9	4	2	7	8

65

2	9	1	4	5	3	8	7	6
6	5	3	8	7	1	4	9	2
7	4	8	2	6	9	3	5	1
4	6	7	3	2	5	1	8	9
8	2	9	7	1	6	5	3	4
1	3	5	9	4	8	6	2	7
3	7	2	6	8	4	9	1	5
9	1	4	5	3	2	7	6	8
5	8	6	1	9	7	2	4	3

63

1	2	4	7	6	5	9	8	3
6	5	3	9	8	2	7	4	1
9	8	7	3	1	4	6	2	5
2	4	9	6	3	8	5	1	7
5	3	1	2	4	7	8	6	9
8	7	6	1	5	9	4	3	2
4	1	2	5	7	6	3	9	8
3	6	5	8	9	1	2	7	4
7	9	8	4	2	3	1	5	6

66

8	1	3	5	7	6	2	9	4
6	9	4	3	2	8	1	5	7
5	7	2	1	9	4	6	3	8
2	6	1	9	5	7	8	4	3
7	4	9	8	6	3	5	1	2
3	5	8	2	4	1	9	7	6
4	2	6	7	1	9	3	8	5
9	3	5	4	8	2	7	6	1
1	8	7	6	3	5	4	2	9

67

9	1	4	7	6	8	5	3	2
5	2	6	4	3	9	8	7	1
3	8	7	1	5	2	4	9	6
6	9	3	8	4	5	2	1	7
4	7	1	3	2	6	9	8	5
8	5	2	9	1	7	6	4	3
1	6	8	5	7	4	3	2	9
2	3	9	6	8	1	7	5	4
7	4	5	2	9	3	1	6	8

70

9	3	7	5	6	2	1	4	8
2	5	4	1	8	3	7	9	6
8	1	6	9	4	7	2	5	3
5	7	3	2	9	4	6	8	1
1	4	8	3	5	6	9	7	2
6	9	2	7	1	8	5	3	4
4	6	1	8	7	5	3	2	9
3	8	5	6	2	9	4	1	7
7	2	9	4	3	1	8	6	5

68

2	9	4	7	6	3	5	1	8
3	1	7	4	5	8	2	9	6
6	5	8	9	1	2	3	7	4
5	7	3	6	2	1	4	8	9
8	4	9	3	7	5	6	2	1
1	2	6	8	4	9	7	3	5
7	3	5	1	8	6	9	4	2
4	6	1	2	9	7	8	5	3
9	8	2	5	3	4	1	6	7

71

9	3	5	4	2	6	1	7	8
4	8	2	3	1	7	6	9	5
6	1	7	5	9	8	2	4	3
3	2	6	1	4	9	5	8	7
1	7	4	8	6	5	3	2	9
5	9	8	7	3	2	4	6	1
8	6	9	2	5	1	7	3	4
2	5	3	9	7	4	8	1	6
7	4	1	6	8	3	9	5	2

69

5	8	9	4	1	7	3	2	6
2	7	6	3	8	9	4	5	1
3	4	1	2	5	6	7	9	8
6	5	2	8	3	4	1	7	9
8	9	7	6	2	1	5	3	4
1	3	4	9	7	5	8	6	2
7	2	5	1	9	8	6	4	3
4	1	3	7	6	2	9	8	5
9	6	8	5	4	3	2	1	7

72

1	2	6	8	7	4	3	9	5
8	4	9	2	3	5	1	6	7
5	3	7	6	1	9	2	8	4
4	1	8	3	9	7	5	2	6
3	7	5	1	2	6	9	4	8
6	9	2	5	4	8	7	1	3
9	5	3	4	6	2	8	7	1
2	6	1	7	8	3	4	5	9
7	8	4	9	5	1	6	3	2

Answers

73

3	9	5	7	8	6	1	4	2
1	4	7	2	9	3	6	8	5
2	8	6	5	1	4	3	9	7
7	2	9	6	5	1	4	3	8
4	6	3	8	7	2	5	1	9
5	1	8	4	3	9	2	7	6
9	5	4	1	6	7	8	2	3
6	7	2	3	4	8	9	5	1
8	3	1	9	2	5	7	6	4

76

8	1	3	7	6	5	4	2	9
2	6	9	1	3	4	7	5	8
7	5	4	2	9	8	3	6	1
4	2	8	3	1	7	5	9	6
6	3	5	8	2	9	1	4	7
9	7	1	4	5	6	2	8	3
5	8	2	6	7	3	9	1	4
1	4	7	9	8	2	6	3	5
3	9	6	5	4	1	8	7	2

74

1	4	8	6	3	9	7	2	5
6	5	3	4	2	7	1	8	9
2	9	7	8	5	1	3	4	6
5	2	1	9	4	6	8	3	7
3	8	9	2	7	5	6	1	4
7	6	4	1	8	3	9	5	2
4	3	5	7	6	8	2	9	1
9	7	2	3	1	4	5	6	8
8	1	6	5	9	2	4	7	3

77

3	5	9	2	4	7	8	6	1
8	1	6	3	5	9	2	4	7
2	7	4	8	6	1	5	3	9
6	8	7	1	3	5	9	2	4
5	2	1	4	9	8	6	7	3
4	9	3	7	2	6	1	8	5
9	4	5	6	8	3	7	1	2
1	3	8	5	7	2	4	9	6
7	6	2	9	1	4	3	5	8

75

5	4	3	8	6	1	2	7	9
9	8	1	4	7	2	3	6	5
6	7	2	3	9	5	1	8	4
2	9	8	5	4	6	7	3	1
4	1	6	9	3	7	8	5	2
7	3	5	1	2	8	9	4	6
1	6	4	2	8	3	5	9	7
8	2	9	7	5	4	6	1	3
3	5	7	6	1	9	4	2	8

78

4	3	1	7	8	2	6	9	5
8	2	5	1	6	9	4	7	3
6	7	9	4	3	5	1	8	2
3	1	6	9	5	8	2	4	7
9	8	2	3	4	7	5	1	6
5	4	7	2	1	6	8	3	9
7	6	8	5	9	1	3	2	4
1	9	3	6	2	4	7	5	8
2	5	4	8	7	3	9	6	1

79

7	3	4	6	2	9	1	8	5
1	9	2	5	7	8	3	6	4
8	5	6	3	4	1	9	2	7
2	1	8	7	5	3	6	4	9
4	6	3	8	9	2	5	7	1
9	7	5	1	6	4	8	3	2
5	8	7	2	1	6	4	9	3
3	2	9	4	8	5	7	1	6
6	4	1	9	3	7	2	5	8

80

9	6	7	1	2	8	3	4	5
1	4	3	6	5	7	9	8	2
2	8	5	4	3	9	6	7	1
6	5	2	8	4	1	7	3	9
4	1	9	5	7	3	2	6	8
3	7	8	2	9	6	5	1	4
5	9	6	7	8	4	1	2	3
8	3	1	9	6	2	4	5	7
7	2	4	3	1	5	8	9	6

81

4	7	8	6	3	1	2	9	5
1	5	6	2	8	9	4	3	7
2	9	3	5	7	4	1	8	6
6	2	1	7	4	8	9	5	3
9	3	4	1	5	6	8	7	2
7	8	5	9	2	3	6	4	1
5	1	9	4	6	7	3	2	8
8	6	2	3	9	5	7	1	4
3	4	7	8	1	2	5	6	9

82

2	7	3	1	8	4	5	6	9
4	1	5	3	6	9	7	2	8
9	6	8	5	7	2	1	4	3
3	5	7	4	2	1	8	9	6
6	2	9	7	5	8	4	3	1
1	8	4	9	3	6	2	7	5
5	9	2	8	4	3	6	1	7
7	3	6	2	1	5	9	8	4
8	4	1	6	9	7	3	5	2

83

6	5	7	8	9	1	2	4	3
2	8	3	7	6	4	9	5	1
9	4	1	2	5	3	6	8	7
4	6	9	3	2	7	5	1	8
1	3	5	6	4	8	7	9	2
8	7	2	9	1	5	4	3	6
5	9	8	1	7	2	3	6	4
3	2	6	4	8	9	1	7	5
7	1	4	5	3	6	8	2	9

84

2	9	7	5	1	3	6	8	4
1	5	8	4	2	6	9	7	3
3	6	4	9	7	8	1	5	2
9	2	1	3	6	7	8	4	5
8	7	5	1	9	4	3	2	6
6	4	3	2	8	5	7	1	9
7	8	2	6	5	9	4	3	1
5	3	6	8	4	1	2	9	7
4	1	9	7	3	2	5	6	8

Answers

85

4	3	6	5	8	1	9	2	7
1	8	2	9	3	7	4	6	5
7	9	5	4	6	2	1	8	3
5	2	1	7	9	3	8	4	6
3	4	7	8	2	6	5	9	1
8	6	9	1	5	4	3	7	2
2	1	4	3	7	9	6	5	8
6	5	3	2	4	8	7	1	9
9	7	8	6	1	5	2	3	4

88

7	8	6	1	3	5	2	4	9
5	9	2	8	4	7	1	3	6
1	3	4	6	9	2	7	8	5
3	2	8	9	5	1	6	7	4
4	1	5	7	8	6	9	2	3
6	7	9	4	2	3	5	1	8
8	5	1	3	7	9	4	6	2
9	4	7	2	6	8	3	5	1
2	6	3	5	1	4	8	9	7

86

1	6	7	8	9	3	5	4	2
8	3	2	5	4	1	9	6	7
4	5	9	6	7	2	3	8	1
2	9	3	1	6	4	7	5	8
6	4	5	2	8	7	1	3	9
7	8	1	3	5	9	4	2	6
9	7	6	4	2	5	8	1	3
5	1	8	9	3	6	2	7	4
3	2	4	7	1	8	6	9	5

89

4	6	9	2	8	5	1	7	3
3	1	8	6	4	7	9	5	2
7	5	2	9	3	1	6	8	4
8	7	4	3	6	2	5	1	9
2	3	5	8	1	9	7	4	6
6	9	1	5	7	4	2	3	8
5	2	3	7	9	8	4	6	1
1	8	7	4	2	6	3	9	5
9	4	6	1	5	3	8	2	7

87

9	2	4	6	7	1	5	8	3
7	3	8	5	9	2	4	6	1
6	5	1	3	4	8	9	2	7
2	8	6	4	3	9	7	1	5
1	4	7	2	5	6	3	9	8
5	9	3	8	1	7	2	4	6
4	6	2	7	8	5	1	3	9
3	7	9	1	6	4	8	5	2
8	1	5	9	2	3	6	7	4

90

1	2	6	4	9	5	8	3	7
7	9	5	3	1	8	4	6	2
3	4	8	2	7	6	5	9	1
6	5	4	8	3	1	7	2	9
2	1	3	9	5	7	6	8	4
8	7	9	6	2	4	3	1	5
4	8	7	1	6	9	2	5	3
9	6	2	5	4	3	1	7	8
5	3	1	7	8	2	9	4	6

91

4	3	6	1	2	8	5	9	7
2	7	8	5	6	9	3	1	4
5	1	9	3	4	7	2	6	8
7	9	3	2	8	6	4	5	1
6	4	2	9	5	1	7	8	3
1	8	5	4	7	3	6	2	9
9	5	1	6	3	4	8	7	2
3	2	7	8	1	5	9	4	6
8	6	4	7	9	2	1	3	5

94

8	6	5	2	3	1	7	9	4
1	2	7	8	9	4	5	3	6
4	9	3	7	5	6	2	1	8
2	5	1	9	6	3	8	4	7
3	4	6	1	8	7	9	2	5
9	7	8	4	2	5	1	6	3
6	1	9	3	7	8	4	5	2
7	3	2	5	4	9	6	8	1
5	8	4	6	1	2	3	7	9

92

6	9	3	4	7	8	1	5	2
1	8	4	2	3	5	7	6	9
7	5	2	1	6	9	8	3	4
8	6	5	7	2	1	9	4	3
4	7	1	9	5	3	2	8	6
2	3	9	6	8	4	5	7	1
5	2	6	3	9	7	4	1	8
3	4	7	8	1	2	6	9	5
9	1	8	5	4	6	3	2	7

95

7	8	1	9	4	3	2	5	6
2	9	3	6	5	8	1	7	4
5	6	4	7	2	1	8	9	3
8	1	2	4	9	6	5	3	7
9	3	5	8	1	7	4	6	2
4	7	6	5	3	2	9	8	1
3	4	8	2	7	9	6	1	5
1	2	9	3	6	5	7	4	8
6	5	7	1	8	4	3	2	9

93

3	5	6	8	9	7	4	1	2
8	4	1	5	2	3	7	6	9
7	2	9	4	6	1	5	8	3
1	9	2	7	3	8	6	4	5
5	3	7	9	4	6	8	2	1
6	8	4	1	5	2	3	9	7
4	7	8	3	1	9	2	5	6
2	1	5	6	7	4	9	3	8
9	6	3	2	8	5	1	7	4

96

4	8	6	5	1	7	2	9	3
5	9	7	8	3	2	6	1	4
2	1	3	4	6	9	7	5	8
8	5	4	6	2	3	9	7	1
1	6	2	9	7	8	3	4	5
3	7	9	1	5	4	8	2	6
9	4	1	7	8	6	5	3	2
6	3	5	2	9	1	4	8	7
7	2	8	3	4	5	1	6	9

97

3	6	8	7	5	1	2	9	4
9	1	7	2	3	4	8	5	6
4	5	2	9	8	6	1	3	7
7	2	3	6	1	5	9	4	8
1	9	5	4	2	8	6	7	3
6	8	4	3	7	9	5	1	2
8	3	1	5	6	7	4	2	9
2	4	6	1	9	3	7	8	5
5	7	9	8	4	2	3	6	1

98

4	5	8	1	9	3	7	6	2
3	7	6	4	5	2	1	8	9
9	1	2	8	6	7	5	3	4
1	4	7	2	8	9	6	5	3
5	6	3	7	1	4	9	2	8
2	8	9	5	3	6	4	7	1
7	9	4	6	2	8	3	1	5
8	3	1	9	7	5	2	4	6
6	2	5	3	4	1	8	9	7

99

1	5	3	6	7	8	9	2	4
6	4	7	2	3	9	1	8	5
2	8	9	1	5	4	6	7	3
9	3	1	7	2	6	4	5	8
5	6	4	8	1	3	7	9	2
7	2	8	4	9	5	3	6	1
3	7	2	5	6	1	8	4	9
4	1	6	9	8	2	5	3	7
8	9	5	3	4	7	2	1	6

100

1	9	8	5	4	6	3	2	7
3	4	2	8	7	9	1	5	6
7	5	6	2	1	3	9	8	4
2	8	1	3	9	7	4	6	5
9	6	4	1	5	2	8	7	3
5	7	3	6	8	4	2	1	9
4	1	9	7	2	5	6	3	8
8	3	5	9	6	1	7	4	2
6	2	7	4	3	8	5	9	1

101

1	6	2	5	4	7	8	9	3
9	3	8	2	6	1	4	7	5
5	4	7	8	9	3	1	2	6
6	1	4	7	5	9	3	8	2
3	2	5	1	8	6	9	4	7
8	7	9	4	3	2	5	6	1
2	8	6	9	1	5	7	3	4
4	5	3	6	7	8	2	1	9
7	9	1	3	2	4	6	5	8

102

9	4	3	6	1	5	8	7	2
5	8	6	2	7	4	3	9	1
1	2	7	8	9	3	5	4	6
4	3	5	7	6	2	9	1	8
6	1	9	3	5	8	7	2	4
8	7	2	1	4	9	6	3	5
3	5	1	4	8	7	2	6	9
2	9	4	5	3	6	1	8	7
7	6	8	9	2	1	4	5	3

103

9	1	7	2	8	4	3	5	6
6	3	2	1	5	7	8	4	9
8	5	4	3	9	6	7	1	2
5	6	9	7	3	8	1	2	4
4	2	8	9	1	5	6	7	3
3	7	1	4	6	2	5	9	8
1	4	5	6	2	3	9	8	7
2	8	3	5	7	9	4	6	1
7	9	6	8	4	1	2	3	5

106

2	3	5	9	7	6	4	1	8
4	7	6	8	1	3	2	9	5
9	1	8	2	5	4	7	3	6
5	9	2	6	4	7	3	8	1
6	4	3	1	8	9	5	2	7
1	8	7	5	3	2	6	4	9
8	6	1	4	2	5	9	7	3
7	5	4	3	9	1	8	6	2
3	2	9	7	6	8	1	5	4

104

5	9	2	3	1	6	4	8	7
4	1	7	2	8	5	6	3	9
3	6	8	4	9	7	2	5	1
7	5	4	9	6	3	1	2	8
8	3	1	7	2	4	9	6	5
6	2	9	1	5	8	3	7	4
9	7	6	8	3	1	5	4	2
2	8	5	6	4	9	7	1	3
1	4	3	5	7	2	8	9	6

107

9	5	8	3	4	2	6	7	1
3	7	4	6	1	9	8	2	5
6	2	1	5	7	8	3	4	9
4	3	5	1	9	7	2	6	8
2	1	9	8	6	4	7	5	3
8	6	7	2	3	5	1	9	4
1	9	3	4	2	6	5	8	7
5	4	6	7	8	1	9	3	2
7	8	2	9	5	3	4	1	6

105

3	5	2	4	1	9	7	8	6
1	8	7	3	6	5	4	9	2
6	4	9	7	2	8	5	1	3
8	3	1	2	7	6	9	5	4
4	9	5	8	3	1	2	6	7
7	2	6	9	5	4	8	3	1
9	7	3	1	8	2	6	4	5
2	6	4	5	9	3	1	7	8
5	1	8	6	4	7	3	2	9

108

1	5	6	2	9	3	4	8	7
7	3	4	8	1	5	2	6	9
2	8	9	4	7	6	1	3	5
8	1	5	3	6	7	9	2	4
4	6	7	9	5	2	3	1	8
3	9	2	1	8	4	5	7	6
9	4	8	7	3	1	6	5	2
6	2	1	5	4	8	7	9	3
5	7	3	6	2	9	8	4	1

109

6	2	9	1	8	4	3	7	5
3	8	7	9	2	5	4	1	6
5	4	1	7	6	3	2	9	8
2	1	6	3	5	9	8	4	7
4	7	5	2	1	8	6	3	9
9	3	8	4	7	6	5	2	1
1	6	2	5	4	7	9	8	3
7	5	3	8	9	2	1	6	4
8	9	4	6	3	1	7	5	2

112

3	1	4	5	6	7	2	8	9
7	6	2	8	9	1	5	3	4
8	9	5	3	4	2	1	6	7
4	5	9	6	1	3	7	2	8
6	7	8	2	5	9	3	4	1
1	2	3	7	8	4	9	5	6
2	3	1	4	7	8	6	9	5
9	4	6	1	3	5	8	7	2
5	8	7	9	2	6	4	1	3

110

5	3	9	1	7	2	8	4	6
1	6	2	3	4	8	9	5	7
7	4	8	6	9	5	3	1	2
3	8	7	2	6	1	4	9	5
9	2	1	5	8	4	6	7	3
4	5	6	7	3	9	1	2	8
8	1	5	4	2	3	7	6	9
6	9	4	8	5	7	2	3	1
2	7	3	9	1	6	5	8	4

113

5	6	7	3	8	4	2	1	9
3	8	1	6	2	9	7	5	4
9	2	4	5	1	7	3	6	8
1	5	2	8	4	3	6	9	7
7	9	6	1	5	2	4	8	3
8	4	3	9	7	6	1	2	5
2	7	9	4	6	8	5	3	1
6	1	8	7	3	5	9	4	2
4	3	5	2	9	1	8	7	6

111

3	7	1	4	9	6	2	5	8
8	2	4	7	1	5	6	3	9
6	5	9	8	2	3	7	4	1
5	9	8	3	7	4	1	6	2
2	3	6	9	8	1	5	7	4
1	4	7	6	5	2	9	8	3
9	8	5	1	4	7	3	2	6
7	1	3	2	6	8	4	9	5
4	6	2	5	3	9	8	1	7

114

9	2	1	7	4	8	5	6	3
4	3	8	5	1	6	9	7	2
6	5	7	3	2	9	1	4	8
7	6	9	4	5	2	3	8	1
8	1	5	9	7	3	6	2	4
2	4	3	6	8	1	7	5	9
5	8	4	1	3	7	2	9	6
1	7	6	2	9	4	8	3	5
3	9	2	8	6	5	4	1	7

115

7	6	2	4	1	5	3	9	8
5	1	3	8	9	2	6	7	4
9	8	4	3	7	6	5	2	1
4	5	1	9	2	3	7	8	6
2	7	6	5	4	8	1	3	9
3	9	8	1	6	7	4	5	2
1	3	5	6	8	9	2	4	7
8	4	7	2	3	1	9	6	5
6	2	9	7	5	4	8	1	3

118

8	4	2	1	6	5	9	3	7
3	5	7	2	9	4	1	6	8
1	9	6	3	8	7	4	2	5
2	6	3	5	7	1	8	4	9
7	1	9	6	4	8	2	5	3
4	8	5	9	2	3	6	7	1
9	3	4	8	5	2	7	1	6
5	2	8	7	1	6	3	9	4
6	7	1	4	3	9	5	8	2

116

5	2	4	9	3	7	1	8	6
7	6	3	1	8	2	4	9	5
1	8	9	4	5	6	2	3	7
3	5	2	6	1	9	8	7	4
6	1	7	3	4	8	9	5	2
9	4	8	2	7	5	3	6	1
8	9	6	7	2	4	5	1	3
2	7	1	5	9	3	6	4	8
4	3	5	8	6	1	7	2	9

119

3	7	9	2	8	6	5	4	1
8	5	4	3	1	7	9	2	6
2	6	1	5	9	4	8	3	7
6	3	5	4	2	1	7	9	8
4	1	7	8	6	9	3	5	2
9	8	2	7	3	5	6	1	4
5	4	6	9	7	2	1	8	3
1	2	3	6	5	8	4	7	9
7	9	8	1	4	3	2	6	5

117

7	5	9	2	3	6	1	4	8
1	3	4	5	8	9	7	2	6
8	6	2	7	4	1	3	9	5
2	7	8	6	1	4	5	3	9
3	4	1	9	5	8	6	7	2
5	9	6	3	2	7	4	8	1
4	1	7	8	6	2	9	5	3
9	2	3	1	7	5	8	6	4
6	8	5	4	9	3	2	1	7

120

4	7	6	1	8	9	3	2	5
3	9	1	6	5	2	7	8	4
5	2	8	3	7	4	1	6	9
7	1	9	5	6	8	2	4	3
2	8	3	4	1	7	9	5	6
6	4	5	2	9	3	8	1	7
9	6	4	8	3	1	5	7	2
1	5	7	9	2	6	4	3	8
8	3	2	7	4	5	6	9	1

121

2	3	1	7	8	6	9	4	5
9	7	4	5	3	2	6	1	8
8	6	5	9	1	4	2	3	7
3	1	6	8	7	5	4	9	2
4	5	8	2	9	1	7	6	3
7	2	9	6	4	3	8	5	1
1	8	7	3	6	9	5	2	4
6	4	2	1	5	7	3	8	9
5	9	3	4	2	8	1	7	6

122

4	8	5	2	9	6	1	7	3
7	3	2	4	1	8	6	9	5
1	9	6	5	3	7	8	4	2
9	2	3	1	8	4	5	6	7
5	1	7	6	2	9	3	8	4
6	4	8	7	5	3	9	2	1
2	6	9	3	4	5	7	1	8
3	7	4	8	6	1	2	5	9
8	5	1	9	7	2	4	3	6

123

6	5	8	2	9	3	7	1	4
7	3	9	8	4	1	6	5	2
4	2	1	5	6	7	3	9	8
3	6	2	1	7	8	9	4	5
9	1	5	4	3	2	8	6	7
8	7	4	9	5	6	1	2	3
2	4	3	7	1	9	5	8	6
5	9	7	6	8	4	2	3	1
1	8	6	3	2	5	4	7	9

124

2	5	7	9	1	6	8	3	4
3	8	9	4	5	7	2	6	1
1	6	4	3	2	8	9	5	7
6	2	3	1	8	4	7	9	5
7	9	8	5	6	3	4	1	2
4	1	5	7	9	2	6	8	3
8	3	6	2	7	1	5	4	9
5	4	2	6	3	9	1	7	8
9	7	1	8	4	5	3	2	6

125

1	8	9	4	5	7	3	6	2
6	3	2	9	1	8	4	5	7
5	7	4	6	3	2	8	1	9
4	1	6	8	2	5	9	7	3
3	9	8	7	6	4	5	2	1
7	2	5	3	9	1	6	4	8
8	6	7	1	4	9	2	3	5
9	5	3	2	7	6	1	8	4
2	4	1	5	8	3	7	9	6

126

2	4	5	7	9	6	3	8	1
6	1	9	3	8	5	4	2	7
3	7	8	1	2	4	9	6	5
9	3	2	6	4	7	5	1	8
7	8	6	9	5	1	2	3	4
1	5	4	2	3	8	6	7	9
5	6	3	8	7	9	1	4	2
8	9	1	4	6	2	7	5	3
4	2	7	5	1	3	8	9	6

127

1	3	9	5	4	6	2	8	7
8	7	2	9	3	1	6	4	5
6	5	4	8	7	2	9	1	3
9	1	3	7	8	5	4	6	2
4	2	5	6	9	3	1	7	8
7	6	8	2	1	4	3	5	9
5	4	1	3	2	7	8	9	6
3	9	6	1	5	8	7	2	4
2	8	7	4	6	9	5	3	1

130

6	4	2	3	9	1	5	7	8
9	5	8	7	6	2	1	4	3
7	3	1	5	8	4	6	9	2
4	1	3	6	7	8	9	2	5
5	8	7	2	1	9	3	6	4
2	6	9	4	5	3	8	1	7
1	9	4	8	3	7	2	5	6
3	2	5	9	4	6	7	8	1
8	7	6	1	2	5	4	3	9

128

7	9	5	6	2	1	4	3	8
4	2	1	3	8	7	5	6	9
3	8	6	4	5	9	2	1	7
6	5	8	2	1	4	9	7	3
2	3	7	5	9	6	1	8	4
1	4	9	8	7	3	6	5	2
9	1	2	7	6	8	3	4	5
8	6	3	9	4	5	7	2	1
5	7	4	1	3	2	8	9	6

131

1	6	3	4	2	5	7	9	8
2	4	9	7	8	3	5	1	6
8	7	5	1	6	9	4	2	3
6	8	2	3	5	1	9	4	7
9	5	4	6	7	8	2	3	1
3	1	7	9	4	2	8	6	5
5	9	8	2	1	6	3	7	4
4	2	1	8	3	7	6	5	9
7	3	6	5	9	4	1	8	2

129

4	6	9	2	7	8	5	3	1
1	5	8	4	9	3	6	2	7
3	2	7	6	5	1	4	8	9
5	3	2	7	4	9	8	1	6
8	9	6	5	1	2	7	4	3
7	4	1	3	8	6	2	9	5
9	1	4	8	6	7	3	5	2
6	8	3	9	2	5	1	7	4
2	7	5	1	3	4	9	6	8

132

4	3	5	7	2	6	9	8	1
1	2	7	9	5	8	4	3	6
9	8	6	4	3	1	2	7	5
2	4	8	3	6	5	1	9	7
3	5	1	8	9	7	6	2	4
7	6	9	1	4	2	3	5	8
8	7	3	6	1	9	5	4	2
6	9	2	5	7	4	8	1	3
5	1	4	2	8	3	7	6	9

Answers

133

8	3	9	1	5	6	7	2	4
4	1	2	3	7	9	8	5	6
7	6	5	2	4	8	1	3	9
3	5	7	4	8	2	9	6	1
1	2	4	9	6	5	3	7	8
6	9	8	7	3	1	2	4	5
5	7	6	8	1	3	4	9	2
9	4	1	6	2	7	5	8	3
2	8	3	5	9	4	6	1	7

136

6	2	8	1	3	5	4	9	7
9	7	3	8	4	2	6	1	5
5	4	1	7	6	9	8	3	2
8	6	5	4	9	7	1	2	3
2	3	9	6	5	1	7	4	8
4	1	7	3	2	8	9	5	6
1	8	2	9	7	3	5	6	4
7	5	6	2	1	4	3	8	9
3	9	4	5	8	6	2	7	1

134

8	1	3	6	4	7	2	9	5
6	2	7	1	5	9	8	3	4
4	9	5	2	3	8	7	1	6
7	8	1	3	9	4	5	6	2
3	4	9	5	6	2	1	7	8
2	5	6	8	7	1	3	4	9
5	7	8	9	1	6	4	2	3
9	3	4	7	2	5	6	8	1
1	6	2	4	8	3	9	5	7

137

5	3	6	9	7	4	2	1	8
8	7	9	1	2	5	3	6	4
4	1	2	3	8	6	5	9	7
3	9	5	4	6	1	7	8	2
7	4	1	8	9	2	6	3	5
6	2	8	5	3	7	9	4	1
1	5	7	6	4	3	8	2	9
2	8	3	7	1	9	4	5	6
9	6	4	2	5	8	1	7	3

135

2	5	8	7	9	1	6	3	4
1	3	7	2	4	6	8	9	5
4	6	9	8	5	3	7	2	1
3	4	1	9	8	2	5	6	7
7	8	5	3	6	4	2	1	9
9	2	6	1	7	5	4	8	3
8	7	2	4	3	9	1	5	6
5	1	3	6	2	7	9	4	8
6	9	4	5	1	8	3	7	2

138

7	1	9	8	6	4	5	2	3
6	2	3	1	5	9	4	7	8
4	5	8	2	3	7	1	6	9
5	4	2	9	1	3	7	8	6
3	8	7	6	4	5	9	1	2
1	9	6	7	2	8	3	4	5
8	3	4	5	7	2	6	9	1
9	6	5	4	8	1	2	3	7
2	7	1	3	9	6	8	5	4

139

2	4	6	3	8	1	9	7	5
5	8	1	9	2	7	3	4	6
7	9	3	5	6	4	1	2	8
3	2	7	4	9	5	8	6	1
8	1	4	6	7	3	2	5	9
9	6	5	8	1	2	7	3	4
1	7	9	2	5	6	4	8	3
6	3	2	1	4	8	5	9	7
4	5	8	7	3	9	6	1	2

142

8	5	6	4	2	7	1	3	9
3	7	1	5	6	9	8	4	2
9	2	4	8	1	3	7	6	5
7	4	3	2	9	8	6	5	1
1	9	8	6	5	4	3	2	7
2	6	5	3	7	1	4	9	8
4	3	9	1	8	2	5	7	6
5	8	7	9	3	6	2	1	4
6	1	2	7	4	5	9	8	3

140

8	5	4	6	7	3	1	2	9
9	7	3	8	2	1	4	6	5
2	1	6	9	4	5	8	3	7
4	2	7	1	5	8	3	9	6
6	8	1	3	9	7	5	4	2
5	3	9	4	6	2	7	8	1
3	6	5	7	8	9	2	1	4
7	9	8	2	1	4	6	5	3
1	4	2	5	3	6	9	7	8

143

7	8	4	1	5	2	3	9	6
5	2	1	3	6	9	7	8	4
6	3	9	4	7	8	1	2	5
1	7	5	9	8	3	6	4	2
3	4	8	2	1	6	9	5	7
2	9	6	5	4	7	8	1	3
4	6	7	8	9	5	2	3	1
8	5	2	6	3	1	4	7	9
9	1	3	7	2	4	5	6	8

141

2	6	4	7	9	3	5	1	8
8	5	1	4	2	6	9	3	7
7	3	9	1	5	8	4	2	6
6	7	2	8	1	5	3	4	9
4	9	8	6	3	2	1	7	5
5	1	3	9	4	7	8	6	2
1	8	7	5	6	4	2	9	3
9	2	5	3	7	1	6	8	4
3	4	6	2	8	9	7	5	1

144

7	3	2	6	5	1	4	9	8
8	1	9	2	3	4	5	7	6
4	5	6	9	7	8	1	3	2
5	7	8	3	1	9	2	6	4
6	4	1	5	2	7	3	8	9
9	2	3	8	4	6	7	1	5
3	9	5	1	6	2	8	4	7
2	6	4	7	8	3	9	5	1
1	8	7	4	9	5	6	2	3

Answers

145

7	5	2	4	1	3	9	8	6
6	4	9	2	8	7	3	1	5
3	1	8	6	9	5	7	4	2
2	3	1	7	5	9	8	6	4
9	8	4	3	2	6	1	5	7
5	6	7	1	4	8	2	9	3
8	2	6	5	7	1	4	3	9
1	7	3	9	6	4	5	2	8
4	9	5	8	3	2	6	7	1

148

6	4	5	7	9	3	8	2	1
3	9	1	4	8	2	7	6	5
2	8	7	5	1	6	4	9	3
9	2	4	3	7	1	6	5	8
8	5	3	9	6	4	1	7	2
1	7	6	2	5	8	9	3	4
4	3	8	6	2	9	5	1	7
5	6	2	1	4	7	3	8	9
7	1	9	8	3	5	2	4	6

146

2	8	3	7	6	5	4	1	9
5	4	1	9	2	3	8	6	7
9	7	6	4	8	1	5	3	2
8	9	5	1	3	7	2	4	6
3	2	4	8	5	6	9	7	1
6	1	7	2	9	4	3	5	8
1	5	9	3	7	8	6	2	4
7	3	2	6	4	9	1	8	5
4	6	8	5	1	2	7	9	3

149

8	9	3	1	2	4	7	5	6
1	6	4	9	5	7	2	8	3
2	7	5	8	3	6	4	9	1
4	1	8	3	6	5	9	7	2
5	3	9	2	7	8	1	6	4
6	2	7	4	1	9	8	3	5
9	8	1	6	4	3	5	2	7
3	5	2	7	8	1	6	4	9
7	4	6	5	9	2	3	1	8

147

9	8	1	4	6	7	2	5	3
4	2	3	8	5	1	9	6	7
7	6	5	2	9	3	1	4	8
2	3	8	1	4	6	5	7	9
1	5	4	9	7	8	6	3	2
6	7	9	5	3	2	4	8	1
8	1	6	3	2	5	7	9	4
5	9	2	7	8	4	3	1	6
3	4	7	6	1	9	8	2	5

150

3	2	4	8	5	7	6	9	1
8	1	6	3	4	9	2	7	5
7	9	5	2	6	1	8	3	4
2	3	1	4	9	5	7	6	8
5	4	9	7	8	6	1	2	3
6	8	7	1	3	2	5	4	9
4	5	2	6	1	3	9	8	7
1	7	3	9	2	8	4	5	6
9	6	8	5	7	4	3	1	2

151

4	5	1	3	7	9	2	8	6
2	8	7	5	6	4	3	9	1
9	6	3	1	8	2	4	7	5
3	1	6	7	2	5	8	4	9
7	9	8	4	3	6	5	1	2
5	4	2	8	9	1	7	6	3
6	3	9	2	4	8	1	5	7
8	2	5	9	1	7	6	3	4
1	7	4	6	5	3	9	2	8

154

4	7	2	1	8	9	5	6	3
9	5	3	2	4	6	8	7	1
8	1	6	5	3	7	4	2	9
5	6	9	3	2	8	7	1	4
1	2	8	6	7	4	9	3	5
7	3	4	9	1	5	6	8	2
2	4	5	7	6	1	3	9	8
6	8	1	4	9	3	2	5	7
3	9	7	8	5	2	1	4	6

152

6	4	7	3	5	2	8	9	1
9	5	8	7	1	6	3	4	2
1	3	2	4	8	9	7	5	6
4	8	5	2	3	7	1	6	9
3	6	1	9	4	5	2	8	7
7	2	9	1	6	8	5	3	4
5	9	6	8	7	1	4	2	3
2	1	3	5	9	4	6	7	8
8	7	4	6	2	3	9	1	5

155

8	3	6	9	4	2	7	1	5
1	9	7	5	6	3	2	8	4
4	2	5	7	8	1	3	9	6
5	6	8	1	3	9	4	7	2
7	4	9	8	2	6	5	3	1
3	1	2	4	5	7	8	6	9
6	7	4	3	9	5	1	2	8
2	8	1	6	7	4	9	5	3
9	5	3	2	1	8	6	4	7

153

8	4	5	1	6	2	9	3	7
9	3	7	4	5	8	2	1	6
2	1	6	3	9	7	4	8	5
6	5	3	8	2	4	7	9	1
1	2	9	5	7	6	3	4	8
4	7	8	9	1	3	5	6	2
7	9	2	6	4	1	8	5	3
5	8	1	2	3	9	6	7	4
3	6	4	7	8	5	1	2	9

156

7	1	9	4	2	5	3	8	6
2	5	6	8	7	3	9	1	4
3	8	4	1	9	6	5	2	7
5	2	8	6	3	7	1	4	9
6	9	7	5	1	4	8	3	2
4	3	1	2	8	9	6	7	5
1	6	3	7	5	2	4	9	8
9	7	5	3	4	8	2	6	1
8	4	2	9	6	1	7	5	3

157

1	8	5	3	2	6	9	7	4
6	4	3	7	9	5	1	2	8
2	9	7	4	8	1	6	3	5
5	2	4	9	1	3	7	8	6
3	7	9	5	6	8	2	4	1
8	1	6	2	4	7	3	5	9
7	6	1	8	3	4	5	9	2
9	3	8	1	5	2	4	6	7
4	5	2	6	7	9	8	1	3

160

6	4	7	9	3	8	5	2	1
5	8	3	7	1	2	9	6	4
1	9	2	5	6	4	7	3	8
4	5	1	2	9	3	6	8	7
7	3	6	4	8	5	2	1	9
8	2	9	6	7	1	3	4	5
3	7	5	8	4	6	1	9	2
2	6	8	1	5	9	4	7	3
9	1	4	3	2	7	8	5	6

158

3	7	4	8	5	9	1	2	6
1	5	9	4	2	6	8	3	7
8	2	6	7	1	3	5	4	9
5	6	7	9	3	4	2	1	8
4	8	2	1	6	7	3	9	5
9	3	1	5	8	2	6	7	4
7	1	5	3	4	8	9	6	2
6	4	3	2	9	5	7	8	1
2	9	8	6	7	1	4	5	3

161

6	1	3	7	9	2	4	5	8
8	5	4	6	1	3	2	9	7
2	7	9	5	4	8	3	6	1
4	9	8	1	5	6	7	3	2
7	6	1	2	3	4	5	8	9
3	2	5	9	8	7	1	4	6
5	8	2	4	7	9	6	1	3
9	4	7	3	6	1	8	2	5
1	3	6	8	2	5	9	7	4

159

3	5	8	2	6	7	4	1	9
7	4	6	9	1	8	5	3	2
9	1	2	4	5	3	6	7	8
1	2	3	6	8	4	7	9	5
6	8	4	7	9	5	1	2	3
5	7	9	1	3	2	8	4	6
4	3	7	8	2	6	9	5	1
8	9	5	3	4	1	2	6	7
2	6	1	5	7	9	3	8	4

SUDOKU

LARGE PRINT

Puzzles That Are Easy on the Eyes, Not on the Brain

8	4			3				
		1		5				
			7				6	9
					8			1
	9	6	5		2	4	8	
5			1					
4	8				7			
				2		7		
				1			3	5

SUDOKU

LARGE PRINT

Publications International, Ltd.

Cover Puzzle: Howard Tomlinson

Puzzle Constructors: Conceptis Puzzles Ltd., Howard Tomlinson

Illustrators: Elizabeth Gerber, Robin Humer, Jen Torche

Brain Games is a trademark of Publications International, Ltd.

Louis Weber, CEO
Publications International, Ltd.
7373 North Cicero Avenue
Lincolnwood, Illinois 60712

Permission is never granted for commercial purposes.

ISBN-13: 978-1-4508-6979-9
ISBN-10: 1-4508-6979-3

Manufactured in U.S.A.

8 7 6 5 4 3 2 1

Easy on the Eyes, Not on the Brain

Join the sudoku puzzle craze without straining your eyes with *Brain Games*™: *Large Print Sudoku*! Including sudoku in the mix of puzzles you do each day will add fresh challenges to your mental workout and help keep your brain cognitively fit, flexible, and young—all while giving your eyes the rest they need. Many gerontologists and physicians recommend working puzzles as one way to keep your mind sharp. Puzzles demand focused attention, help increase mental flexibility, and require the use of problem-solving skills, all of which are important cognitive functions. We can think of puzzles as mini brain workouts. And don't let all the numbers scare you off: There's no math involved in these brain exercises—only logic.

This book is loaded with more than 160 sudoku puzzles of varying difficulty, beginning with easier puzzles in the first level, moving on to medium, and then finally to the most challenging ones that will really build your mental muscle. Each puzzle takes up an entire page so you can strain your brain—not your eyes—as you work each one. If you've never worked a sudoku puzzle before, you may want to start with a few easier puzzles before working your way up to

the more challenging levels. Once you've learned the ropes, skip around the book and try your hand at the tougher ones. You will be a sudoku pro before you know it!

With all this in mind, now is a great time to start solving! A sudoku puzzle is basically a 9 by 9 grid of squares; the challenge is to place the numbers 1 through 9 once in each horizontal row, vertical column, and 3 by 3 box of squares (indicated by heavy outline). The puzzles have some numbers filled in—you work out the rest. And don't forget that you'll never have to guess, as all the puzzles can be solved by logic.

Getting Started

First, look at the numbers already placed in the grid; by using a process of elimination, you should be able to fill in some of the empty squares. Study the rows, columns, and boxes, especially those that have the most numbers already in place. Find situations where only a single number can fit into a single square. For instance, in the puzzle example shown (see next page), the number 4 is missing from the top right box. To place this missing 4 correctly in one of the box's empty squares, start by examining the rows and columns that

3

intersect with this box. If you check the third row from the top, you'll see that a 4 already appears over in the top left box. Because each number can appear only once in any row (or column, or box), you know you can't put the missing 4 between the 2 and the 7 in the top right box.

Now take a look at the columns. If you examine the third column from the right, you'll see a 4 way down in the bottom row of the puzzle; you can therefore eliminate the empty square between the 2 and the 6 as a place for the missing 4 in the top right box. The only spot now left for the 4 is the empty square between the 3 and the 7 in the rightmost column. (Remember, discovering where numbers *cannot* be placed will help you discover where they *can* be placed.)

Congratulations—you've just placed your first number!

Pencil in Possibilities

If, after using the aforementioned method, you still have empty squares, try using pencil marks. In each empty square, pencil in every number that could go in that square; make the numbers very small. Before writing in these tiny numbers, check the rest of that square's row, column, and box to rule out any numbers that already appear.

Start by working on rows, columns, and boxes with the most numbers already correctly positioned—you may be able to fill in a few of the remaining squares quickly. If you find a number that appears only once in the pencil marks for any row, column, or box, you know that number must be in that square. Be sure to erase that number from the pencil marks in the other squares of that row, column, or box.

As you can see, much of sudoku solving is a process of elimination. As you work more sudoku puzzles, you'll discover your own techniques for solving them. For more advanced methods, go to www.conceptispuzzles.com, and click on "Sudoku" and then "Sudoku techniques."

Now that you have the basic information, it's time to grab your pencil and start giving your brain a good, healthy workout and your eyes a rest—the sudoku way!

I

	9	1						4
7			6			1	2	
4		5	7	8	1		9	
	1	3		6		9		
		7	4		9	5		
		2		1		7	6	
	7		1	4	5	6		3
	5	6			8			9
1						2	5	

Answer on page 166.

2

9		1		3		4	2
8					2	1		9
		1	9		7		5	
1		6				2	8	7
				2				
2	3	4				5		6
	4		6		5	8		
5		8	2					4
7	6		8		1		3	

Answer on page 166.

3

	1			5			8	
3			1		2			4
8		2	6	9	4	5		3
			9	6	5			
4	6						5	7
			4	7	8			
9		5	7	1	6	4		2
1			5		3			8
	4			2			6	

Answer on page 166.

4

	7			9			3	
9					3			6
	6	4	5	8		1	7	
	1		4		8	9		
7		6				5		8
		5	1		7		2	
	5	2		7	1	6	9	
1			9					5
	3			4			8	

Answer on page 166.

5

5			4	7	2		6	9
	1	9			6			8
	4			9		7	3	
1	6		3		4			
			9		5		8	1
	7	6		2			1	
2			7			8	9	
4	8		6	5	9			7

Answer on page 166.

6

5	6		3			9		2
9		3		4				
	4		2	9	6			3
6		8			1	5		
	7	4				2	6	
		5	8			4		1
7			5	3	4		9	
				1		3		5
3		9			2		1	4

Answer on page 166.

7

	6					3	9	
7			3	5	8			2
8					6			
	4	8		9			3	
	7						5	
	2			1		8	6	
			5					4
6			4	7	2			3
	9	2					7	

Answer on page 167.

8

5				9			1	
	7		1		8		9	
1		8		7	5		4	3
				3			5	
9								7
	8			4				
7	6		8	5		4		9
	4		9		2		7	
	3			1				5

Answer on page 167.

9

		3		6	2	1	4	7
	4				3			2
7		2	9					3
		6	5				7	9
5				3				8
3	8				9	5		
6					8	2		5
2			1				8	
8	7	1	2	4		9		

Answer on page 167.

10

				6	7			
7		1	3		9	5		
		8	5	4		7	1	3
	7		6	2			5	8
4	1			9	3		6	
2	3	6		7	5	1		
		7	2		8	6		5
			9	1				

Answer on page 167.

11

		4		8	9	2		3
	5		3		1			
9		1		6				8
	1				3		6	2
3		9		5		7		1
4	8		2				5	
7				9		4		5
			7		4		8	
1		8	6	2		9		

Answer on page 167.

12

5		1	4		9	2		6
		2		6		3		
	9		3		7		1	
3		7		4		9		1
	5		6		2		8	
1		8		7		4		2
	4		1		8		3	
		3		5		8		
7		6	2		4	1		5

Answer on page 167.

13

	4	1						
				3				5
9	3	6	4	8			7	2
8	6		9			7		
1		7	6		8	5		9
		5			1		2	8
7	1			2	9	3	8	6
6				1				
						2	1	

Answer on page 168.

14

	9		6		3		7	8
8		3		5	2			9
	6	1			7	2		
9						6	3	1
	3			2			5	
1	8	5						4
		8	2			3	1	
2			3	6		7		5
3	5		8		1		9	

Answer on page 168.

15

	1		8	3		2	4	
3					5			8
8		2	6			7		
	9		3	7	2	4		5
7								1
4		5	1	6	8		9	
		4			6	1		2
6			4					9
	5	3		1	9		8	

Answer on page 168.

16

7	2			1	3			
1			2	5	9			6
5	3		7	8		1		
2	7						6	
			9		5			
	9						4	7
		2		9	7		1	8
4			5	3	6			9
			8	2			5	3

Answer on page 168.

17

			8	5	2			
	9		7		6		8	
		8				3		
8	4		9		7		1	5
9								3
6	5		3		1		7	9
		5				7		
	1		5		9		2	
			4	6	8			

Answer on page 168.

18

	7		2		3	1	9	4
			7			8		
2				4	8			7
		8				9	7	
	1	9	3		6	2	4	
	5	4				6		
9			6	7				8
		7			9			
5	4	6	8		2		3	9

Answer on page 168.

19

2		4		5		3		
		3	2		7		6	
7	1				4			9
	6			1		8	2	
3			5		6			1
	4	5		2			7	
6			1				3	8
	3		7		8	5		
		2		3		4		6

Answer on page 169.

20

7	9			8		4	6	
4		2	3			9		8
	5	6					3	1
	3			7	6			
6			4	5	1			3
			8	9			7	
3	6					2	8	
1		7			2	5		4
	2	5		4			1	6

Answer on page 169.

21

6			5		9			4
	5	2		3		8	7	
			2					
1						7		6
	9						1	
8		7						5
				7				
	2	4		8		5	6	
5			9		4			1

Answer on page 169.

22

5					1	6		
3		6	4	8			5	
	1			2			3	4
2	7		5		9			8
	3						2	
6			2		3		4	9
1	5			6			9	
	4			5	8	2		6
		8	1					5

Answer on page 169.

23

		3	7	9		8		
		1	2	5	4	3		
9					1			5
	9	2					6	8
4	8			7			9	3
3	7					4	5	
			4					1
		4	8	6	9	2		
		8		2	5	9		

Answer on page 169.

24

	4			5			8	
8			7		9			2
		1	2		8	6		
	1	6	3		4	8	5	
9								3
	8	2	9		5	4	7	
		8	5		6	7		
1			4		2			5
	9			7			4	

Answer on page 169.

25

		7		3	6	4		2
		4	8		9	3	5	
	8				4			
	4				5			6
	5	8	3		2	1	9	
2			4				7	
			1				3	
	3	5	6		7	2		
8		9	2	4		6		

Answer on page 170.

26

	1		7		2		3	
7		4				6		9
	2		4	3	9		5	
5		7		8		2		3
		1				7		
4		2		1		8		5
	7		5	4	1		8	
2		9				5		1
	5		9		6		7	

Answer on page 170.

27

	8		7		5			
	7	2	4		9	3		
			6			8	4	7
1	5	9	3					
8			9		6			3
					2	5	9	4
9	1	6			8			
		5	1		4	2	6	
			5		3		7	

Answer on page 170.

28

2					4			5
				9		2		1
			1		3	8	4	9
1	7	5	2		9	6		
3								2
		2	4		6	1	3	7
7	3	1	9		5			
9		8		7				
5			8					3

Answer on page 170.

29

4	7		5					
3	6			1	9		2	
			8		4			7
2	1	6		9	8			4
		9				2		
7			2	5		9	8	1
6			1		2		3	
	5		9	4			1	6
					5		7	2

Answer on page 170.

30

6					9			2
	5	8	1	3		9	7	
	9	3			7	6		
	8	6					9	
	3		7		8		6	
	2					7	8	
		5	6			1	2	
	7	2		1	4	8	5	
9			2					7

Answer on page 170.

31

	8				4	7		
	4		7	3	5			
9			6		8			5
						8		
6								1
		7						
5			8		7			6
			9	6	3		7	
		2	5				9	

Answer on page 171.

32

		1		8	7		6	
	5		2					9
7			5		6	4		2
	1			6		7	9	5
	6	9				1	8	
5	8	7		4			3	
6		5	1		8			7
8					4		2	
	4		7	3		6		

Answer on page 171.

33

	4	2				9	3	7
		6	7	2	3			
7		5						8
8		7	4				1	6
			3		8			
3	5				6	7		4
5						4		1
			9	8	1	5		
6	1	3				8	9	

Answer on page 171.

34

4	7	5		3	6			
	6				1	5		
	9				5	6		
					4		1	7
			6	1	3			
1	5		2					
		7	1				4	
		2	3				8	
			4	7		9	2	6

Answer on page 171.

35

		3	5					4
8			1		9	5		
	6	4			3	1	7	
			9	5				1
				3				
1				7	2			
	5	6	3			9	1	
		9	6		4			5
3					5	2		

Answer on page 171.

36

		3		9			6	
5						1		
	1			7	4			8
		7						
2		4				5		6
						9		
3			9	4			5	
		6						1
	9			3		7		

Answer on page 171.

37

				5		7		
		4			7		8	
7	2					3		6
			9	4				
	1	3	2		5	9	4	
			3	8				
5		2					3	8
	3		1			4		
		1		2				

Answer on page 172.

38

				7		4		
	9		2	6			7	
		8			1		5	
9	7	3				5		
	4						3	
		6				7	8	4
	6		5			3		
	8			2	6		1	
		7		9				

Answer on page 172.

39

3	7		2				6	
8				6				
		9	8		3			
						9	2	6
6		7				3		1
1	9	5						
			6		5	2		
				9				8
	4				2		3	5

Answer on page 172.

40

	4		3			2		
				7		5	8	
9			4		8		3	
6	3				2			8
				8				
4			5				7	2
	5		9		7			6
	9	4		2				
		2			3		4	

Answer on page 172.

41

		4		8				
	9			3	6			
3		7				2		
					9		7	
9	1						3	2
	7		2					
		3				9		8
			3	4			1	
			1		5			

Answer on page 172.

42

3		1					4	
	7		9			1	3	
								5
1		5			6	2		4
			7		2			
4		7	5			8		6
8								
	1	2			7		5	
	6					4		9

Answer on page 172.

43

			2		9			
		9				4		
	4		6		8		3	
9		8		5		7		1
5		7		3		8		4
	5		3		2		8	
		6				9		
			1		5			

Answer on page 173.

44

		7	3					
		4			5			3
3	6	1			8			2
1		6		8				
5								9
				1		3		6
9			4			6	8	7
4			9			2		
					3	9		

Answer on page 173.

45

			2		1	9		
		1				6	2	
	7	2		6			8	
					3	8		1
	8	3	1		7	5	6	
1		9	5					
	2			9		4	1	
	5	6				7		
		4	8		2			

Answer on page 173.

46

8	5	7	6					
	9				4			1
2		1			8			
		3				7	1	
	8		5	4	7		6	
	6	4				5		
			4			1		7
4			1				5	
					3	9	4	8

Answer on page 173.

47

8		6						4
			9			3		
3		9	5					1
			7				8	6
			4		3			
7	5				1			
5					6	8		9
1		8			9			
9						7		2

Answer on page 173.

48

	8		7		5			
				4			8	7
			6				9	5
2					4			3
	4	8				9	2	
3			9					4
4	9				6			
6	1			7				
			2		1		5	

Answer on page 173.

49

8	5		3		4			1
3		7			8		6	
						3	8	
	8				3			5
4		1				9		8
5			7				4	
	4	3						
	9		5			4		7
7			9		1		2	3

Answer on page 174.

50

7	8	1	2		4			5
		9	8					7
					5		1	
			4	1	7	3		
	4						8	
		3	5	2	8			
	7		3					
4					9	8		
8			1		6	9	7	2

Answer on page 174.

51

	8		9					1
9			1		6	4		5
		4				3		9
8				6	7		1	
		1				8		
	7		8	5				3
2		6				1		
4		8	5		9			7
7					4		9	

Answer on page 174.

52

	8				4		5	2
	6					4		
4					5		9	
	7	8		4	3			
	9	4	7		1	6	8	
			5	9		7	4	
	3		4					8
		2					6	
8	4		2				1	

Answer on page 174.

53

4				9	5		6	8
	5							9
					4	2		5
3			7				9	6
				4				
9	6				1			4
6		9	2					
8							1	
5	2		9	1				7

Answer on page 174.

54

9			3	5	1			6
						1	5	
		8			9			2
		4			7	5		
	1	3	9		8	2	6	
		9	6			8		
8			4			9		
	7	1						
4			5	1	2			8

Answer on page 174.

55

	4	7				5	6	
9								7
8				5				1
			1		7			
		3				8		
			3		4			
6				2				4
4								8
	8	1				7	9	

Answer on page 175.

56

		6	4		5		
4			2					
7		8		9		4		
		3		6	4		9	
5								4
	4		1	8		6		
		2		7		1		6
					8			5
		5		1		7		

Answer on page 175.

57

				9		2	8	6
4		6	8				5	
	8							
		3	1					8
6	4		9		8		3	5
1					3	9		
							7	
	6				4	5		2
2	9	1		5				

Answer on page 175.

58

1					4		3	
9		3		7		2		
	2				3	7		6
	8	1				5		
6			2		8			1
		2				3	6	
4		7	9				5	
		5		1		8		7
	3		7					9

Answer on page 175.

59

				3		7		
		9						4
	2		4	5	9			6
	3	7			2			
	9		5		7		6	
			9			4	7	
3			8	1	6		4	
1						3		
		4		7				

Answer on page 175.

60

			8					9
1	7		6		5		8	
			2					1
			5				6	
7	8		3		4		1	2
	3				9			
2					6			
	9		7		1		4	6
8					2			

Answer on page 175.

61

		4	8			3	9	1
	1	3	9	7			5	
		8			6			4
	2		5					
				4				
					3		6	
1			6			7		
	4			9	1	5	3	
5	9	7			2	6		

Answer on page 176.

62

					3	8	5	
6		2			3	8	5	
5	7	9	6					
7	5		9			4	8	
2			7		4			5
	9	4			5		3	2
					7	6	1	8
	4	7	8			5		9

Answer on page 176.

63

		9			8			
7		4						
					5	3	9	8
	7		6	5		1		
9			4		1			3
		6		8	9		5	
3	1	2	5					
						4		1
			2			5		

Answer on page 176.

64

					4	6		8
	9		1					
			5		8			3
	2	5	6			3		1
8		9			1	4	6	
7			4		3			
					7		2	
2		6	9					

Answer on page 176.

65

	9		3				8	2
	5			2	6	7		
6			9				3	5
	6		7					8
	4						2	
9					8		7	
5	8				7			3
		1	6	5			9	
7	2				1		6	

Answer on page 176.

66

		5	4				7	
		6	9		2	4		1
						3		
	7		8	4				3
8								6
6				5	1		2	
		1						
5		3	2		7	9		
	9				4	1		

Answer on page 176.

67

			3		6		5	
1	3			5			8	
		6						
			7				9	2
	8	9				3	1	
4	5				9			
						1		
	4			1			3	7
	7		9		8			

Answer on page 177.

68

		3			9		
			8		3	4		5
			6	2	1	3	7	
			2				8	
	9					7		
7				9				
8	6	1	4	7				
9		7	3		2			
	2					1		

Answer on page 177.

69

8	4			3				
		1		5				
			7				6	9
					8			1
	9	6	5		2	4	8	
5			1					
4	8				7			
				2		7		
				1			3	5

Answer on page 177.

70

7	9				6			
	6	8	1					
		3	4					
	5				9			2
8	3			4			6	9
1			8				7	
					4	3		
					3	7	2	
			7				5	8

Answer on page 177.

71

				4	3	7		
	7							9
		5		9			2	
4	6		9	5				2
5				7	4		1	9
	2			8		5		
	9						6	
		7	4	1				

Answer on page 177.

72

		8					4	
4				6		8		
	1	7			9	5		
	2		3	9				
8								9
				1	5		3	
		6	1			4	9	
		2		7				1
	5					3		

Answer on page 177.

73

			4	5	3		7	6
		4		2	6			
							1	
2	4		9				6	8
6	9				7		3	5
	5							
			5	6		7		
8	1		7	9	4			

Answer on page 178.

74

4			1	2	8		5	
				5		3		
	6					7	1	
		3						
6			5		9			3
						8		
	5	6					4	
		2		9				
	7		6	4	5			9

Answer on page 178.

75

		1			4			
2						6		8
	7		5				1	
3				2			8	
		2	1		9	4		
	6			5				3
	2				5		9	
8		3						7
			8			1		

Answer on page 178.

76

					8			
				6	5		4	
	8	6	2			5		1
	6		1					2
5								6
4					2		1	
1		3			7	9	6	
	4		3	9				
			8					

Answer on page 178.

77

3					2		8	
5		7						2
				4	8			
		1		9	7		3	8
4	9		8	3		1		
			9	7				
2						4		7
	7		2					9

Answer on page 178.

78

	6			3			8	5
	3		7	9				
	7	1		5	8			
				2		6		
	2							1
		6		1				
			5	7		1	9	
				8	9		5	
9	8			6			4	

Answer on page 178.

79

9	5				7			
		2	4					
3	1		5				6	
4			6			9		
		7			9			1
	6				1		5	8
					2	4		
			9				3	6

Answer on page 179.

80

	1		7	5				4
	5			4			2	
2	7					9		
	9	2						3
			9		6			
8						2	9	
		3					7	8
	8			6			4	
4				3	5		6	

Answer on page 179.

81

				8		2		1
			2		3		7	5
		6		7			9	
	8					1	6	3
5	3	7					4	
	5			1		3		
2	4		7		9			
8		1		3				

Answer on page 179.

82

9	6							5
		5		1	7			
1	4					2		
	5		4		6	8		
				5				
		4	9		1		3	
		8					7	2
			7	6		9		
2							5	1

Answer on page 179.

83

							8	
	5			6	3	9	1	
	8		2					5
	1			5				3
3			9		8			1
5				7			4	
8					7		9	
	6	1	5	9			3	
	9							

Answer on page 179.

84

8					1	3	6	9
	2		1		5		7		
	6	3						5	2
		9	7					6
1		2				4		7
3				4	8			
7	1					6	2	
		5		1		9		4
9	3	8	4					1

Answer on page 179.

85

	7		5	8				4
	3			6		1		
					9	5		
			7			8	4	
				3				
	4	7			8			
		2	1					
		5		4			7	
8				9	7		6	

Answer on page 180.

86

4								3
		1						
	5			6			4	
		5		3	6		2	9
1	2						6	8
9	6		5	1		4		
	9			4			5	
						8		
6								1

Answer on page 180.

87

2		4	3		7			
	6							3
					5	4	9	
1				5			8	
		9				6		
	2			9				7
	7	8	1					
4							2	
			4		3	8		9

Answer on page 180.

88

		7						
2				5	1			
		1	9		2			4
			4			8		7
	5		1		7	6		
9		6			5			
3			6		9	4		
			8	7				5
						2		

Answer on page 180.

89

8			4	2			5	
						4		
		5			1	7		
5	3				6	8		
	8		5		7		1	
		1	8				7	5
		2	1			5		
		8						
	4			3	5			2

Answer on page 180.

90

							8	
	9	7		3	6		1	
	8		1			4		3
								5
1			9		5			8
9								
2		1			9		4	
	7		3	5		8	9	
	3							

Answer on page 180.

91

	1			3		7	9	
			7	5				8
6								
		5				6	8	3
			3		2			
1	3	8				4		
								1
9				2	3			
	8	6		4			2	

Answer on page 181.

92

3		7					1	
	5							2
			6	7	2			
					4	9		
6			1	8	7			4
		8	9					
			2	3	6			
9							5	
	4					3		8

Answer on page 181.

93

	4	1	5					3
5			4				9	2
			8					
4				5	8	9		
		9				4		
		2	3	4				6
				6				
1	8				2			5
2					4	7	6	

Answer on page 181.

94

1		5	7					
9			2					
3	7					1		4
7		8	1					
				9				
					3	5		6
8		6					4	7
					8			5
					1	8		3

Answer on page 181.

95

		3		6	1			
	7					5		
					7	1	4	
7			1				8	5
	4						3	
8	6				9			7
	5	6	9					
		4					7	
			4	1		3		

Answer on page 181.

96

	4			1	6	2		
					9			3
2	8		4					
	5					8	9	
1								4
	3	8					7	
					5		6	7
7			3					
		6	9	8			3	

Answer on page 181.

97

	6					5	7	4
		1	9		7		6	
			1					7
8			6	4	2			1
4					3			
	3		5		6	2		
9	7	4					1	

Answer on page 182.

98

9		2	1	4		5		
	4				6			1
5					2			
	5					1		
	2						4	
		9					3	
			8					3
2			5				7	
		7		2	1	6		8

Answer on page 182.

99

4								3
		7				9		
	8		6		9		5	
		6	8		3	1		
				7				
		9	1		6	5		
	6		4		2		3	
		2				6		
8								2

Answer on page 182.

100

	3			9				
	6	2	4		7			
4	8				6			
1		6						9
		8				3		
3						4		1
			1				3	2
			6		5	8	1	
				4			5	

Answer on page 182.

101

3	2				1		7	9
				9		6		
				8			5	1
			1			2		
		8		5				
	7		3					
9	4	7						
		8	2					
7	6	5				9	8	

Answer on page 182.

102

7		2			6			3
			2			8		
	5				3			4
5		3					4	
	1					6		7
2			3				9	
		7		4				
4			8			1		5

Answer on page 182.

103

		8			1			
1		4	9					3
					5		4	
3					6	5		
	2			1			8	
		1	7					9
	1		5					
9					7	2		4
			4			8		

Answer on page 183.

104

			5			3	7	9
9		3			2			1
6		5						
		2		1				
1	6						8	4
				4		6		
						1		2
3			6			8		7
7	2	1			5			

Answer on page 183.

105

		8		7				
		9				5		2
	5						9	
4		5		2				
			4	6	9			
				1		6		4
	8						5	
6		2				7		
				4		3		

Answer on page 183.

106

		3	2		4			
	9	8		3				7
							4	
			9			7		6
		9	6		7	2		
5		7			2			
	5							
2				7		1	9	
			1		3	8		

Answer on page 183.

107

			9		4			
		3				5		
	1	9				2	7	
5				7				2
			3		8			
4				1				6
	8	5				9	1	
		7				3		
			1		7			

Answer on page 183.

108

	3			4		9		
								5
			5			3	2	
5					6			7
	2		7	9	1		5	
4			3					1
	4	3			7			
9								
		8		2			6	

Answer on page 183.

109

9				2			6	8
1	6						9	
		4			3		5	
					4	9	2	
	4	3	5					
	7		3			6		
	9						1	3
3	1			7				9

Answer on page 184.

110

	1				6			
7					5	6		
	6		2			8		7
			7	2				4
		5				3		
4				8	1			
1		7			2		6	
		2	6					5
			3				7	

Answer on page 184.

III

				1				
		9	2		3	4		
8		7				3		1
	1						8	
7			9					2
	2						5	
4		8				2		9
		3	9		2	1		
			7					

Answer on page 184.

112

			4		5	1		9
	9		1					2
6						4		
	7				1		4	
			9		4			
	5		8				2	
		8						3
7					8		5	
1		3	5		9			

Answer on page 184.

113

9	3		2			4		
2			5	4	7			
	4						5	
				4				6
7								3
6			8					
	2						8	
			7	8	5			1
		1			3		4	5

Answer on page 184.

114

	5						3	
6		9			7			5
	8		6					
		5		6			9	
			2	3	9			
	4			8		7		
					6		4	
5			9			6		8
	2						7	

Answer on page 184.

115

	1			6		4	8	
				8			5	1
		9				3		
	6	5			3			
			5		2			
			8			2	9	
		1				7		
4	5			2				
	3	8		9			1	

Answer on page 185.

116

					3			
1		7		9				2
	3	4			1			
		2		4		9		
3	9						8	1
		1		3		6		
			5			2	6	
2				1		7		5
			9					

Answer on page 185.

117

9	5			2				
6			7				8	
		7		8	6			
					8	2	6	
	7						5	
	3	6	5					
			2	7		9		
	8				3			4
			6				7	1

Answer on page 185.

118

2				4				8
	1				9	7		
					7		9	
			3			4	1	
1								9
	2	7			6			
	3		7					
		8	2				5	
5				9				4

Answer on page 185.

119

5	3							9
4	8		2				1	
					7	2		
	4				9	6		
		1	6				7	
		6	8					
	5				6		8	1
9							6	5

Answer on page 185.

120

	3		4		2		5	
5				3				8
		1				9		
7								9
	2			5			8	
3								4
		6				2		
2				6				3
	1		8		9		7	

Answer on page 185.

121

4		1				3		
	2		5					
6		7						1
		4		3	7	6		
				1				
		8	6	4		5		
8						4		5
					9		3	
		9				8		6

Answer on page 186.

122

		9			1		4	8
		8		7				
7						3		
		5			8	9		
	9			5			7	
		2	3			5		
		6						1
				2		4		
3	5		4			2		

Answer on page 186.

123

		5			8			7
					4		8	
3				5		9		
					9		4	1
		7				5		
8	9		1					
		6		9				2
	1		2					
2			7			6		

Answer on page 186.

124

			7					
6		2				1	9	
		8		4	6	2		
						3	8	
8			2		3			9
	6	9						
		3	5	8		6		
	7	5				8		2
					4			

Answer on page 186.

125

					1			
	4			5	2		9	
		9				6		
3	6		5		7			
	1			3			2	
			1		4		8	7
		5				8		
	2		8	4			5	
			2					

Answer on page 186.

126

2	6							5
		8			5	7	9	
			4	6				
1					3		5	
		9				3		
	2		5					9
				4	7			
	7	3	8			1		
5							7	2

Answer on page 186.

127

9					5			2
	5			9			1	
		6	4			5		
1						6		
	7						2	
		4						8
		5			3	4		
	9			7			8	
4			6					1

Answer on page 187.

128

6			1		9			
7	9						6	
				5		9		8
			9					1
	2	9		6		4	7	
4					2			
8		4		2				
	6						5	2
			3		8			7

Answer on page 187.

129

		8		7				
		5	9			3		
	4				1		6	9
		6					9	
1								5
	8					2		
3	6		4				7	
		7			8	6		
				2		4		

Answer on page 187.

130

6			5					1
	9							
5	4		8					
1		2	7	8			4	
4	7						2	8
	6			2	4	3		9
					3		8	6
							1	
2				6				4

Answer on page 187.

131

				3				6
					7	9		
4	8		2			3		
5					3		9	8
			1					
2	9		8					4
		7			4		6	5
		9	6					
1				2				

Answer on page 187.

132

	7			4			8	
4								2
	1	6	9			3		
		8	2	9				
	6						9	
				8	4	2		
		3			8	1	6	
7								4
	4			5			3	

Answer on page 187.

133

							8	
8		1			6		5	3
				8	2			
	6		5			7	1	
	5	2				3	6	
	7	9			4		2	
			6	5				
7	1		8			2		5
	3							

Answer on page 188.

134

			6	9		4		
1		8	5					9
				7		5	6	
4		9	7	2				
				5	6	1		4
	2	1		8				
8					7	2		3
		6		1	3			

Answer on page 188.

135

2	5				3		6	
		1		4	6		8	
						5		
				8		6	3	
		5	3		7	9		
	8	3		1				
		2						
	4		2	7		8		
	9		6				4	2

Answer on page 188.

136

7			9					4
	6				7			
	1	3					5	
			7	1				5
		5				8		
1				6	4			
	2					9	3	
			8				4	
8					1			7

Answer on page 188.

137

	2				9		4	
	8			7				
		5	4					7
		8		2			1	9
				8				
1	4			9		8		
7					5	6		
				4			2	
	1		8				7	

Answer on page 188.

138

5				4				6
	3				9		7	
			8		1			
	1	8				2		
2				6				5
		6				8	9	
			1		6			
	6		7				5	
7				8				4

Answer on page 188.

139

		9	2	6		1		
2			4			3	7	
					9			
	7			8	4			
6								5
			5	2			1	
			1					
	3	7			6			4
		8		7	2	6		

Answer on page 189.

140

				6				
		6	2		4	9		
	7						4	
	3		9		1		8	
2				3				4
	9		6		2		5	
	8						7	
		9	8		3	1		
				2				

Answer on page 189.

141

4				1				7
				8	6	2		3
	5		3					
		9						
		5	7		3	9		
						1		
					1		7	
7		6	8	9				
3				7				5

Answer on page 189.

142

2							5	
	7			6	8	2		
4			5					
		8		3		1		
	5						7	
		9		7		8		
					6			7
		1	7	2			9	
	9							8

Answer on page 189.

143

7			1		4			
							7	
	9		8	2		5		
	2							8
4		1		6		9		7
6							5	
		6		4	9		1	
	3							
			7		3			9

Answer on page 189.

144

1	4			6		9		
			2		8			
		9					3	7
						7	6	
			6	2	4			
	9	1						
2	7					1		
			8		9			
		3		1			4	8

Answer on page 189.

145

		7	8					
		2		3	5			
					2		1	4
	1	8						7
	4						3	
2						4	6	
7	8		5					
			2	9		6		
					4	9		

Answer on page 190.

146

					3	2		
	8			2		7	5	
			5				6	9
		7						4
	9			5			3	
3						8		
6	7				4			
	5	8		3			9	
		1	6					

Answer on page 190.

147

		3	8		7	2		
	4						8	
			6		1			
2		4				7		8
				9				
5		8				3		4
			2		3			
	6						7	
		7	9		6	1		

Answer on page 190.

148

2					4		7	
		7						8
		3	1	6				
		5			3		8	
		9		2		3		
	6		5			2		
				7	6	1		
1						8		
	5		9					2

Answer on page 190.

149

			8		6		7	
8								
9	3				2			5
1		9			3			
	6	8				9	1	
			6			3		8
5			4				6	2
								1
	4		3		8		5	

Answer on page 190.

150

	2			3				6
	6			4	1	5		
		1	9					
6	9	5				7		
		7				6	3	9
					3	2		
		3	7	6			1	
4				1			5	

Answer on page 190.

151

	7		9		8		5	
6				3				4
3			5		2			7
	2			9			4	
8			4		3			6
1				7				2
	5		8		1		7	

Answer on page 191.

152

						6		2
5								7
			6	5			4	
7				4	2		9	
	6		9		1		3	
	8		3	6				4
	5			8	3			
6								1
1		9						

Answer on page 191.

153

							1	
4							1	
	7		2					
				1	4			5
	2				7			9
		8		9		6		
9			5				7	
1			3	8				
					6		5	
	8							7

Answer on page 191.

154

	8				1			
	2		9	3				6
		4					5	
	3			9				8
2								4
7				5			3	
	6					2		
4				1	5		7	
			2				1	

Answer on page 191.

155

			7		2			
		5		9		6		
	4			3			8	
5								8
	2	1				9	3	
9								4
	6			5			7	
		4		1		2		
			8		3			

Answer on page 191.

156

6	3		1				2	5
		1	2	9		3		
							6	2
	6			8			1	
8	7							
		4		5	9	2		
2	5				4		3	1

Answer on page 191.

157

			7				3	
			8			9		5
				1	5		8	
7	8					5		
		3		4		1		
		6					9	2
	3		1	6				
1		9			7			
	6				9			

Answer on page 192.

158

			5					
							1	2
	2	5				9	4	
		1	6		5		2	
	4			7			8	
	6		2		8	3		
	8	4				6	9	
9	1							
					9			

Answer on page 192.

159

			2					
	2			8		4	5	9
4	6				3			
2		1						
	4						2	
						5		6
			4				1	5
1	5	9		3			4	
					7			

Answer on page 192.

160

					6	3	8	
	1		3	7				
5								6
	8		2		7			
		5				4		
			6		1		9	
8								7
				9	8		3	
	3	4	5					

Answer on page 192.

161

			6		3		7	
4					5			
		2		9		3		
9	3							1
		8				9		
7							6	3
		5		6		8		
			7					2
	1		9		2			

Answer on page 192.

1

6	9	1	3	5	2	8	7	4
7	3	8	6	9	4	1	2	5
4	2	5	7	8	1	3	9	6
5	1	3	8	6	7	9	4	2
8	6	7	4	2	9	5	3	1
9	4	2	5	1	3	7	6	8
2	7	9	1	4	5	6	8	3
3	5	6	2	7	8	4	1	9
1	8	4	9	3	6	2	5	7

4

5	7	1	6	9	4	8	3	2
9	2	8	7	1	3	4	5	6
3	6	4	5	8	2	1	7	9
2	1	3	4	5	8	9	6	7
7	4	6	3	2	9	5	1	8
8	9	5	1	6	7	3	2	4
4	5	2	8	7	1	6	9	3
1	8	7	9	3	6	2	4	5
6	3	9	2	4	5	7	8	1

2

6	9	5	1	8	3	7	4	2
8	7	3	4	5	2	1	6	9
4	2	1	9	6	7	3	5	8
1	5	6	3	9	4	2	8	7
9	8	7	5	2	6	4	1	3
2	3	4	7	1	8	5	9	6
3	4	9	6	7	5	8	2	1
5	1	8	2	3	9	6	7	4
7	6	2	8	4	1	9	3	5

5

5	3	8	4	7	2	1	6	9
7	1	9	5	3	6	2	4	8
6	4	2	1	9	8	7	3	5
1	6	5	3	8	4	9	7	2
8	9	4	2	1	7	6	5	3
3	2	7	9	6	5	4	8	1
9	7	6	8	2	3	5	1	4
2	5	3	7	4	1	8	9	6
4	8	1	6	5	9	3	2	7

3

6	1	4	3	5	7	2	8	9
3	5	9	1	8	2	6	7	4
8	7	2	6	9	4	5	1	3
2	3	7	9	6	5	8	4	1
4	6	8	2	3	1	9	5	7
5	9	1	4	7	8	3	2	6
9	8	5	7	1	6	4	3	2
1	2	6	5	4	3	7	9	8
7	4	3	8	2	9	1	6	5

6

5	6	1	3	7	8	9	4	2
9	2	3	1	4	5	6	8	7
8	4	7	2	9	6	1	5	3
6	3	8	4	2	1	5	7	9
1	7	4	9	5	3	2	6	8
2	9	5	8	6	7	4	3	1
7	1	2	5	3	4	8	9	6
4	8	6	7	1	9	3	2	5
3	5	9	6	8	2	7	1	4

7

2	6	5	1	4	7	3	9	8
7	1	9	3	5	8	6	4	2
8	3	4	9	2	6	7	1	5
1	4	8	6	9	5	2	3	7
9	7	6	2	8	3	4	5	1
5	2	3	7	1	4	8	6	9
3	8	7	5	6	9	1	2	4
6	5	1	4	7	2	9	8	3
4	9	2	8	3	1	5	7	6

10

5	2	3	1	6	7	8	9	4
7	4	1	3	8	9	5	2	6
9	6	8	5	4	2	7	1	3
3	7	9	6	2	1	4	5	8
6	8	2	7	5	4	9	3	1
4	1	5	8	9	3	2	6	7
2	3	6	4	7	5	1	8	9
1	9	7	2	3	8	6	4	5
8	5	4	9	1	6	3	7	2

8

5	2	6	3	9	4	7	1	8
4	7	3	1	2	8	5	9	6
1	9	8	6	7	5	2	4	3
6	1	2	7	3	9	8	5	4
9	5	4	2	8	6	1	3	7
3	8	7	5	4	1	9	6	2
7	6	1	8	5	3	4	2	9
8	4	5	9	6	2	3	7	1
2	3	9	4	1	7	6	8	5

11

6	7	4	5	8	9	2	1	3
8	5	2	3	7	1	6	9	4
9	3	1	4	6	2	5	7	8
5	1	7	9	4	3	8	6	2
3	2	9	8	5	6	7	4	1
4	8	6	2	1	7	3	5	9
7	6	3	1	9	8	4	2	5
2	9	5	7	3	4	1	8	6
1	4	8	6	2	5	9	3	7

9

9	5	3	8	6	2	1	4	7
1	4	8	7	5	3	6	9	2
7	6	2	9	1	4	8	5	3
4	2	6	5	8	1	3	7	9
5	1	9	6	3	7	4	2	8
3	8	7	4	2	9	5	6	1
6	9	4	3	7	8	2	1	5
2	3	5	1	9	6	7	8	4
8	7	1	2	4	5	9	3	6

12

5	3	1	4	8	9	2	7	6
8	7	2	5	6	1	3	4	9
6	9	4	3	2	7	5	1	8
3	2	7	8	4	5	9	6	1
4	5	9	6	1	2	7	8	3
1	6	8	9	7	3	4	5	2
2	4	5	1	9	8	6	3	7
9	1	3	7	5	6	8	2	4
7	8	6	2	3	4	1	9	5

Answers

13

5	4	1	2	9	7	8	6	3
2	7	8	1	3	6	4	9	5
9	3	6	4	8	5	1	7	2
8	6	3	9	5	2	7	4	1
1	2	7	6	4	8	5	3	9
4	9	5	3	7	1	6	2	8
7	1	4	5	2	9	3	8	6
6	8	2	7	1	3	9	5	4
3	5	9	8	6	4	2	1	7

16

7	2	9	6	1	3	5	8	4
1	8	4	2	5	9	7	3	6
5	3	6	7	8	4	1	9	2
2	7	1	3	4	8	9	6	5
6	4	3	9	7	5	8	2	1
8	9	5	1	6	2	3	4	7
3	5	2	4	9	7	6	1	8
4	1	8	5	3	6	2	7	9
9	6	7	8	2	1	4	5	3

14

4	9	2	6	1	3	5	7	8
8	7	3	4	5	2	1	6	9
5	6	1	9	8	7	2	4	3
9	2	7	5	4	8	6	3	1
6	3	4	1	2	9	8	5	7
1	8	5	7	3	6	9	2	4
7	4	8	2	9	5	3	1	6
2	1	9	3	6	4	7	8	5
3	5	6	8	7	1	4	9	2

17

1	3	7	8	5	2	9	6	4
5	9	4	7	3	6	1	8	2
2	6	8	1	9	4	3	5	7
8	4	3	9	2	7	6	1	5
9	7	1	6	8	5	2	4	3
6	5	2	3	4	1	8	7	9
4	8	5	2	1	3	7	9	6
3	1	6	5	7	9	4	2	8
7	2	9	4	6	8	5	3	1

15

5	1	9	8	3	7	2	4	6
3	6	7	2	4	5	9	1	8
8	4	2	6	9	1	7	5	3
1	9	8	3	7	2	4	6	5
7	3	6	9	5	4	8	2	1
4	2	5	1	6	8	3	9	7
9	7	4	5	8	6	1	3	2
6	8	1	4	2	3	5	7	9
2	5	3	7	1	9	6	8	4

18

8	7	5	2	6	3	1	9	4
4	6	3	7	9	1	8	5	2
2	9	1	5	4	8	3	6	7
6	2	8	1	5	4	9	7	3
7	1	9	3	8	6	2	4	5
3	5	4	9	2	7	6	8	1
9	3	2	6	7	5	4	1	8
1	8	7	4	3	9	5	2	6
5	4	6	8	1	2	7	3	9

19

2	9	4	6	5	1	3	8	7
5	8	3	2	9	7	1	6	4
7	1	6	3	8	4	2	5	9
9	6	7	4	1	3	8	2	5
3	2	8	5	7	6	9	4	1
1	4	5	8	2	9	6	7	3
6	5	9	1	4	2	7	3	8
4	3	1	7	6	8	5	9	2
8	7	2	9	3	5	4	1	6

22

5	2	4	3	9	1	6	8	7
3	9	6	4	8	7	1	5	2
8	1	7	6	2	5	9	3	4
2	7	1	5	4	9	3	6	8
4	3	9	8	7	6	5	2	1
6	8	5	2	1	3	7	4	9
1	5	2	7	6	4	8	9	3
7	4	3	9	5	8	2	1	6
9	6	8	1	3	2	4	7	5

20

7	9	3	1	8	5	4	6	2
4	1	2	3	6	7	9	5	8
8	5	6	9	2	4	7	3	1
5	3	8	2	7	6	1	4	9
6	7	9	4	5	1	8	2	3
2	4	1	8	9	3	6	7	5
3	6	4	5	1	9	2	8	7
1	8	7	6	3	2	5	9	4
9	2	5	7	4	8	3	1	6

23

2	5	3	7	9	6	8	1	4
8	6	1	2	5	4	3	7	9
9	4	7	3	8	1	6	2	5
1	9	2	5	4	3	7	6	8
4	8	5	6	7	2	1	9	3
3	7	6	9	1	8	4	5	2
6	2	9	4	3	7	5	8	1
5	1	4	8	6	9	2	3	7
7	3	8	1	2	5	9	4	6

21

6	3	8	5	7	9	1	2	4
4	5	2	1	3	6	8	7	9
7	1	9	2	4	8	6	5	3
1	4	5	8	9	2	7	3	6
2	9	3	7	6	5	4	1	8
8	6	7	4	1	3	2	9	5
3	8	1	6	5	7	9	4	2
9	2	4	3	8	1	5	6	7
5	7	6	9	2	4	3	8	1

24

2	4	9	6	5	1	3	8	7
8	6	3	7	4	9	5	1	2
5	7	1	2	3	8	6	9	4
7	1	6	3	2	4	8	5	9
9	5	4	8	6	7	1	2	3
3	8	2	9	1	5	4	7	6
4	2	8	5	9	6	7	3	1
1	3	7	4	8	2	9	6	5
6	9	5	1	7	3	2	4	8

Answers

25

9	1	7	5	3	6	4	8	2
6	2	4	8	1	9	3	5	7
5	8	3	7	2	4	9	6	1
3	4	1	9	7	5	8	2	6
7	5	8	3	6	2	1	9	4
2	9	6	4	8	1	5	7	3
4	6	2	1	5	8	7	3	9
1	3	5	6	9	7	2	4	8
8	7	9	2	4	3	6	1	5

28

2	1	9	6	8	4	3	7	5
4	8	3	5	9	7	2	6	1
6	5	7	1	2	3	8	4	9
1	7	5	2	3	9	6	8	4
3	6	4	7	1	8	9	5	2
8	9	2	4	5	6	1	3	7
7	3	1	9	6	5	4	2	8
9	4	8	3	7	2	5	1	6
5	2	6	8	4	1	7	9	3

26

9	1	5	7	6	2	4	3	8
7	3	4	1	5	8	6	2	9
8	2	6	4	3	9	1	5	7
5	9	7	6	8	4	2	1	3
3	8	1	2	9	5	7	4	6
4	6	2	3	1	7	8	9	5
6	7	3	5	4	1	9	8	2
2	4	9	8	7	3	5	6	1
1	5	8	9	2	6	3	7	4

29

4	7	1	5	2	3	6	9	8
3	6	8	7	1	9	4	2	5
9	2	5	8	6	4	1	3	7
2	1	6	3	9	8	7	5	4
5	8	9	4	7	1	2	6	3
7	4	3	2	5	6	9	8	1
6	3	7	1	8	2	5	4	9
8	5	2	9	4	7	3	1	6
1	9	4	6	3	5	8	7	2

27

4	8	1	7	3	5	9	2	6
6	7	2	4	8	9	3	5	1
5	9	3	6	2	1	8	4	7
1	5	9	3	4	7	6	8	2
8	2	4	9	5	6	7	1	3
3	6	7	8	1	2	5	9	4
9	1	6	2	7	8	4	3	5
7	3	5	1	9	4	2	6	8
2	4	8	5	6	3	1	7	9

30

6	1	7	8	4	9	5	3	2
2	5	8	1	3	6	9	7	4
4	9	3	5	2	7	6	1	8
7	8	6	3	5	2	4	9	1
1	3	4	7	9	8	2	6	5
5	2	9	4	6	1	7	8	3
8	4	5	6	7	3	1	2	9
3	7	2	9	1	4	8	5	6
9	6	1	2	8	5	3	4	7

31

1	8	5	2	9	4	7	6	3
2	4	6	7	3	5	1	8	9
9	7	3	6	1	8	2	4	5
4	9	1	3	5	6	8	2	7
6	5	8	4	7	2	9	3	1
3	2	7	1	8	9	6	5	4
5	3	9	8	2	7	4	1	6
8	1	4	9	6	3	5	7	2
7	6	2	5	4	1	3	9	8

34

4	7	5	8	3	6	1	9	2
3	6	8	9	2	1	5	7	4
2	9	1	7	4	5	6	3	8
8	3	6	5	9	4	2	1	7
7	2	4	6	1	3	8	5	9
1	5	9	2	8	7	4	6	3
9	8	7	1	6	2	3	4	5
6	4	2	3	5	9	7	8	1
5	1	3	4	7	8	9	2	6

32

9	2	1	4	8	7	5	6	3
4	5	6	2	1	3	8	7	9
7	3	8	5	9	6	4	1	2
3	1	4	8	6	2	7	9	5
2	6	9	3	7	5	1	8	4
5	8	7	9	4	1	2	3	6
6	9	5	1	2	8	3	4	7
8	7	3	6	5	4	9	2	1
1	4	2	7	3	9	6	5	8

35

9	1	3	5	6	7	8	2	4
8	7	2	1	4	9	5	6	3
5	6	4	2	8	3	1	7	9
2	4	8	9	5	6	7	3	1
6	9	7	8	3	1	4	5	2
1	3	5	4	7	2	6	9	8
4	5	6	3	2	8	9	1	7
7	2	9	6	1	4	3	8	5
3	8	1	7	9	5	2	4	6

33

1	4	2	8	6	5	9	3	7
9	8	6	7	2	3	1	4	5
7	3	5	1	9	4	6	2	8
8	2	7	4	5	9	3	1	6
4	6	1	3	7	8	2	5	9
3	5	9	2	1	6	7	8	4
5	9	8	6	3	2	4	7	1
2	7	4	9	8	1	5	6	3
6	1	3	5	4	7	8	9	2

36

7	8	3	1	9	2	4	6	5
5	4	2	3	6	8	1	7	9
6	1	9	5	7	4	2	3	8
9	6	7	4	1	5	8	2	3
2	3	4	7	8	9	5	1	6
8	5	1	6	2	3	9	4	7
3	7	8	9	4	1	6	5	2
4	2	6	8	5	7	3	9	1
1	9	5	2	3	6	7	8	4

Answers

37

1	6	8	3	5	2	7	9	4
3	5	4	6	9	7	2	8	1
7	2	9	8	1	4	3	5	6
2	7	5	9	4	1	8	6	3
8	1	3	2	6	5	9	4	7
9	4	6	7	3	8	5	1	2
5	9	2	4	7	6	1	3	8
6	3	7	1	8	9	4	2	5
4	8	1	5	2	3	6	7	9

40

5	4	8	3	6	1	2	9	7
3	1	6	2	7	9	5	8	4
9	2	7	4	5	8	6	3	1
6	3	1	7	9	2	4	5	8
2	7	5	1	8	4	3	6	9
4	8	9	5	3	6	1	7	2
1	5	3	9	4	7	8	2	6
8	9	4	6	2	5	7	1	3
7	6	2	8	1	3	9	4	5

38

6	1	2	8	7	5	4	9	3
4	9	5	2	6	3	1	7	8
7	3	8	9	4	1	6	5	2
9	7	3	4	8	2	5	6	1
8	4	1	6	5	7	2	3	9
5	2	6	1	3	9	7	8	4
2	6	9	5	1	8	3	4	7
3	8	4	7	2	6	9	1	5
1	5	7	3	9	4	8	2	6

41

5	6	4	7	8	2	3	9	1
2	9	1	5	3	6	4	8	7
3	8	7	4	9	1	2	6	5
6	3	2	1	5	9	8	7	4
9	1	5	8	7	4	6	3	2
4	7	8	2	6	3	1	5	9
1	5	3	6	2	7	9	4	8
8	2	9	3	4	5	7	1	6
7	4	6	9	1	8	5	2	3

39

3	7	4	2	5	1	8	6	9
8	1	2	4	6	9	5	7	3
5	6	9	8	7	3	1	4	2
4	3	8	5	1	7	9	2	6
6	2	7	9	4	8	3	5	1
1	9	5	3	2	6	4	8	7
7	8	1	6	3	5	2	9	4
2	5	3	7	9	4	6	1	8
9	4	6	1	8	2	7	3	5

42

3	8	1	6	2	5	9	4	7
5	7	6	9	8	4	1	3	2
2	4	9	3	7	1	6	8	5
1	3	5	8	9	6	2	7	4
6	9	8	7	4	2	5	1	3
4	2	7	5	1	3	8	9	6
8	5	4	2	3	9	7	6	1
9	1	2	4	6	7	3	5	8
7	6	3	1	5	8	4	2	9

43

3	7	5	2	4	9	6	1	8
6	8	9	5	1	3	4	7	2
1	4	2	6	7	8	5	3	9
9	3	8	4	5	6	7	2	1
4	6	1	8	2	7	3	9	5
5	2	7	9	3	1	8	6	4
7	5	4	3	9	2	1	8	6
2	1	6	7	8	4	9	5	3
8	9	3	1	6	5	2	4	7

44

2	5	7	3	4	6	1	9	8
8	9	4	1	2	5	7	6	3
3	6	1	7	9	8	4	5	2
1	3	6	2	8	9	5	7	4
5	4	2	6	3	7	8	1	9
7	8	9	5	1	4	3	2	6
9	1	3	4	5	2	6	8	7
4	7	8	9	6	1	2	3	5
6	2	5	8	7	3	9	4	1

45

6	3	8	2	5	1	9	7	4
4	9	1	7	3	8	6	2	5
5	7	2	4	6	9	1	8	3
7	6	5	9	2	3	8	4	1
2	8	3	1	4	7	5	6	9
1	4	9	5	8	6	2	3	7
3	2	7	6	9	5	4	1	8
8	5	6	3	1	4	7	9	2
9	1	4	8	7	2	3	5	6

46

8	5	7	6	3	1	4	9	2
3	9	6	2	5	4	8	7	1
2	4	1	9	7	8	6	3	5
5	2	3	8	9	6	7	1	4
1	8	9	5	4	7	2	6	3
7	6	4	3	1	2	5	8	9
9	3	8	4	6	5	1	2	7
4	7	2	1	8	9	3	5	6
6	1	5	7	2	3	9	4	8

47

8	1	6	3	2	7	9	5	4
2	7	5	9	1	4	3	6	8
3	4	9	5	6	8	2	7	1
4	9	3	7	5	2	1	8	6
6	8	1	4	9	3	5	2	7
7	5	2	6	8	1	4	9	3
5	2	7	1	4	6	8	3	9
1	3	8	2	7	9	6	4	5
9	6	4	8	3	5	7	1	2

48

9	8	6	7	3	5	1	4	2
5	2	3	1	4	9	6	8	7
1	7	4	6	8	2	3	9	5
2	6	9	8	1	4	5	7	3
7	4	8	5	6	3	9	2	1
3	5	1	9	2	7	8	6	4
4	9	2	3	5	6	7	1	8
6	1	5	4	7	8	2	3	9
8	3	7	2	9	1	4	5	6

49

8	5	6	3	2	4	7	9	1
3	2	7	1	9	8	5	6	4
9	1	4	6	5	7	3	8	2
6	8	9	4	1	3	2	7	5
4	7	1	2	6	5	9	3	8
5	3	2	7	8	9	1	4	6
1	4	3	8	7	2	6	5	9
2	9	8	5	3	6	4	1	7
7	6	5	9	4	1	8	2	3

52

7	8	9	3	6	4	1	5	2
1	6	5	9	8	2	4	3	7
4	2	3	1	7	5	8	9	6
5	7	8	6	4	3	9	2	1
3	9	4	7	2	1	6	8	5
2	1	6	5	9	8	7	4	3
6	3	1	4	5	9	2	7	8
9	5	2	8	1	7	3	6	4
8	4	7	2	3	6	5	1	9

50

7	8	1	2	3	4	6	9	5
5	2	9	8	6	1	4	3	7
3	6	4	9	7	5	2	1	8
6	5	8	4	1	7	3	2	9
2	4	7	6	9	3	5	8	1
1	9	3	5	2	8	7	4	6
9	7	6	3	8	2	1	5	4
4	1	2	7	5	9	8	6	3
8	3	5	1	4	6	9	7	2

53

4	3	2	1	9	5	7	6	8
7	5	8	3	6	2	1	4	9
1	9	6	8	7	4	2	3	5
3	4	1	7	2	8	5	9	6
2	8	5	6	4	9	3	7	1
9	6	7	5	3	1	8	2	4
6	1	9	2	8	7	4	5	3
8	7	3	4	5	6	9	1	2
5	2	4	9	1	3	6	8	7

51

3	8	5	9	4	2	7	6	1
9	2	7	1	3	6	4	8	5
1	6	4	7	8	5	3	2	9
8	3	9	4	6	7	5	1	2
5	4	1	2	9	3	8	7	6
6	7	2	8	5	1	9	4	3
2	9	6	3	7	8	1	5	4
4	1	8	5	2	9	6	3	7
7	5	3	6	1	4	2	9	8

54

9	4	2	3	5	1	7	8	6
3	6	7	2	8	4	1	5	9
1	5	8	7	6	9	4	3	2
6	8	4	1	2	7	5	9	3
5	1	3	9	4	8	2	6	7
7	2	9	6	3	5	8	1	4
8	3	5	4	7	6	9	2	1
2	7	1	8	9	3	6	4	5
4	9	6	5	1	2	3	7	8

55

1	4	7	2	3	8	5	6	9
9	3	5	4	1	6	2	8	7
8	2	6	7	5	9	4	3	1
5	6	4	1	8	7	9	2	3
7	1	3	5	9	2	8	4	6
2	9	8	3	6	4	1	7	5
6	7	9	8	2	1	3	5	4
4	5	2	9	7	3	6	1	8
3	8	1	6	4	5	7	9	2

58

1	7	8	6	2	4	9	3	5
9	6	3	5	7	1	2	8	4
5	2	4	8	9	3	7	1	6
3	8	1	4	6	7	5	9	2
6	5	9	2	3	8	4	7	1
7	4	2	1	5	9	3	6	8
4	1	7	9	8	2	6	5	3
2	9	5	3	1	6	8	4	7
8	3	6	7	4	5	1	2	9

56

3	2	6	8	4	1	5	7	9
4	9	1	2	5	7	3	6	8
7	5	8	3	9	6	4	2	1
8	1	3	5	6	4	2	9	7
5	6	9	7	3	2	8	1	4
2	4	7	1	8	9	6	5	3
9	3	2	4	7	5	1	8	6
1	7	4	6	2	8	9	3	5
6	8	5	9	1	3	7	4	2

59

5	4	8	6	3	1	7	2	9
6	1	9	7	2	8	5	3	4
7	2	3	4	5	9	1	8	6
4	3	7	1	6	2	8	9	5
8	9	1	5	4	7	2	6	3
2	6	5	9	8	3	4	7	1
3	5	2	8	1	6	9	4	7
1	7	6	2	9	4	3	5	8
9	8	4	3	7	5	6	1	2

57

3	1	5	4	9	7	2	8	6
4	2	6	8	3	1	7	5	9
7	8	9	5	6	2	3	1	4
9	7	3	1	2	5	4	6	8
6	4	2	9	7	8	1	3	5
1	5	8	6	4	3	9	2	7
5	3	4	2	8	9	6	7	1
8	6	7	3	1	4	5	9	2
2	9	1	7	5	6	8	4	3

60

3	5	4	8	1	7	6	2	9
1	7	2	6	9	5	3	8	4
9	6	8	2	4	3	7	5	1
4	2	1	5	7	8	9	6	3
7	8	9	3	6	4	5	1	2
6	3	5	1	2	9	4	7	8
2	1	7	4	3	6	8	9	5
5	9	3	7	8	1	2	4	6
8	4	6	9	5	2	1	3	7

61

7	6	4	8	2	5	3	9	1
2	1	3	9	7	4	8	5	6
9	5	8	3	1	6	2	7	4
3	2	1	5	6	9	4	8	7
6	8	5	1	4	7	9	2	3
4	7	9	2	8	3	1	6	5
1	3	2	6	5	8	7	4	9
8	4	6	7	9	1	5	3	2
5	9	7	4	3	2	6	1	8

64

3	1	7	2	9	4	6	5	8
5	9	8	1	3	6	2	4	7
6	4	2	5	7	8	9	1	3
4	2	5	6	8	9	3	7	1
1	6	3	7	4	2	5	8	9
8	7	9	3	5	1	4	6	2
7	5	1	4	2	3	8	9	6
9	3	4	8	6	7	1	2	5
2	8	6	9	1	5	7	3	4

62

4	8	3	5	7	1	2	9	6
6	1	2	4	9	3	8	5	7
5	7	9	6	2	8	1	4	3
7	5	6	9	3	2	4	8	1
2	3	1	7	8	4	9	6	5
8	9	4	1	6	5	7	3	2
9	2	5	3	4	7	6	1	8
3	4	7	8	1	6	5	2	9
1	6	8	2	5	9	3	7	4

65

1	9	4	3	7	5	6	8	2
3	5	8	1	2	6	7	4	9
6	7	2	9	8	4	1	3	5
2	6	3	7	1	9	4	5	8
8	4	7	5	6	3	9	2	1
9	1	5	2	4	8	3	7	6
5	8	6	4	9	7	2	1	3
4	3	1	6	5	2	8	9	7
7	2	9	8	3	1	5	6	4

63

5	3	9	1	2	8	6	7	4
7	8	4	9	3	6	2	1	5
2	6	1	7	4	5	3	9	8
8	7	3	6	5	2	1	4	9
9	2	5	4	7	1	8	6	3
1	4	6	3	8	9	7	5	2
3	1	2	5	6	4	9	8	7
6	5	7	8	9	3	4	2	1
4	9	8	2	1	7	5	3	6

66

9	1	5	4	8	3	6	7	2
3	8	6	9	7	2	4	5	1
4	2	7	1	6	5	3	8	9
1	7	2	8	4	6	5	9	3
8	5	4	3	2	9	7	1	6
6	3	9	7	5	1	8	2	4
7	4	1	6	9	8	2	3	5
5	6	3	2	1	7	9	4	8
2	9	8	5	3	4	1	6	7

67

8	9	7	3	4	6	2	5	1
1	3	4	2	5	7	6	8	9
5	2	6	8	9	1	7	4	3
6	1	3	7	8	4	5	9	2
7	8	9	5	6	2	3	1	4
4	5	2	1	3	9	8	7	6
9	6	5	4	7	3	1	2	8
2	4	8	6	1	5	9	3	7
3	7	1	9	2	8	4	6	5

70

7	9	2	5	3	6	8	4	1
4	6	8	1	9	7	2	3	5
5	1	3	4	2	8	6	9	7
6	5	4	3	7	9	1	8	2
8	3	7	2	4	1	5	6	9
1	2	9	8	6	5	4	7	3
2	7	5	9	8	4	3	1	6
9	8	1	6	5	3	7	2	4
3	4	6	7	1	2	9	5	8

68

8	2	3	7	5	4	9	1	6
7	6	1	8	9	3	4	2	5
4	9	5	6	2	1	3	7	8
1	3	4	2	7	6	5	8	9
6	5	9	4	1	8	7	3	2
2	7	8	5	3	9	6	4	1
5	8	6	1	4	7	2	9	3
9	1	7	3	6	2	8	5	4
3	4	2	9	8	5	1	6	7

71

9	1	6	2	4	3	7	8	5
2	7	8	5	6	1	4	9	3
3	4	5	8	9	7	1	2	6
4	6	1	9	5	8	3	7	2
7	3	9	1	2	6	8	5	4
5	8	2	3	7	4	6	1	9
1	2	3	6	8	9	5	4	7
8	9	4	7	3	5	2	6	1
6	5	7	4	1	2	9	3	8

69

8	4	9	6	3	1	2	5	7
7	6	1	2	5	9	3	4	8
3	5	2	7	8	4	1	6	9
2	3	4	9	6	8	5	7	1
1	9	6	5	7	2	4	8	3
5	7	8	1	4	3	9	2	6
4	8	5	3	9	7	6	1	2
6	1	3	8	2	5	7	9	4
9	2	7	4	1	6	8	3	5

72

2	6	8	7	5	1	9	4	3
4	9	5	2	6	3	8	1	7
3	1	7	8	4	9	5	2	6
5	2	1	3	9	8	7	6	4
8	4	3	6	2	7	1	5	9
6	7	9	4	1	5	2	3	8
7	8	6	1	3	2	4	9	5
9	3	2	5	7	4	6	8	1
1	5	4	9	8	6	3	7	2

Answers

73

9	8	1	4	5	3	2	7	6
5	7	4	1	2	6	8	9	3
3	6	2	8	7	9	5	1	4
2	4	7	9	3	5	1	6	8
1	3	5	6	4	8	9	2	7
6	9	8	2	1	7	4	3	5
7	5	9	3	8	2	6	4	1
4	2	3	5	6	1	7	8	9
8	1	6	7	9	4	3	5	2

76

3	5	4	7	1	8	6	2	9
2	7	1	9	6	5	8	4	3
9	8	6	2	3	4	5	7	1
8	6	7	1	5	3	4	9	2
5	1	2	4	7	9	3	8	6
4	3	9	6	8	2	7	1	5
1	2	3	5	4	7	9	6	8
6	4	8	3	9	1	2	5	7
7	9	5	8	2	6	1	3	4

74

4	3	7	1	2	8	9	5	6
2	1	9	7	5	6	3	8	4
8	6	5	9	3	4	7	1	2
7	8	3	4	1	2	6	9	5
6	2	1	5	8	9	4	7	3
5	9	4	3	6	7	8	2	1
9	5	6	2	7	3	1	4	8
3	4	2	8	9	1	5	6	7
1	7	8	6	4	5	2	3	9

77

3	1	4	7	6	2	9	8	5
5	8	7	3	1	9	6	4	2
9	2	6	5	4	8	7	1	3
6	5	1	4	9	7	2	3	8
7	3	8	6	2	1	5	9	4
4	9	2	8	3	5	1	7	6
8	4	5	9	7	6	3	2	1
2	6	9	1	8	3	4	5	7
1	7	3	2	5	4	8	6	9

75

6	5	1	2	8	4	3	7	9
2	3	4	9	7	1	6	5	8
9	7	8	5	6	3	2	1	4
3	4	5	7	2	6	9	8	1
7	8	2	1	3	9	4	6	5
1	6	9	4	5	8	7	2	3
4	2	7	3	1	5	8	9	6
8	1	3	6	9	2	5	4	7
5	9	6	8	4	7	1	3	2

78

2	6	9	1	3	4	7	8	5
5	3	8	7	9	2	4	6	1
4	7	1	6	5	8	9	3	2
1	9	4	8	2	5	6	7	3
8	2	7	3	4	6	5	1	9
3	5	6	9	1	7	8	2	4
6	4	2	5	7	3	1	9	8
7	1	3	4	8	9	2	5	6
9	8	5	2	6	1	3	4	7

79

9	5	6	1	3	7	8	2	4
8	7	2	4	9	6	5	1	3
3	1	4	5	2	8	7	6	9
4	2	1	6	8	3	9	7	5
5	9	3	7	1	4	6	8	2
6	8	7	2	5	9	3	4	1
7	6	9	3	4	1	2	5	8
1	3	5	8	6	2	4	9	7
2	4	8	9	7	5	1	3	6

82

9	6	7	2	4	3	1	8	5
8	2	5	6	1	7	4	9	3
1	4	3	5	8	9	2	6	7
3	5	2	4	7	6	8	1	9
6	1	9	3	5	8	7	2	4
7	8	4	9	2	1	5	3	6
4	9	8	1	3	5	6	7	2
5	3	1	7	6	2	9	4	8
2	7	6	8	9	4	3	5	1

80

6	1	9	7	5	2	8	3	4
3	5	8	6	4	9	7	2	1
2	7	4	3	8	1	9	5	6
5	9	2	4	7	8	6	1	3
7	3	1	9	2	6	4	8	5
8	4	6	5	1	3	2	9	7
1	6	3	2	9	4	5	7	8
9	8	5	1	6	7	3	4	2
4	2	7	8	3	5	1	6	9

83

6	3	9	7	1	5	2	8	4
4	5	2	8	6	3	9	1	7
1	8	7	2	4	9	3	6	5
9	1	8	4	5	6	7	2	3
3	7	4	9	2	8	6	5	1
5	2	6	3	7	1	8	4	9
8	4	5	6	3	7	1	9	2
7	6	1	5	9	2	4	3	8
2	9	3	1	8	4	5	7	6

81

4	7	5	9	8	6	2	3	1
1	9	8	2	4	3	6	7	5
3	2	6	1	7	5	4	9	8
9	8	4	5	2	7	1	6	3
6	1	2	3	9	4	5	8	7
5	3	7	8	6	1	9	4	2
7	5	9	6	1	8	3	2	4
2	4	3	7	5	9	8	1	6
8	6	1	4	3	2	7	5	9

84

8	5	7	2	4	1	3	6	9
2	9	1	6	5	3	7	4	8
4	6	3	8	7	9	1	5	2
5	4	9	7	3	8	2	1	6
1	8	2	5	9	6	4	3	7
3	7	6	1	2	4	8	9	5
7	1	4	9	8	5	6	2	3
6	2	5	3	1	7	9	8	4
9	3	8	4	6	2	5	7	1

Answers

85

2	7	6	5	8	1	9	3	4
5	3	9	4	6	2	1	8	7
4	8	1	3	7	9	5	2	6
6	2	3	7	1	5	8	4	9
9	5	8	6	3	4	7	1	2
1	4	7	9	2	8	6	5	3
7	6	2	1	5	3	4	9	8
3	9	5	8	4	6	2	7	1
8	1	4	2	9	7	3	6	5

88

6	9	7	3	4	8	5	1	2
2	8	4	7	5	1	3	9	6
5	3	1	9	6	2	7	8	4
1	2	3	4	9	6	8	5	7
8	4	5	1	3	7	6	2	9
9	7	6	2	8	5	1	4	3
3	5	8	6	2	9	4	7	1
4	1	2	8	7	3	9	6	5
7	6	9	5	1	4	2	3	8

86

4	8	6	2	5	7	9	1	3
2	7	1	3	9	4	6	8	5
3	5	9	1	6	8	7	4	2
7	4	5	8	3	6	1	2	9
1	2	3	4	7	9	5	6	8
9	6	8	5	1	2	4	3	7
8	9	2	7	4	1	3	5	6
5	1	7	6	2	3	8	9	4
6	3	4	9	8	5	2	7	1

89

8	7	3	4	2	9	6	5	1
6	1	9	7	5	8	4	2	3
4	2	5	3	6	1	7	9	8
5	3	7	2	1	6	8	4	9
2	8	4	5	9	7	3	1	6
9	6	1	8	4	3	2	7	5
3	9	2	1	8	4	5	6	7
1	5	8	6	7	2	9	3	4
7	4	6	9	3	5	1	8	2

87

2	9	4	3	1	7	5	6	8
5	6	1	9	4	8	2	7	3
3	8	7	2	6	5	4	9	1
1	3	6	7	5	2	9	8	4
7	4	9	8	3	1	6	5	2
8	2	5	6	9	4	1	3	7
9	7	8	1	2	6	3	4	5
4	1	3	5	8	9	7	2	6
6	5	2	4	7	3	8	1	9

90

3	1	6	5	2	4	7	8	9
4	9	7	8	3	6	5	1	2
5	8	2	1	9	7	4	6	3
7	4	8	6	1	3	9	2	5
1	2	3	9	4	5	6	7	8
9	6	5	2	7	8	1	3	4
2	5	1	7	8	9	3	4	6
6	7	4	3	5	2	8	9	1
8	3	9	4	6	1	2	5	7

91

8	1	2	6	3	4	7	9	5
3	4	9	7	5	1	2	6	8
6	5	7	2	9	8	1	3	4
2	9	5	4	1	7	6	8	3
7	6	4	3	8	2	5	1	9
1	3	8	9	6	5	4	7	2
4	2	3	8	7	6	9	5	1
9	7	1	5	2	3	8	4	6
5	8	6	1	4	9	3	2	7

94

1	8	5	7	3	4	2	6	9
9	6	4	2	1	5	7	3	8
3	7	2	6	8	9	1	5	4
7	5	8	1	4	6	3	9	2
6	2	3	5	9	7	4	8	1
4	9	1	8	2	3	5	7	6
8	1	6	3	5	2	9	4	7
2	3	9	4	7	8	6	1	5
5	4	7	9	6	1	8	2	3

92

3	2	7	5	9	8	4	1	6
8	5	6	4	1	3	7	9	2
1	9	4	6	7	2	8	3	5
5	7	2	3	6	4	9	8	1
6	3	9	1	8	7	5	2	4
4	1	8	9	2	5	6	7	3
7	8	5	2	3	6	1	4	9
9	6	3	8	4	1	2	5	7
2	4	1	7	5	9	3	6	8

95

4	2	3	5	6	1	7	9	8
1	7	8	2	9	4	5	6	3
6	9	5	8	3	7	1	4	2
7	3	2	1	4	6	9	8	5
5	4	9	7	2	8	6	3	1
8	6	1	3	5	9	4	2	7
2	5	6	9	7	3	8	1	4
3	1	4	6	8	5	2	7	9
9	8	7	4	1	2	3	5	6

93

9	4	1	5	2	6	8	7	3
5	6	8	4	7	3	1	9	2
3	2	7	9	8	1	6	5	4
4	1	3	6	5	8	9	2	7
6	5	9	2	1	7	4	3	8
8	7	2	3	4	9	5	1	6
7	3	4	1	6	5	2	8	9
1	8	6	7	9	2	3	4	5
2	9	5	8	3	4	7	6	1

96

3	4	7	5	1	6	2	8	9
5	6	1	8	2	9	7	4	3
2	8	9	4	7	3	5	1	6
6	5	4	7	3	2	8	9	1
1	7	2	6	9	8	3	5	4
9	3	8	1	5	4	6	7	2
8	1	3	2	4	5	9	6	7
7	9	5	3	6	1	4	2	8
4	2	6	9	8	7	1	3	5

97

7	8	5	3	6	4	1	9	2
3	6	9	8	2	1	5	7	4
2	4	1	9	5	7	3	6	8
6	9	3	1	8	5	4	2	7
8	5	7	6	4	2	9	3	1
4	1	2	7	9	3	8	5	6
1	3	8	5	7	6	2	4	9
9	7	4	2	3	8	6	1	5
5	2	6	4	1	9	7	8	3

98

9	3	2	1	4	8	5	6	7
7	4	8	3	5	6	9	2	1
5	1	6	7	9	2	3	8	4
8	5	4	6	3	7	1	9	2
1	2	3	9	8	5	7	4	6
6	7	9	2	1	4	8	3	5
4	6	5	8	7	9	2	1	3
2	8	1	5	6	3	4	7	9
3	9	7	4	2	1	6	5	8

99

4	9	1	7	5	8	2	6	3
6	5	7	2	3	4	9	1	8
2	8	3	6	1	9	4	5	7
5	2	6	8	4	3	1	7	9
1	4	8	9	7	5	3	2	6
3	7	9	1	2	6	5	8	4
7	6	5	4	9	2	8	3	1
9	1	2	3	8	7	6	4	5
8	3	4	5	6	1	7	9	2

100

7	3	1	8	9	2	6	4	5
5	6	2	4	3	7	1	9	8
4	8	9	5	1	6	2	7	3
1	7	6	3	2	4	5	8	9
2	4	8	9	5	1	3	6	7
3	9	5	7	6	8	4	2	1
6	5	4	1	8	9	7	3	2
9	2	3	6	7	5	8	1	4
8	1	7	2	4	3	9	5	6

101

3	2	6	4	5	1	8	7	9
1	8	5	3	9	7	6	4	2
4	9	7	2	6	8	3	5	1
8	5	3	6	1	4	9	2	7
2	1	9	8	7	5	4	3	6
6	7	4	9	3	2	1	8	5
9	4	2	7	8	6	5	1	3
5	3	8	1	2	9	7	6	4
7	6	1	5	4	3	2	9	8

102

7	4	2	5	8	6	9	1	3
3	9	1	2	4	7	8	5	6
8	5	6	1	9	3	7	2	4
5	7	3	6	1	8	2	4	9
6	2	4	7	3	9	5	8	1
9	1	8	4	2	5	6	3	7
2	6	5	3	7	1	4	9	8
1	8	7	9	5	4	3	6	2
4	3	9	8	6	2	1	7	5

103

2	3	8	6	4	1	9	7	5
1	5	4	9	7	8	6	2	3
7	9	6	2	3	5	1	4	8
3	4	7	8	9	6	5	1	2
5	2	9	3	1	4	7	8	6
8	6	1	7	5	2	4	3	9
4	1	2	5	8	9	3	6	7
9	8	3	1	6	7	2	5	4
6	7	5	4	2	3	8	9	1

104

2	1	4	5	6	8	3	7	9
9	8	3	4	7	2	5	6	1
6	7	5	1	3	9	4	2	8
4	3	2	8	1	6	7	9	5
1	6	7	9	5	3	2	8	4
5	9	8	2	4	7	6	1	3
8	5	6	7	9	4	1	3	2
3	4	9	6	2	1	8	5	7
7	2	1	3	8	5	9	4	6

105

2	3	8	9	7	5	4	6	1
7	4	9	1	8	6	5	3	2
1	5	6	2	3	4	8	9	7
4	6	5	8	2	7	9	1	3
8	1	3	4	6	9	2	7	5
9	2	7	5	1	3	6	8	4
3	8	4	7	9	2	1	5	6
6	9	2	3	5	1	7	4	8
5	7	1	6	4	8	3	2	9

106

7	1	3	2	6	4	5	8	9
4	9	8	5	3	1	6	2	7
6	2	5	7	8	9	3	4	1
1	4	2	9	5	8	7	3	6
8	3	9	6	1	7	2	5	4
5	6	7	3	4	2	9	1	8
3	5	1	8	9	6	4	7	2
2	8	6	4	7	5	1	9	3
9	7	4	1	2	3	8	6	5

107

7	5	6	9	2	4	1	8	3
2	4	3	7	8	1	5	6	9
8	1	9	6	3	5	2	7	4
5	6	1	4	7	9	8	3	2
9	7	2	3	6	8	4	5	1
4	3	8	5	1	2	7	9	6
6	8	5	2	4	3	9	1	7
1	2	7	8	9	6	3	4	5
3	9	4	1	5	7	6	2	8

108

1	3	5	2	4	8	9	7	6
8	9	2	6	7	3	4	1	5
6	7	4	5	1	9	3	2	8
5	1	9	4	8	6	2	3	7
3	2	6	7	9	1	8	5	4
4	8	7	3	5	2	6	9	1
2	4	3	1	6	7	5	8	9
9	6	1	8	3	5	7	4	2
7	5	8	9	2	4	1	6	3

Answers

109

9	3	5	1	2	7	4	6	8
1	6	7	4	5	8	3	9	2
2	8	4	9	6	3	1	5	7
8	5	1	7	3	4	9	2	6
7	2	9	6	8	1	5	3	4
6	4	3	5	9	2	8	7	1
4	7	2	3	1	9	6	8	5
5	9	8	2	4	6	7	1	3
3	1	6	8	7	5	2	4	9

112

2	3	7	4	8	5	1	6	9
8	9	4	1	7	6	5	3	2
6	1	5	2	9	3	4	8	7
9	7	2	6	5	1	3	4	8
3	8	6	9	2	4	7	1	5
4	5	1	8	3	7	9	2	6
5	4	8	7	1	2	6	9	3
7	6	9	3	4	8	2	5	1
1	2	3	5	6	9	8	7	4

110

3	1	4	8	7	6	2	5	9
7	2	8	1	9	5	6	4	3
5	6	9	2	3	4	8	1	7
6	8	1	7	2	3	5	9	4
2	7	5	4	6	9	3	8	1
4	9	3	5	8	1	7	2	6
1	3	7	9	5	2	4	6	8
8	4	2	6	1	7	9	3	5
9	5	6	3	4	8	1	7	2

113

9	3	5	2	6	1	4	7	8
2	6	8	5	4	7	1	3	9
1	4	7	3	9	8	6	5	2
3	8	2	1	7	4	5	9	6
7	1	4	9	5	6	8	2	3
6	5	9	8	3	2	7	1	4
5	2	6	4	1	9	3	8	7
4	9	3	7	8	5	2	6	1
8	7	1	6	2	3	9	4	5

111

6	3	2	4	1	7	8	9	5
1	5	9	2	8	3	4	6	7
8	4	7	6	5	9	3	2	1
3	1	5	7	2	6	9	8	4
7	8	4	3	9	5	6	1	2
9	2	6	1	4	8	7	5	3
4	6	8	5	3	1	2	7	9
5	7	3	9	6	2	1	4	8
2	9	1	8	7	4	5	3	6

114

2	5	7	4	9	8	1	3	6
6	1	9	3	2	7	4	8	5
3	8	4	6	5	1	9	2	7
8	3	5	7	6	4	2	9	1
7	6	1	2	3	9	8	5	4
9	4	2	1	8	5	7	6	3
1	9	8	5	7	6	3	4	2
5	7	3	9	4	2	6	1	8
4	2	6	8	1	3	5	7	9

115

5	1	2	3	6	9	4	8	7
3	4	6	2	8	7	9	5	1
7	8	9	4	5	1	3	2	6
2	6	5	9	1	3	8	7	4
8	9	4	5	7	2	1	6	3
1	7	3	8	4	6	2	9	5
9	2	1	6	3	5	7	4	8
4	5	7	1	2	8	6	3	9
6	3	8	7	9	4	5	1	2

118

2	7	9	5	4	1	6	3	8
3	1	6	8	2	9	7	4	5
8	5	4	6	3	7	1	9	2
6	9	5	3	8	2	4	1	7
1	8	3	4	7	5	2	6	9
4	2	7	9	1	6	5	8	3
9	3	1	7	5	4	8	2	6
7	4	8	2	6	3	9	5	1
5	6	2	1	9	8	3	7	4

116

8	2	9	4	7	3	5	1	6
1	5	7	6	9	8	3	4	2
6	3	4	2	5	1	8	7	9
7	8	2	1	4	6	9	5	3
3	9	6	7	2	5	4	8	1
5	4	1	8	3	9	6	2	7
9	1	3	5	8	7	2	6	4
2	6	8	3	1	4	7	9	5
4	7	5	9	6	2	1	3	8

119

5	3	2	1	6	8	7	4	9
4	8	7	2	9	3	5	1	6
1	6	9	5	4	7	2	3	8
8	4	3	7	1	9	6	5	2
6	7	5	4	8	2	1	9	3
2	9	1	6	3	5	8	7	4
3	1	6	8	5	4	9	2	7
7	5	4	9	2	6	3	8	1
9	2	8	3	7	1	4	6	5

117

9	5	8	3	2	1	7	4	6
6	4	3	7	5	9	1	8	2
1	2	7	4	8	6	3	9	5
5	1	4	9	3	8	2	6	7
8	7	9	6	1	2	4	5	3
2	3	6	5	4	7	8	1	9
4	6	1	2	7	5	9	3	8
7	8	5	1	9	3	6	2	4
3	9	2	8	6	4	5	7	1

120

9	3	8	4	1	2	7	5	6
5	7	2	9	3	6	4	1	8
6	4	1	5	7	8	9	3	2
7	6	4	3	8	1	5	2	9
1	2	9	6	5	4	3	8	7
3	8	5	2	9	7	1	6	4
8	5	6	7	4	3	2	9	1
2	9	7	1	6	5	8	4	3
4	1	3	8	2	9	6	7	5

121

4	5	1	7	2	8	3	6	9
9	2	3	5	6	1	7	8	4
6	8	7	3	9	4	2	5	1
5	1	4	9	3	7	6	2	8
2	7	6	8	1	5	9	4	3
3	9	8	6	4	2	5	1	7
8	3	2	1	7	6	4	9	5
7	6	5	4	8	9	1	3	2
1	4	9	2	5	3	8	7	6

124

5	3	1	7	9	2	4	6	8
6	4	2	8	3	5	1	9	7
7	9	8	1	4	6	2	5	3
2	5	4	9	7	1	3	8	6
8	1	7	2	6	3	5	4	9
3	6	9	4	5	8	7	2	1
9	2	3	5	8	7	6	1	4
4	7	5	6	1	9	8	3	2
1	8	6	3	2	4	9	7	5

122

5	6	9	2	3	1	7	4	8
1	3	8	9	7	4	6	5	2
7	2	4	8	6	5	3	1	9
6	1	5	7	4	8	9	2	3
8	9	3	6	5	2	1	7	4
4	7	2	3	1	9	5	8	6
2	4	6	5	9	7	8	3	1
9	8	7	1	2	3	4	6	5
3	5	1	4	8	6	2	9	7

125

5	8	6	7	9	1	2	3	4
1	4	3	6	5	2	7	9	8
2	7	9	4	8	3	6	1	5
3	6	8	5	2	7	9	4	1
7	1	4	9	3	8	5	2	6
9	5	2	1	6	4	3	8	7
4	9	5	3	1	6	8	7	2
6	2	7	8	4	9	1	5	3
8	3	1	2	7	5	4	6	9

123

9	4	5	3	2	8	1	6	7
6	7	2	9	1	4	3	8	5
3	8	1	6	5	7	9	2	4
5	2	3	8	6	9	7	4	1
1	6	7	4	3	2	5	9	8
8	9	4	1	7	5	2	3	6
4	3	6	5	9	1	8	7	2
7	1	9	2	8	6	4	5	3
2	5	8	7	4	3	6	1	9

126

2	6	1	7	3	9	4	8	5
4	3	8	1	2	5	7	9	6
7	9	5	4	6	8	2	1	3
1	4	6	2	9	3	8	5	7
8	5	9	6	7	4	3	2	1
3	2	7	5	8	1	6	4	9
6	1	2	9	4	7	5	3	8
9	7	3	8	5	2	1	6	4
5	8	4	3	1	6	9	7	2

127

9	4	8	1	3	5	7	6	2
3	5	2	7	9	6	8	1	4
7	1	6	4	2	8	5	9	3
1	8	9	3	5	2	6	4	7
6	7	3	8	4	1	9	2	5
5	2	4	9	6	7	1	3	8
8	6	5	2	1	3	4	7	9
2	9	1	5	7	4	3	8	6
4	3	7	6	8	9	2	5	1

130

6	2	8	5	3	7	4	9	1
7	9	1	6	4	2	8	5	3
5	4	3	8	9	1	2	6	7
1	3	2	7	8	9	6	4	5
4	7	9	3	6	5	1	2	8
8	6	5	1	2	4	3	7	9
9	1	4	2	5	3	7	8	6
3	5	6	4	7	8	9	1	2
2	8	7	9	1	6	5	3	4

128

6	5	8	1	3	9	7	2	4
7	9	1	2	8	4	5	6	3
3	4	2	7	5	6	9	1	8
5	3	6	9	4	7	2	8	1
1	2	9	8	6	3	4	7	5
4	8	7	5	1	2	3	9	6
8	7	4	6	2	5	1	3	9
9	6	3	4	7	1	8	5	2
2	1	5	3	9	8	6	4	7

131

9	7	2	1	3	8	5	4	6
6	3	1	5	4	7	9	8	2
4	8	5	2	6	9	3	7	1
5	1	6	4	7	3	2	9	8
7	4	8	9	1	2	6	5	3
2	9	3	8	5	6	7	1	4
8	2	7	3	9	4	1	6	5
3	5	9	6	8	1	4	2	7
1	6	4	7	2	5	8	3	9

129

9	1	8	6	7	3	5	2	4
6	7	5	9	4	2	3	8	1
2	4	3	5	8	1	7	6	9
5	2	6	8	3	4	1	9	7
1	3	9	2	6	7	8	4	5
7	8	4	1	5	9	2	3	6
3	6	2	4	1	5	9	7	8
4	5	7	3	9	8	6	1	2
8	9	1	7	2	6	4	5	3

132

9	7	2	5	4	3	6	8	1
4	3	5	8	6	1	9	7	2
8	1	6	9	2	7	3	4	5
3	5	8	2	9	6	4	1	7
2	6	4	7	1	5	8	9	3
1	9	7	3	8	4	2	5	6
5	2	3	4	7	8	1	6	9
7	8	1	6	3	9	5	2	4
6	4	9	1	5	2	7	3	8

133

6	9	7	4	3	5	1	8	2
8	2	1	9	7	6	4	5	3
5	4	3	1	8	2	6	9	7
3	6	8	5	2	9	7	1	4
4	5	2	7	1	8	3	6	9
1	7	9	3	6	4	5	2	8
2	8	4	6	5	7	9	3	1
7	1	6	8	9	3	2	4	5
9	3	5	2	4	1	8	7	6

136

7	8	2	9	5	3	6	1	4
5	6	4	1	2	7	3	8	9
9	1	3	4	8	6	7	5	2
2	3	9	7	1	8	4	6	5
6	4	5	2	3	9	8	7	1
1	7	8	5	6	4	2	9	3
4	2	1	6	7	5	9	3	8
3	5	7	8	9	2	1	4	6
8	9	6	3	4	1	5	2	7

134

5	7	2	6	9	1	4	3	8
1	6	8	5	3	4	7	2	9
9	3	4	8	7	2	5	6	1
4	1	9	7	2	8	3	5	6
6	5	3	1	4	9	8	7	2
2	8	7	3	5	6	1	9	4
3	2	1	9	8	5	6	4	7
8	9	5	4	6	7	2	1	3
7	4	6	2	1	3	9	8	5

137

6	2	7	3	5	9	1	4	8
4	8	1	2	7	6	3	5	9
9	3	5	4	1	8	2	6	7
3	5	8	6	2	4	7	1	9
2	7	9	5	8	1	4	3	6
1	4	6	7	9	3	8	5	2
7	9	2	1	3	5	6	8	4
8	6	3	9	4	7	5	2	1
5	1	4	8	6	2	9	7	3

135

2	5	8	7	9	3	1	6	4
7	3	1	5	4	6	2	8	9
9	6	4	1	2	8	5	7	3
1	7	9	4	8	2	6	3	5
4	2	5	3	6	7	9	1	8
6	8	3	9	1	5	4	2	7
5	1	2	8	3	4	7	9	6
3	4	6	2	7	9	8	5	1
8	9	7	6	5	1	3	4	2

138

5	8	9	3	4	7	1	2	6
1	3	4	6	2	9	5	7	8
6	2	7	8	5	1	3	4	9
9	1	8	4	7	5	2	6	3
2	7	3	9	6	8	4	1	5
4	5	6	2	1	3	8	9	7
3	4	5	1	9	6	7	8	2
8	6	2	7	3	4	9	5	1
7	9	1	5	8	2	6	3	4

139

3	4	9	2	6	7	1	5	8
2	8	6	4	1	5	3	7	9
7	1	5	8	3	9	4	6	2
5	7	1	6	8	4	9	2	3
6	2	3	7	9	1	8	4	5
8	9	4	5	2	3	7	1	6
9	6	2	1	4	8	5	3	7
1	3	7	9	5	6	2	8	4
4	5	8	3	7	2	6	9	1

142

2	8	6	3	1	7	4	5	9
9	7	5	4	6	8	2	3	1
4	1	3	5	9	2	7	8	6
7	4	8	2	3	9	1	6	5
6	5	2	8	4	1	9	7	3
1	3	9	6	7	5	8	4	2
5	2	4	9	8	6	3	1	7
8	6	1	7	2	3	5	9	4
3	9	7	1	5	4	6	2	8

140

9	4	8	1	6	7	5	2	3
3	5	6	2	8	4	9	1	7
1	7	2	3	9	5	8	4	6
6	3	4	9	5	1	7	8	2
2	1	5	7	3	8	6	9	4
8	9	7	6	4	2	3	5	1
5	8	3	4	1	6	2	7	9
4	2	9	8	7	3	1	6	5
7	6	1	5	2	9	4	3	8

143

7	6	5	1	3	4	8	9	2
8	4	2	9	5	6	3	7	1
1	9	3	8	2	7	5	4	6
3	2	9	4	7	5	1	6	8
4	5	1	2	6	8	9	3	7
6	7	8	3	9	1	2	5	4
2	8	6	5	4	9	7	1	3
9	3	7	6	1	2	4	8	5
5	1	4	7	8	3	6	2	9

141

4	6	3	2	1	9	5	8	7
9	1	7	5	8	6	2	4	3
8	5	2	3	4	7	6	9	1
6	3	9	1	2	4	7	5	8
1	8	5	7	6	3	9	2	4
2	7	4	9	5	8	1	3	6
5	2	8	6	3	1	4	7	9
7	4	6	8	9	5	3	1	2
3	9	1	4	7	2	8	6	5

144

1	4	2	3	6	7	9	8	5
7	3	5	2	9	8	4	1	6
8	6	9	1	4	5	2	3	7
5	2	4	9	8	1	7	6	3
3	8	7	6	2	4	5	9	1
6	9	1	5	7	3	8	2	4
2	7	8	4	3	6	1	5	9
4	1	6	8	5	9	3	7	2
9	5	3	7	1	2	6	4	8

145

4	3	7	8	1	9	5	2	6
1	6	2	4	3	5	7	8	9
8	9	5	6	7	2	3	1	4
5	1	8	3	4	6	2	9	7
9	4	6	1	2	7	8	3	5
2	7	3	9	5	8	4	6	1
7	8	9	5	6	3	1	4	2
3	5	4	2	9	1	6	7	8
6	2	1	7	8	4	9	5	3

148

2	1	6	8	9	4	5	7	3
4	9	7	3	5	2	6	1	8
5	8	3	1	6	7	4	2	9
7	2	5	6	4	3	9	8	1
8	4	9	7	2	1	3	6	5
3	6	1	5	8	9	2	4	7
9	3	8	2	7	6	1	5	4
1	7	2	4	3	5	8	9	6
6	5	4	9	1	8	7	3	2

146

1	6	5	9	7	3	2	4	8
9	8	3	4	2	6	7	5	1
7	4	2	5	8	1	3	6	9
5	2	7	3	6	8	9	1	4
8	9	4	1	5	7	6	3	2
3	1	6	2	4	9	8	7	5
6	7	9	8	1	4	5	2	3
4	5	8	7	3	2	1	9	6
2	3	1	6	9	5	4	8	7

149

2	5	4	8	9	6	1	7	3
8	1	6	5	3	7	2	9	4
9	3	7	1	4	2	6	8	5
1	2	9	7	8	3	5	4	6
3	6	8	2	5	4	9	1	7
4	7	5	6	1	9	3	2	8
5	9	3	4	7	1	8	6	2
7	8	2	9	6	5	4	3	1
6	4	1	3	2	8	7	5	9

147

6	5	3	8	4	7	2	1	9
7	4	1	3	2	9	6	8	5
8	2	9	6	5	1	4	3	7
2	9	4	1	3	5	7	6	8
3	7	6	4	9	8	5	2	1
5	1	8	7	6	2	3	9	4
1	8	5	2	7	3	9	4	6
9	6	2	5	1	4	8	7	3
4	3	7	9	8	6	1	5	2

150

7	2	4	5	3	8	1	9	6
3	6	9	2	4	1	5	7	8
5	8	1	9	7	6	3	4	2
6	9	5	3	8	4	7	2	1
1	3	2	6	9	7	4	8	5
8	4	7	1	2	5	6	3	9
9	1	8	4	5	3	2	6	7
2	5	3	7	6	9	8	1	4
4	7	6	8	1	2	9	5	3

151

4	7	3	9	2	8	6	5	1
6	8	5	1	3	7	2	9	4
9	1	2	6	5	4	7	3	8
3	4	6	5	8	2	9	1	7
5	2	1	7	9	6	8	4	3
8	9	7	4	1	3	5	2	6
7	3	8	2	4	9	1	6	5
1	6	9	3	7	5	4	8	2
2	5	4	8	6	1	3	7	9

154

6	8	3	5	2	1	4	9	7
5	2	7	9	3	4	1	8	6
9	1	4	7	6	8	3	5	2
1	3	6	4	9	7	5	2	8
2	5	9	1	8	3	7	6	4
7	4	8	6	5	2	9	3	1
8	6	1	3	7	9	2	4	5
4	9	2	8	1	5	6	7	3
3	7	5	2	4	6	8	1	9

152

3	9	7	4	1	8	6	5	2
5	4	6	2	3	9	8	1	7
8	2	1	6	5	7	9	4	3
7	1	3	8	4	2	5	9	6
4	6	5	9	7	1	2	3	8
9	8	2	3	6	5	1	7	4
2	5	4	1	8	3	7	6	9
6	7	8	5	9	4	3	2	1
1	3	9	7	2	6	4	8	5

155

1	9	8	7	6	2	3	4	5
3	7	5	4	9	8	6	1	2
6	4	2	1	3	5	7	8	9
5	3	7	2	4	9	1	6	8
4	2	1	5	8	6	9	3	7
9	8	6	3	7	1	5	2	4
2	6	3	9	5	4	8	7	1
8	5	4	6	1	7	2	9	3
7	1	9	8	2	3	4	5	6

153

4	9	5	6	7	3	8	1	2
8	7	1	2	5	9	4	6	3
3	6	2	8	1	4	7	9	5
6	2	4	1	3	7	5	8	9
7	5	8	4	9	2	6	3	1
9	1	3	5	6	8	2	7	4
1	4	7	3	8	5	9	2	6
2	3	9	7	4	6	1	5	8
5	8	6	9	2	1	3	4	7

156

6	3	9	1	4	8	7	2	5
7	4	1	2	9	5	3	8	6
5	2	8	7	6	3	1	4	9
1	9	5	4	3	7	8	6	2
4	6	3	9	8	2	5	1	7
8	7	2	5	1	6	4	9	3
9	8	7	3	2	1	6	5	4
3	1	4	6	5	9	2	7	8
2	5	6	8	7	4	9	3	1

157

5	2	8	7	9	4	6	3	1
6	7	1	8	2	3	9	4	5
3	9	4	6	1	5	2	8	7
7	8	2	9	3	1	5	6	4
9	5	3	2	4	6	1	7	8
4	1	6	5	7	8	3	9	2
8	3	7	1	6	2	4	5	9
1	4	9	3	5	7	8	2	6
2	6	5	4	8	9	7	1	3

160

9	4	7	1	2	6	3	8	5
6	1	8	3	7	5	2	4	9
5	2	3	9	8	4	7	1	6
3	8	9	2	4	7	6	5	1
1	6	5	8	3	9	4	7	2
4	7	2	6	5	1	8	9	3
8	9	1	4	6	3	5	2	7
2	5	6	7	9	8	1	3	4
7	3	4	5	1	2	9	6	8

158

4	9	3	5	2	1	8	6	7
6	7	8	3	9	4	5	1	2
1	2	5	8	6	7	9	4	3
8	3	1	6	4	5	7	2	9
5	4	2	9	7	3	1	8	6
7	6	9	2	1	8	3	5	4
3	8	4	7	5	2	6	9	1
9	1	7	4	8	6	2	3	5
2	5	6	1	3	9	4	7	8

161

1	5	9	6	4	3	2	7	8
4	8	3	2	7	5	6	1	9
6	7	2	8	9	1	3	4	5
9	3	4	5	2	6	7	8	1
5	6	8	3	1	7	9	2	4
7	2	1	4	8	9	5	6	3
2	9	5	1	6	4	8	3	7
3	4	6	7	5	8	1	9	2
8	1	7	9	3	2	4	5	6

159

9	1	8	2	4	5	7	6	3
3	2	7	6	8	1	4	5	9
4	6	5	7	9	3	1	8	2
2	7	1	9	5	6	8	3	4
5	4	6	3	7	8	9	2	1
8	9	3	1	2	4	5	7	6
7	8	2	4	6	9	3	1	5
1	5	9	8	3	2	6	4	7
6	3	4	5	1	7	2	9	8

Recipes from Grandma's Kitchen™

Slow Cooker
Casseroles
One Dish Meals

Publications International, Ltd.

Favorite Brand Name Recipes at www.fbnr.com

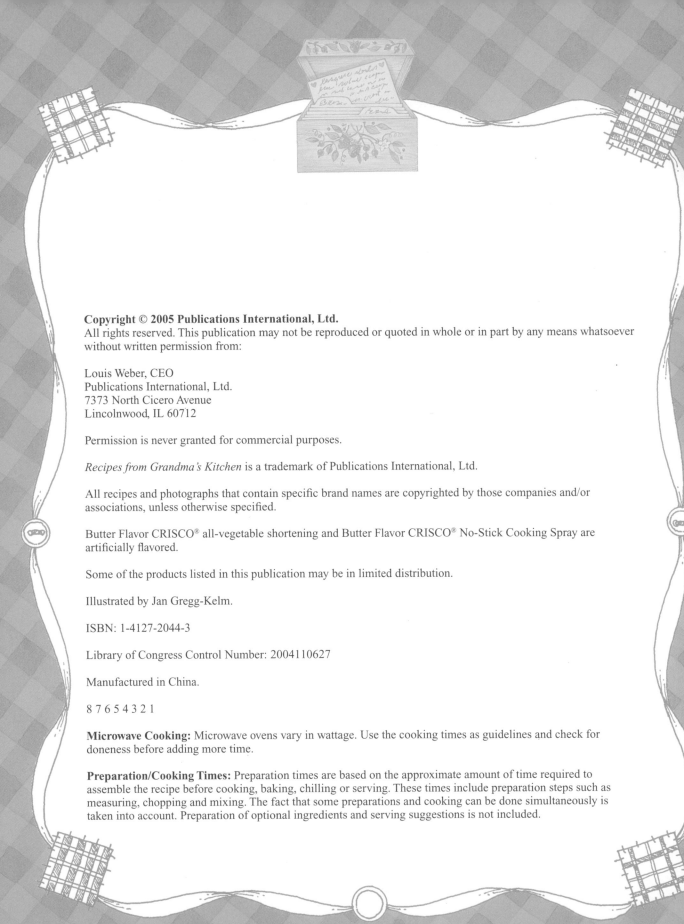

ISBN: 1-4127-2044-3

Library of Congress Control Number: 2004110627

Manufactured in China.

8 7 6 5 4 3 2 1

Microwave Cooking: Microwave ovens vary in wattage. Use the cooking times as guidelines and check for doneness before adding more time.

Preparation/Cooking Times: Preparation times are based on the approximate amount of time required to assemble the recipe before cooking, baking, chilling or serving. These times include preparation steps such as measuring, chopping and mixing. The fact that some preparations and cooking can be done simultaneously is taken into account. Preparation of optional ingredients and serving suggestions is not included.

Table of Contents

Just the Basics

Slow Cooker Basics

Slow cookers were introduced in the 1970's and found a renewed popularity in the mid 1990's that continues into the new century. Considering the hectic pace of today's lifestyles, it's no wonder so many people have rediscovered this time-saving kitchen helper. Spend a few minutes preparing the ingredients, turn on the slow cooker and relax. Low heat and long cooking times take the stress out of meal preparation. Leave for work or a day of leisure and come home four, eight or even ten hours later to a hot, delicious meal.

The recipes in this cookbook can be prepared in a 3-, 3½- or 4-quart slow cooker. There are two types of slow cookers. The most common models have heat coils circling the crockery insert, allowing heat to surround the food and cook evenly. Two settings, LOW (about 200°F) and HIGH (about 300°F) regulate cooking temperatures. One hour on HIGH equals 2 to 2½ hours on LOW. Less common models have heat coils on the bottom and have adjustable thermostats. If you own this type, consult your manufacturer's instructions for advice on converting the recipes in this publication.

Tips and Techniques

Filling the Slow Cooker: Manufacturers recommend that slow cookers should be one-half to three-quarters full for best results.

Keep a Lid On It: A slow cooker can take as long as twenty minutes to regain heat lost when the cover is removed. If the recipe calls for stirring or checking the dish near the end of the cooking time, replace the cover as quickly as you can. Otherwise, resist the urge to remove the cover.

Cleaning Your Slow Cooker: To clean your slow cooker, follow the manufacturer's instructions. To make cleanup even easier, spray with nonstick cooking spray before adding food.

Tasting: Always taste the finished dish before serving to adjust seasonings to your preference. Consider adding a dash of the following: salt, freshly ground pepper, seasoned salt, seasoned herb blends, lemon juice, soy sauce, Worcestershire sauce, flavored vinegar or minced herbs.

Adapting Recipes: If you'd like to adapt your own favorite recipe to a slow cooker, you'll need to follow a few guidelines. First, try to find a similar slow cooker recipe in this publication or the manufacturer's guide. Note the cooking times, amount of liquid, and quantity and size of meat and vegetable pieces. Because the slow cooker captures moisture, you will want to reduce the amount of liquid, often by as much as half. Add dairy products toward the end of the cooking time so they do not curdle. Follow this chart to estimate the cooking time you will need:

Cooking Guidelines		
Conventional Recipe	Cook on LOW	Cook on HIGH
30 to 45 minutes	6 to 10 hours	3 to 4 hours
50 minutes to 3 hours	8 to 15 hours	4 to 6 hours

Selecting the Right Meat: A good tip to keep in mind is that you can, and in fact should, use tougher, inexpensive cuts of meat. Top-quality cuts, such as loin chops or filet mignon, fall apart during long cooking periods and therefore are not good choices to use in the slow cooker. Keep those cuts for roasting, broiling or grilling, and save money when using your slow cooker. Even the toughest cuts of meat will come out fork-tender and flavorful.

Reducing the Fat: The slow cooker can help you make lower-fat meals because you won't be cooking in oil or butter as you do when you sauté and stir-fry. And tougher, inexpensive cuts of meat have less fat than prime cuts. Many recipes call for trimming excess fat from meat. If you do use fatty cuts of meat, such as ribs, consider browning them first on top of the range to cook off excess fat before adding them to the slow cooker.

You can also remove most of the fat from accumulated juices and soups. The simplest way is to refrigerate the liquid for several hours or overnight. The fat will float on the top and congeal for easy removal. If you plan to serve the liquid right away, ladle it into a bowl or measuring cup. Let it stand about 5 minutes so the fat can rise to the surface. Skim with a large spoon or lightly pull a paper towel over the surface, letting it absorb the fat.

Cutting Your Vegetables: Vegetables often take longer to cook than meats. Cut vegetables into small, thin pieces and place them near the bottom or side of the slow cooker. Pay careful attention to the recipe instructions in order to cut vegetables to the proper size so they will cook in the amount of time given.

Food Safety Tips: If you do any advance preparation, such as trimming meat or cutting vegetables, make sure to cover and refrigerate the food until you are ready to start cooking. Store uncooked meats and vegetables separately. If you are preparing meat, poultry or fish, remember to wash your cutting board, utensils and hands with hot, soapy water before touching other food.

Once the food is cooked, don't keep it in the slow cooker for very long. Foods need to be kept cooler than 40°F or hotter than 140°F to avoid growth of harmful bacteria. Remove food to a clean container, cover and refrigerate as soon as possible. For large amounts of leftovers, it is best to divide them into several containers so they will cool faster. Do not reheat leftovers in the slow cooker. Use a microwave oven, the range top or the oven for reheating.

Casserole Basics

Whether you are making an everyday meal or planning for company, casseroles are perfect for any occasion. These warm, satisfying meals take you back to comforting memories of home-style cooking and are sure to have your family asking for more. Take advantage of the convenience of cooking casseroles and enjoy warm, home-cooked meals, especially when you don't have a lot of time to cook.

Tips and Techniques

Cookware: Casserole cookware comes in a variety of shapes, sizes and materials that fall into two general descriptions. They can be either deep, round containers with handles and sometimes tight-fitting lids or square and rectangular baking dishes.

Casseroles are made of glass, ceramic or metal. When making a casserole, it's important to bake the casserole in the proper size dish so that the ingredients cook evenly in the time specified.

How to determine dish size: If the size of the casserole or baking dish isn't marked on the bottom of the dish, it can be measured to determine the size.

•Round and oval casseroles are generally measured by volume, not inches, and are listed by quart capacity. Fill a measuring cup with water and pour it into the empty casserole. Repeat until the casserole is filled with water, keeping track of the amount of water added. The amount of water is equivalent to the size of the dish.

•Square and retangular baking dishes are usually measured in inches. If the dimensions are not marked on the bottom of a baking dish, use a ruler to measure on top from inside of one edge to the inside of the opposite edge. Repeat to determine the other dimension.

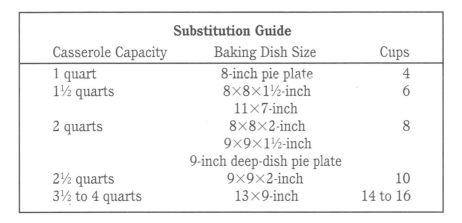

Substitution Guide		
Casserole Capacity	Baking Dish Size	Cups
1 quart	8-inch pie plate	4
1½ quarts	8×8×1½-inch	6
	11×7-inch	
2 quarts	8×8×2-inch	8
	9×9×1½-inch	
	9-inch deep-dish pie plate	
2½ quarts	9×9×2-inch	10
3½ to 4 quarts	13×9-inch	14 to 16

Cooking Meat and Poultry

Two cooking methods commonly used when assembling casseroles are sautéing and poaching.

•Sautéing is a quick-cooking method that can be used to partially cook meat, poultry and vegetables. It promotes even cooking and produces a crisp, brown surface on meat and poultry that locks in flavorful juices. Food to be sautéed should be dry and cut into even-size pieces, such as cubes or strips, so that they cook in the same amount of time.

Heat a small amount of cooking oil or other fat in a skillet over medium-high heat until hot. (Make sure the skillet is large enough so that the food is not overcrowded.) Add the meat, poultry or vegetables. Large pieces should be turned when brown and small pieces should be stirred frequently for even cooking. To test for chicken doneness, cut a few pieces to make sure they are no longer pink in centers.

•Poaching is a cooking method suitable for preparing chicken especially when a casserole recipe calls for cooked chicken. Fill a saucepan or stockpot with enough liquid, such as cold water or broth, to completely cover the chicken pieces. Bring the water to a gentle simmer and add the chicken. Maintain an even, gentle simmer and make sure the chicken is fully submerged. *Do not allow the water to boil.* Remove the chicken when it is completely cooked and no longer pink in the center. Meat from poached chicken is mild in flavor and tender and juicy in texture.

Topping It Off: Buttery, golden brown bread crumbs are a popular choice when it comes to topping a casserole but the selections shouldn't end there. Be creative with the many choices available to jazz up an old favorite or just vary how they are used. Crispy toppings can be crushed, partially crushed, broken into bite-size pieces or left whole. They add a nice texture to casseroles. Choose from crushed unsweetened cereals; potato, corn, tortilla or bagel chips; pretzels; flour or corn tortilla strips; plain or flavored croutons; flavored

crackers; crumbled bacon; ramen or chow mein noodles; sesame seeds; French fried onions and various nuts. As a guide, add 1 tablespoon melted butter to ½ cup crushed crumbs. Sprinkle over the casserole and bake to add buttery flavor.

•Homemade bread crumbs are a great way to use up leftover bread. To make bread crumbs, preheat the oven to 300°F. Place a single layer of bread slices on a baking sheet and bake 5 to 8 minutes or until the bread is completely dry and lightly browned. Cool completely. Process in the food processor or crumble in a resealable plastic food storage bag until crumbs are very fine. For additional flavor, season with salt, pepper and a small amount of dried herbs, ground spices or grated cheese as desired. Generally, 1 slice of bread equals ⅓ cup bread crumbs.

•Croutons may also be made from leftover bread, either by baking or sautéing. To make croutons by using the baking method, cut the bread into cubes and follow the above directions for making bread crumbs, except after cooling the croutons, add them to the casserole; do not crumble. One of the fastest ways to make croutons is sautéing, first cut the bread into cubes. Heat a small amount of vegetable oil or butter in a skillet over medium-high heat until hot. Add the bread cubes to the skillet and stir the cubes constantly until they are browned on all sides; cool completely. Top the casserole with the croutons.

•Toasting nuts intensifies their flavor and gives a boost to any casserole. Because nuts have a high fat content, they become rancid quickly. Therefore, purchase small amounts at a time and use them as soon as possible. To toast nuts, preheat the oven to 350°F. Place a single layer of nuts on a baking sheet and bake until golden brown, stirring occasionally. Bake almonds, pecans and walnuts 5 to 10 minutes; hazelnuts 8 to 10 minutes and pine nuts 3 to 6 minutes. Sprinkle the toasted nuts over the baked casserole.

•Fruits, vegetables and other toppings add a burst of color to casseroles, along with nutrients. Add green, red or white onions; orange or lemon peel; mushrooms; dried or fresh fruits, such as apples, apricots, cranberries, dates, oranges, pineapple and raisins; olives; bell or chili peppers; tomatoes; avocados; celery; corn; coconut; carrots; fresh herbs and shredded cheeses.

•Fruits, vegetables and other toppings can be chopped, sliced or shredded. Sprinkle a new spice or herb in place of another one. All the toppings can be placed on top of the casserole in a variety of ways—a small amount in the center, around the edges as a border or in straight or diagonal lines across the top.

Freezing Convenience: Most casseroles freeze very well and are popular for that reason. With today's hectic lifestyles, the convenience of casseroles is very appealing. Prepare the casserole when you have time, then cover and freeze it. All you need to do is defrost and cook the casserole in order to serve a well-balanced meal with relative ease at your convenience.

To Freeze:
1. Line a casserole or baking dish with plastic wrap, folding plastic wrap over the edges of the casserole. Spray it with nonstick cooking spray.
2. Add the combined casserole ingredients to the lined casserole. Place the casserole in the freezer.
3. When it is frozen, lift the food from the casserole by lifting the plastic wrap by the edges. Wrap the casserole contents airtight in freezer paper or place it in resealable plastic freezer storage bags, removing as much air as possible to prevent freezer burn.
4. Return the casserole to the freezer.

To Cook:
1. Remove the casserole from the freezer; discard all plastic wrap.
2. Place it in the original container; cover and place it in the refrigerator to defrost.*
3. Bake the thawed casserole in a preheated oven as the recipe directs.

Some casseroles can be placed directly in the oven without defrosting. Generally, the baking time needs to be doubled, but begin checking for doneness 15 minutes before the final time.

Freezing Tips
•Casseroles made with condensed soup freeze well.
•Cook pasta and rice just until tender, but still chewy, to avoid overcooking during reheating.
•Cooked pasta and rice freeze well in resealable plastic food storage bags. These are convenient to have on hand when preparing casseroles.
•Freeze the casserole in individual serving size containers for a quick meal anytime.
•Double the recipe and freeze the second casserole for another meal.

Cooking Pasta
•For every pound of pasta, bring 4 to 6 quarts of water to a full, rolling boil. Gradually add the pasta, allowing the water to return to a boil. Stir the pasta frequently to prevent it from sticking together.
•Pasta is finished cooking when it is tender but still firm to the bite, or al dente. The pasta continues to cook when the casserole is placed in the oven, so it is important that the pasta be slightly undercooked. Otherwise, the more the pasta cooks, the softer it becomes and, eventually, it will fall apart. Immediately drain pasta in a colander to prevent overcooking. For best results, combine pasta with the other recipe ingredients immediately after draining.

Cooking Rice
The different types of rice require different amounts of water and cooking times. Follow the package instructions for the best results. Here are some general tips to keep in mind when cooking rice.

•Measure the amount of water specified on the package and pour it into a medium saucepan. Bring to a boil over medium-high heat. Slowly add the rice and return to a boil. Reduce heat to low. Cover and simmer for the time specified on the package or until the rice is tender and most of the water has been absorbed.

•To test the rice for doneness, bite into a grain or squeeze a grain between your thumb and index finger. The rice is done when it is tender and the center is not hard.

Skillet Dish Basics

Skillet dishes are complete meals prepared in a skillet. They consist of a protein source, usually rice or pasta, and vegetables and seasonings. They are a convenient method of preparing dinner and cleanup is minimized. Skillets are round and shallow with straight or slightly sloping sides. When choosing a skillet, it is best to choose one that is heavy, conducts heat evenly and has a tight-fitting cover. Skillets range in size from 6 to 12 inches in diameter. Some large skillets will have a second short handle on the opposite side of the long handle, making them much easier to lift.

Tips for Preparing Skillet Dishes

•Use a deep skillet that is large enough to contain all the ingredients.

•Keep cooked pasta and rice in the freezer for quick additions to skillet dishes.

•A well-stocked pantry and freezer will make meal planning easier. They also eliminate last-minute dashes to the grocery store to pick up extra items.

Stir-Fry Basics

Stir-fry cooking is done by rapidly cooking small pieces of food over high heat, usually in hot oil. They are often cooked in a wok, but a large skillet can be substituted. Preparing the ingredients and cooking them are the two major steps in stir-frying. While cooking stir-fries, they require constant attention which makes it important to have ingredients cleaned, cut up, measured and arranged for easy access before you even begin.

A wok has a high, sloping side which allows for a hot surface area, ensuring even cooking. It is usually used for stir-frying. Woks range in size from 12 to 24 inches in diameter. The most ideal choice for a wok is 14 inches; this will accommodate typical amounts of ingredients without taking up too much space on the stove.

Many kinds of woks are available: round- or flat-bottomed woks made of thin or heavy rolled steel, aluminum, stainless steel or copper as well as electric woks with nonstick finishes and thermostatic controls. Just remember to follow the manufacturer's instructions for using and taking care of any wok you choose.

Tips for Preparing Stir-Fries

- Carefully read the entire recipe and prepare all ingredients before beginning to cook.
- Cut ingredients into similar-size pieces so they cook at the same rate.
- A consistent, easily controlled heat source is important when stir-frying.
- Stir-fry with oils that can withstand high temperatures without burning, such as peanut, corn and soybean oils.

Soups & Stew Basics

A soup is a liquid, usually hot, but sometimes cold, that has been cooked with added ingredients, such as meat and vegetables. The simplest are clear liquids, such as consommés and bouillons, which may be served plain or garnished with bits of vegetables, meat or dumplings. Most soups are heartier, filled with a number of ingredients, such as meat, fish, poultry, vegetables, pasta, dumplings or rice. Soups may be served as smooth purées or left chunky. Depending on the ingredients, they can be served as a main course or a first course.

A stew is a dish of meat, chicken or fish and vegetables that is prepared by long simmering in a covered pan. This method is called stewing. Stewing blends flavors and tenderizes less tender but economical cuts of meat.

A good soup/stew pot is one that is heavy and conducts and distributes heat evenly, such as aluminum, or stainless steel with a copper or aluminum core.

Tips for Preparing Soups & Stews

- Cut vegetables and meats into equal bite-size pieces.
- Cook pasta and rice separately and add them to the soup when it is ready to serve. This prevents the pasta or rice from overcooking and making the soup cloudy.
- Make an extra-large batch and freeze it in separate containers for quick meals.

Pasta Creations

Michigan Goulash

2 tablespoons vegetable oil
1 pound lean ground beef or ground turkey
1 medium onion, chopped
1 large green bell pepper, seeded and diced
3 ribs celery, cut into thin slices
1 small zucchini, cut into thin slices
1 jalapeño pepper,* seeded and minced
1 can (8 ounces) tomato sauce
1 cup water
¾ cup barbecue sauce
1 package (8 to 10 ounces) egg noodles, cooked and kept warm
2 cups (8 ounces) shredded Cheddar cheese

Jalapeño peppers can sting and irritate the skin; wear rubber gloves when handling peppers and do not touch eyes. Wash hands after handling peppers.

1. Preheat oven to 350°F. Grease 13×9-inch baking dish.

2. Heat oil in large skillet over medium-high heat. Add beef, stirring to break up meat. Add onion, bell pepper, celery, zucchini and jalapeño pepper; cook and stir until meat is no longer pink. Add tomato sauce, water and barbecue sauce; stir to combine. Reduce heat to medium-low and simmer 20 minutes.

3. Combine meat mixture and noodles in prepared dish; top with cheese.

4. Bake 10 to 15 minutes or until cheese is melted.

Makes 8 servings

Triple Cheese & Turkey Tetrazzini

  1 (12-ounce) package extra broad egg noodles
  2 (10¾-ounce) cans cheddar cheese condensed soup
1½ cups skim milk
  4 teaspoons HERB-OX® chicken flavored bouillon granules, divided
  3 cups diced, cooked turkey breast
  1 medium onion, chopped
1½ cups finely shredded Monterey Jack and Cheddar cheeses
1½ cups sourdough cheese-flavored croutons, crushed
  3 tablespoons butter, melted

Preheat oven to 350°F. Prepare noodles as package directs. Meanwhile, in saucepan, combine soup, milk and 3 teaspoons bouillon; heat over medium heat until warmed through. In large bowl, combine prepared egg noodles, turkey, onion and soup mixture. Stir to combine ingredients thoroughly. Place turkey mixture into 13×9-inch baking dish which has been lightly sprayed with nonstick cooking spray. In small bowl, toss crushed croutons with melted butter and remaining bouillon. Sprinkle cheese over noodles and top with crouton mixture. Bake 40 to 45 minutes or until warmed through and golden brown.

Makes 12 servings

Prep Time: 20 minutes
Total Time: 1 hour

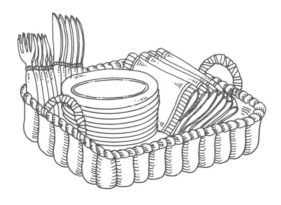

Italian Antipasto Bake

2 cups rotini or elbow macaroni, cooked in unsalted water and drained
1 bag (16 ounces) frozen vegetable combination (broccoli, water chestnuts, red pepper), thawed and drained
2 chicken breast halves, skinned, boned and cut into strips
⅔ cup bottled Italian salad dressing
½ cup drained garbanzo beans (optional)
¼ cup sliced pitted ripe olives (optional)
¼ cup (1 ounce) grated Parmesan cheese
½ teaspoon Italian seasoning
1 cup (4 ounces) shredded mozzarella cheese, divided
1⅓ cups *French's*® French Fried Onions, divided

Preheat oven to 350°F. In 13×9-inch baking dish, combine hot pasta, vegetables, chicken, salad dressing, garbanzo beans, olives, Parmesan cheese and Italian seasoning. Stir in ½ cup mozzarella cheese and *⅔ cup* French Fried Onions. Bake, covered, at 350°F for 35 minutes or until chicken is done. Top with remaining mozzarella cheese and *⅔ cup* onions; bake, uncovered, 5 minutes or until onions are golden brown.

Makes 4 to 6 servings

Microwave Directions: In 12×8-inch microwave-safe dish, combine ingredients, except chicken strips, as above. Arrange uncooked chicken strips around edges of dish. Cook, covered, on HIGH 6 minutes. Stir center of casserole; rearrange chicken and rotate dish. Cook, covered, 5 to 6 minutes or until chicken is done. Stir casserole to combine chicken and pasta mixture. Top with remaining mozzarella cheese and onions; cook, uncovered, 1 minute or until cheese melts. Let stand 5 minutes.

Four Cheese Mac & Cheese

    1 package (16 ounces) uncooked macaroni
    4 cups milk
    4 cups (16 ounces) sharp white Cheddar cheese, shredded
    4 cups (16 ounces) American cheese, shredded
    2 cups (8 ounces) Muenster cheese, shredded
    2 cups (8 ounces) mozzarella cheese, shredded
    ½ cup bread crumbs

1. Preheat oven to 350°F. Cook macaroni according to package directions. Drain; set aside and keep warm.

2. Heat milk in large saucepan over medium heat, to almost boiling. *Reduce heat to low.* Gradually add cheeses, stirring constantly. Cook; about 5 minutes until all cheese has melted.

3. Place macaroni in 4-quart casserole or individual ovenproof dishes. Pour cheese sauce over pasta and stir until well blended. Sprinkle with bread crumbs. Bake 50 to 60 minutes or until browned and bubbly. *Makes 8 servings*

Baked Manicotti

    1 jar (1 pound 10 ounces) RAGÚ® Old World Style® Pasta Sauce
    8 fresh or frozen prepared manicotti
    ½ cup (about 2 ounces) shredded mozzarella cheese
    2 tablespoons grated Parmesan cheese

Preheat oven to 450°F. In 13×9-inch baking dish, spread ½ of the Ragú Old World Style Pasta Sauce; arrange manicotti over sauce. Top with remaining sauce. Sprinkle with cheeses. Bake covered 20 minutes. Remove cover and continue baking 5 minutes or until heated through. *Makes 4 servings*

Warm Chicken & Couscous Salad

1 tablespoon olive oil
1 package (about 12 ounces) chicken tenders or boneless skinless chicken breasts,
    cut into strips
2 teaspoons Cajun or blackened seasoning
1 teaspoon minced garlic
1 can (about 14 ounces) chicken broth
2 cups frozen broccoli, carrot and red bell pepper blend
1 cup uncooked couscous
3 cups packed torn spinach leaves
¼ cup poppy seed dressing

1. Heat oil in large nonstick skillet over medium-high heat. Toss chicken with Cajun seasoning. Add chicken and garlic to skillet; cook and stir 3 minutes or until chicken is no longer pink.

2. Add broth and vegetables to skillet; bring to a boil. Stir in couscous; cover and let stand 5 minutes. Stir in spinach; transfer to plates. Drizzle with dressing.   *Makes 4 servings*

Serve It With Style: A side of fresh fruit, such as melon wedges, makes this quick salad into a satisfying meal.

Prep and Cook Time: 20 minutes

Cousin Arlene's Spaghetti Lasagna

8 ounces uncooked spaghetti or other thin pasta
1 tablespoon butter
1 clove garlic, finely chopped
2 pounds 90% lean ground beef
1 teaspoon sugar
    Salt and black pepper
2 cans (8 ounces each) tomato sauce
1 can (6 ounces) tomato paste
1 cup (8 ounces) sour cream
1 package (3 ounces) cream cheese, softened
6 green onions, chopped
¼ cup grated Parmesan cheese

1. Preheat oven to 350°F. Cook spaghetti in large saucepan of salted boiling water until almost tender. Drain and set aside.

2. Melt butter in large skillet over medium heat. Add garlic; cook and stir 1 minute. Add ground beef and sugar; season with salt and pepper. Cook and stir until beef is no longer pink; drain fat. Add tomato sauce and tomato paste; simmer 20 minutes, stirring occasionally.

3. Meanwhile beat sour cream and cream cheese in medium bowl until smooth. Add green onions; mix well.

4. Spread some meat sauce in 2-quart casserole to prevent noodles from sticking. Layer half of spaghetti, half of sour cream mixture and half of meat mixture. Repeat layers. Sprinkle Parmesan cheese over top. Bake 35 minutes or until heated through.

Makes 6 servings

Tip: This casserole can be frozen and baked later, however, thaw it in the refrigerator overnight, making sure it is completely thawed before baking.

Mexican Turkey Stuffed Shells

 1 pound ground turkey
½ cup chopped onions
¼ cup chopped fresh cilantro
 1 teaspoon minced garlic
 1 teaspoon dried oregano leaves
½ teaspoon cumin
½ teaspoon salt
 1 cup non-fat ricotta cheese
18 large pasta shells, uncooked
 2 cans (10 ounces each) mild enchilada sauce
¼ cup (1 ounce) shredded reduced-fat Monterey Jack cheese

1. In large bowl, combine turkey, onions, cilantro, garlic, oregano, cumin and salt. Blend in ricotta. Stuff each shell with 1 heaping tablespoon turkey mixture.

2. In 2-quart oblong, glass baking dish, pour 1 can of enchilada sauce. Arrange shells in baking dish; dot any remaining turkey mixture over shells. Pour remaining can of sauce over shells and cover tightly with foil. Bake at 375°F 1 to 1¼ hours or until shells are tender. Sprinkle cheese over top. Re-cover and allow to stand 10 minutes.

Makes 6 servings

Favorite recipe from **National Turkey Federation**

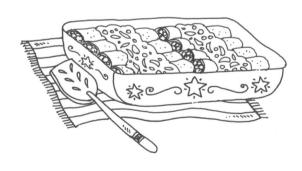

Spaghetti Rolls

1 package (8 ounces) manicotti shells
2 pounds ground beef
1 tablespoon onion powder
1 teaspoon salt
½ teaspoon black pepper
2 cups spaghetti sauce, divided
1 cup (4 ounces) shredded pizza-flavored cheese blend or mozzarella cheese

1. Cook pasta according to package directions. Drain in colander, then rinse under warm running water. Drain well.

2. Preheat oven to 350°F. Grease 13×9-inch baking pan.

3. Brown beef in large skillet over medium-high heat, stirring to separate meat; drain drippings. Stir in onion powder, salt and pepper. Stir in 1 cup spaghetti sauce; cool and set aside.

4. Reserve ½ cup ground beef mixture. Combine remaining beef mixture with cheese in large bowl; fill shells with beef mixture using spoon.

5. Arrange shells in prepared pan. Combine remaining 1 cup spaghetti sauce and reserved beef mixture in small bowl; blend well. Pour over shells. Cover with foil.

6. Bake 20 to 30 minutes or until hot.

Makes 4 servings

Cheesy Pasta Swirls

    4 ounces fettuccine, cooked in unsalted water and drained
    1 bag (16 ounces) frozen vegetable combination (peas, carrots, cauliflower), thawed
        and drained
    1 cup (4 ounces) shredded mozzarella cheese
    ½ cup (2 ounces) cubed provolone cheese
 1⅓ cups *French's®* French Fried Onions, divided
    1 can (10¾ ounces) condensed cream of mushroom soup
    ¾ cup milk
    ½ teaspoon garlic salt
    ⅓ cup (about 1½ ounces) grated Parmesan cheese

Preheat oven to 350°F. In 12×8-inch baking dish, combine vegetables, mozzarella, provolone and *⅔ cup* French Fried Onions. Twirl a few strands of hot fettuccine around long-tined fork to form a pasta swirl. Remove pasta swirl from fork; stand upright on top of vegetable mixture. Repeat process to form 5 more swirls. In medium bowl, stir together soup, milk and garlic salt; pour over pasta swirls and vegetable mixture. Bake, loosely covered, at 350°F for 30 minutes or until vegetables are done. Top pasta swirls with Parmesan cheese; sprinkle remaining *⅔ cup* onions around swirls. Bake, uncovered, 5 minutes or until onions are golden brown.   *Makes 6 servings*

Microwave Directions: In 12×8-inch microwave-safe dish, prepare vegetable mixture as above. Form pasta swirls and place on vegetables as above. Prepare soup mixture as above; pour over pasta and vegetables. Cook, loosely covered, on HIGH 14 to 16 minutes or until vegetables are done. Rotate dish halfway through cooking time. Top pasta swirls with Parmesan cheese and remaining onions as above; cook, uncovered, 1 minute. Let stand 5 minutes.

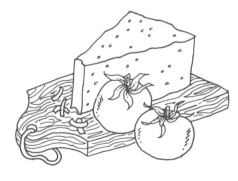

One-Pan Chicken Alfredo

1¼ pounds skinless, chicken breasts
2 tablespoons CRISCO® Oil*
2 cans (14½ ounces each) chicken broth
1 package (8 ounces) uncooked rotini pasta
1½ cups baby carrots, sliced into thin rounds
1 tablespoon plus 1½ teaspoons cornstarch
1 package (1.6 ounces) garlic-herb pasta sauce mix
1½ cups skim milk
1 package (10 ounces) frozen chopped broccoli, thawed, drained and squeezed dry
⅓ cup Parmesan cheese

Use your favorite Crisco Oil product.

Rinse chicken; pat dry. Cut into ¾-inch pieces. Heat oil in deep nonstick 12-inch skillet or Dutch oven on medium-high heat. Add chicken. Cook and stir for 3 minutes or until no longer pink in center. Stir in broth and rotini. Bring to a boil. Reduce heat to medium. Cover. Simmer 5 minutes. Add carrots. Stir and cover. Cook 4 to 5 minutes longer.

Place cornstarch and pasta sauce mix in small bowl. Whisk in milk until smooth. Add gradually to chicken mixture, stirring constantly. Mix in broccoli. Cook and stir for 3 to 5 minutes or until sauce comes to a boil and is thickened. Remove from heat. Sprinkle with cheese. Cover. Let stand 5 minutes. Serve.   *Makes 6 servings*

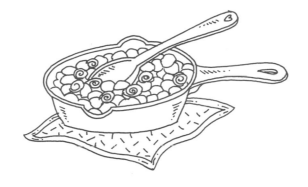

One Pot Creamy Chicken and Noodles

3 cups water
1 tablespoon HERB-OX® chicken flavored bouillon granules
8 ounces wide egg noodles
1 cup frozen mixed vegetables
⅓ cup chopped onion
1 (10¾-ounce) can condensed cream of mushroom soup, undiluted
1 cup (4 ounces) shredded Cheddar cheese
½ cup milk
2 (5-ounce) cans HORMEL® chunk breast of chicken, drained and flaked*
⅛ to ¼ teaspoon pepper

You may substitute 2 (5-ounce) cans HORMEL® chunk turkey or chunk lean ham. (If using ham, omit bouillon; proceed as above.)

In medium saucepan, bring water and bouillon to a boil. Stir in uncooked noodles. Cover; simmer 5 minutes, stirring occasionally. Add vegetables and onion. Cover; simmer 5 minutes, or until noodles are tender and most liquid is absorbed. Add soup, cheese and milk; mix well. Stir in chicken and pepper. Heat through.   *Makes about 6 servings*

Prep Time: 10 minutes
Total Time: 25 minutes

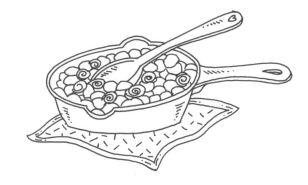

Colorful Turkey Pasta Bake

　2 cups (about 8 ounces) uncooked mixed vegetable rotini pasta*
　1 tablespoon margarine
　1 tablespoon all-purpose flour
　¼ teaspoon salt
　⅛ teaspoon pepper
1⅓ cups skim milk
　1 cup (4 ounces) shredded natural Swiss cheese, divided
　2 cups cubed cooked turkey

*If desired, substitute elbow macaroni, rotelle, small shells or ziti for rotini.

1. Cook pasta according to package directions; drain. In 2-quart saucepan, melt margarine over medium heat. Stir in flour, salt and pepper. Blend in milk; cook, stirring constantly, until thickened and bubbly. Add ¾ cup cheese; stir until melted. Stir in turkey and pasta.

2. Spray 8-inch square baking dish with nonstick vegetable spray. Add pasta mixture; sprinkle with remaining ¼ cup cheese. Bake at 350°F until heated through, about 30 minutes. To serve, cut into squares.　　　　　　　　　　　　　*Makes 4 servings*

Favorite recipe from **National Turkey Federation**

Italian Tomato Bake

1 pound sweet Italian sausage, cut into ½-inch slices
2 tablespoons margarine or butter
1 cup chopped onion
4 cups cooked egg noodles
2 cups frozen broccoli florets, thawed and drained
2 cups prepared pasta sauce
½ cup diced tomatoes
2 cloves garlic, minced
3 plum tomatoes, sliced
1 cup (8 ounces) ricotta cheese
⅓ cup grated Parmesan cheese
1 teaspoon dried oregano leaves

1. Preheat oven to 350°F. Cook sausage in large skillet over medium heat about 10 minutes or until barely pink in center. Drain on paper towels; set aside. Drain fat from skillet.

2. Add margarine and onion to skillet; cook and stir until onion is tender. Combine onion, noodles, broccoli, pasta sauce, diced tomatoes and garlic in large bowl; mix well. Transfer to 13×9-inch baking dish.

3. Top mixture with prepared sausage and arrange tomato slices over top. Place 1 heaping tablespoonful ricotta cheese on each tomato slice. Sprinkle casserole with Parmesan cheese and oregano. Bake 35 minutes or until hot and bubbly. *Makes 6 servings*

Macaroni & Cheese with Bacon

  3 cups (8 ounces) uncooked rotini pasta
  2 tablespoons butter or margarine
  2 tablespoons all-purpose flour
  ¼ teaspoon salt
  ¼ teaspoon dry mustard
  ⅛ teaspoon black pepper
1½ cups milk
  2 cups (8 ounces) shredded sharp Cheddar cheese
  8 ounces bacon, crisply cooked and crumbled*
  2 medium tomatoes, sliced

*You may substitute 1 cup of cubed cooked ham for the bacon.

1. Preheat oven to 350°F. Lightly grease 1½-quart shallow casserole.

2. Cook pasta according to package directions; drain and return to saucepan.

3. Melt butter over medium-low heat in 2-quart saucepan. Whisk in flour, salt, mustard and pepper; cook and stir 1 minute. Whisk in milk. Bring to a boil over medium heat, stirring frequently. Reduce heat and simmer 2 minutes. Remove from heat. Add cheese; stir until melted.

4. Add cheese mixture and bacon to pasta; stir until well blended. Transfer to prepared casserole. Bake uncovered 20 minutes. Arrange tomato slices on casserole. Bake additional 5 to 8 minutes or until casserole is bubbly and tomatoes are hot.

Makes 4 servings

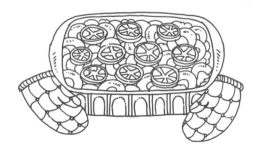

Chicken Parisienne

6 boneless skinless chicken breasts (about 1½ pounds), cubed
½ teaspoon salt
½ teaspoon black pepper
½ teaspoon paprika
1 can (10¾ ounces) condensed cream of mushroom or cream of chicken soup, undiluted
2 cans (4 ounces each) sliced mushrooms, drained
½ cup dry white wine
1 cup sour cream
6 cups hot cooked egg noodles

Slow Cooker Directions

1. Place chicken in slow cooker. Sprinkle with salt, pepper and paprika.

2. Add soup, mushrooms and wine to slow cooker; mix well. Cover and cook on HIGH 2 to 3 hours. Add sour cream during last 30 minutes of cooking. Serve over noodles.

Makes 6 servings

Tip: For a taste-pleasing variation, try this dish over rice instead of noodles.

Italian Lasagna Rolls

     8 ounces lasagna noodles (about 12 noodles)
     2 (10-ounce) packages frozen spinach, thawed and well drained
    16 ounces nonfat cottage cheese
   2½ cups shredded mozzarella cheese, divided
   1½ cups grated Parmesan cheese, divided
     1 package (8 ounces) non-fat cream cheese, softened
    ½ teaspoon dried basil leaves
    ¼ teaspoon *each* salt, black pepper and dried oregano leaves
       Light Tomato Sauce (recipe follows)

Cook lasagna noodles according to package directions; drain and cool slightly. Combine
spinach, cottage cheese, 2 cups mozzarella cheese, 1 cup Parmesan cheese, cream cheese,
basil, salt, pepper and oregano in large bowl; stir well. Spread scant ½ cup spinach mixture
on each lasagna noodle; roll up jelly-roll fashion, starting at narrow end. Place lasagna
rolls, seam side down, in 13×9×2-inch baking dish. Pour Light Tomato Sauce evenly over
rolls; sprinkle with ½ cup Parmesan cheese and ½ cup mozzarella cheese. Bake at 350°F
for 50 to 60 minutes, covering baking dish with foil for first 30 minutes. (To prevent
mozzarella cheese from sticking, coat foil with cooking spray.)   *Makes 5 to 6 servings*

Light Tomato Sauce

     1 large onion, chopped
    ¼ cup finely chopped green bell pepper
     3 cloves garlic, minced
     3 tablespoons low-fat margarine
     2 (28-ounce) cans crushed tomatoes in tomato puree
     1 (15-ounce) can tomato sauce
     2 tablespoons sugar
     2 teaspoons *each* dried basil leaves and dried Italian seasoning
    ¼ teaspoon *each* salt and black pepper

Sauté onion, bell pepper and garlic in margarine in large skillet until tender. Add remaining
ingredients; simmer 30 minutes.

Favorite recipe from **North Dakota Wheat Commission**

Dilled Turkey Noodle Bake

　　1 cup chopped celery
　　½ cup chopped onion
　　⅓ cup chopped green bell pepper
　　1 tablespoon margarine
　　2 tablespoons all-purpose flour
1¾ cups skim milk
　　2 teaspoons dried parsley flakes
　　1 teaspoon dried dill
　　¾ teaspoon salt
　　½ teaspoon black pepper
　　4 cups egg noodles, cooked according to package directions
　　2 cups ½-inch cubed cooked turkey
　　1 cup non-fat sour cream
　　¼ cup seasoned dry bread crumbs

1. In large nonstick skillet over medium heat, sauté celery, onion and green pepper in margarine 5 minutes or until vegetables are tender. Reduce heat to low; stir in flour. Cook 1 minute, stirring constantly. Gradually add milk, stirring constantly. Stir in parsley, dill, salt and black pepper; cook 1 to 2 minutes or until sauce is thickened. Remove from heat.

2. Add noodles, turkey and sour cream to ingredients in skillet; mix well. Spray 11×7-inch baking dish with vegetable cooking spray. Add noodle mixture; sprinkle with bread crumbs. Bake at 350°F 30 minutes or until hot and bubbly. *Makes 4 servings*

Favorite recipe from **National Turkey Federation**

Skillet Pasta Roma

½ pound Italian sausage, sliced or crumbled
1 large onion, coarsely chopped
1 large clove garlic, minced
2 cans (14½ ounces each) DEL MONTE® Diced Tomatoes with Basil, Garlic & Oregano
1 can (8 ounces) DEL MONTE Tomato Sauce
1 cup water
8 ounces uncooked rotini or other spiral pasta
8 mushrooms, sliced (optional)
  Grated Parmesan cheese and fresh parsley sprigs (optional)

1. Brown sausage in large skillet. Add onion and garlic. Cook until onion is soft; drain. Stir in undrained tomatoes, tomato sauce, water and pasta.

2. Cover and bring to a boil; reduce heat. Simmer, covered, 25 to 30 minutes or until pasta is tender, stirring occasionally.

3. Stir in mushrooms, if desired; simmer 5 minutes. Serve in skillet garnished with cheese and parsley, if desired. *Makes 4 servings*

Mediterranean Pasta & Chicken

1 tablespoon olive oil
8 ounces boneless, skinless chicken breasts, cut into thin strips
1 jar (1 pound 10 ounces) RAGÚ® Chunky Gardenstyle Pasta Sauce
1 jar (7 ounces) roasted red peppers, drained and sliced
1 jar (6 ounces) marinated artichoke hearts, drained and coarsely chopped
⅔ cup sliced pitted ripe olives
¼ to ½ teaspoon crushed red pepper flakes
8 ounces rotelle or spiral pasta, cooked and drained

In 12-inch skillet, heat olive oil over medium-high heat and cook chicken, stirring frequently, 4 minutes or until thoroughly cooked. Remove chicken and set aside.

In same skillet, stir in Pasta Sauce, roasted red peppers, artichokes, olives and red pepper flakes. Bring to a boil over high heat. Reduce heat to low and simmer uncovered, stirring occasionally, 10 minutes. Return chicken to skillet and heat through. Toss hot pasta with sauce and sprinkle, if desired, with grated Parmesan cheese. *Makes 4 servings*

Mom's Spaghetti Sauce

7½ cups water
3 cans (15 ounces each) tomato purée
3 cans (6 ounces each) tomato paste*
1 can (14½ ounces) tomatoes, undrained
2 large onions, chopped
3 tablespoons sugar
2 tablespoons salt
1½ tablespoons Italian seasoning
1½ tablespoons dried oregano
1 tablespoon black pepper
6 large cloves garlic, minced
3 bay leaves
2 to 2½ pounds Italian hot or sweet sausage (optional)
3 pounds ground beef, shaped into about 35 meatballs and browned (optional)

Add more tomato paste if sauce is not thick enough for your taste.

Slow Cooker Directions
1. Combine all ingredients, except optional sausage and meatballs, in slow cooker; mix well. If using optional sausage and meatballs, divide sauce between two slow cookers.

2. Cover; cook on HIGH 1 hour. Add meatballs and sausages to each slow cooker, if desired. Cover; cook on LOW 6 to 8 hours.   *Makes 10 to 12 servings*

Serving Suggestion: Serve over hot spaghetti or your favorite pasta. Any leftover meatless sauce can be served over cooked boneless, skinless chicken breasts or used to make a flavorful base for a pot of vegetable soup.

Noodly Chicken

1 (1- to 2-pound) boneless, skinless chicken breasts
2 tablespoons CRISCO® Oil*
4 ounces egg noodles
¼ cup all-purpose flour
1 cup milk
1 cup cut-up fresh vegetables or frozen vegetables, thawed
½ cup chicken broth
½ cup grated Parmesan cheese
1 tablespoon chopped parsley
¼ teaspoon salt
⅛ to ¼ teaspoon pepper

Use your favorite Crisco Oil product.

Rinse chicken; pat dry.

Heat oil in large skillet on medium heat. Add chicken. Cook a few minutes on each side, turning once, until chicken is no longer pink in center. Remove from skillet. Cut into bite-size pieces. Remove skillet from heat.

Cook noodles according to package directions. Drain. Keep warm.

Stir flour into drippings in skillet. Stir in milk. Cook and stir on medium-high heat until mixture begins to thicken. Stir in vegetables, chicken broth, cheese, parsley, salt, pepper and chicken. Cook a few minutes longer until vegetables are desired consistency. Combine with noodles. Serve.

Makes 4 servings

Easy Microwave Turkey Lasagna

1 pound ground turkey
1 clove garlic, chopped
1 cup onion, chopped
1 can (14½ ounces) tomatoes, chopped
1 can (6 ounces) tomato paste
2½ teaspoons Italian seasoning or dried oregano leaves
8 uncooked lasagna noodles
1 container (12 ounces) low-fat cottage cheese
2 cups (8 ounces) part-skim mozzarella cheese, shredded

1. In 2-quart microwave-safe casserole dish, combine turkey, garlic and onion; cover with plastic wrap. Microwave at HIGH (100% power) 5 minutes, stirring halfway through cooking time. Add tomatoes, tomato paste and Italian seasoning. Microwave, uncovered, at HIGH (100% power) 5 minutes.

2. Spoon ⅓ of the tomato sauce (about 1⅓ cups) over bottom of oblong 2-quart casserole dish. Top with 4 lasagna noodles, breaking noodles to fit. Spoon cottage cheese over noodles; sprinkle mozzarella over top of cottage cheese. Spoon ⅓ more sauce over cheese; top with remaining noodles. Spoon remaining sauce over noodles; cover with vented plastic wrap.

3. Microwave at HIGH (100% power) 5 minutes. Microwave at MEDIUM (50% power) 20 to 25 minutes or until noodles are tender. Let stand, covered, 10 minutes.

Makes 8 servings

Tip: To absorb any spill overs in microwave, set lasagna dish on several layers of paper toweling.

*Favorite recipe from **National Turkey Federation***

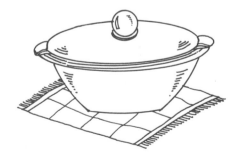

Wild Rice Tetrazzini

1 cup chopped green bell pepper
1 cup chopped onion
1 jar (8 ounces) sliced mushrooms, drained
¼ cup butter or margarine
1 package (about 1¼ pounds) fresh lean ground turkey
½ cup grated Parmesan cheese
3 tablespoons all-purpose flour
2 teaspoons garlic powder
1 teaspoon salt
1 teaspoon black pepper
2 cups chicken broth
2 cups cream or milk
½ cup cooking sherry
2 cups cooked and drained spaghetti
3 cups cooked wild rice
2 cups shredded mozzarella cheese, divided
  Parsley flakes

Preheat oven to 350°F. Sauté green pepper, onion and mushrooms in butter. Add turkey; brown. Add parmesan cheese, flour and seasonings; stir and cook 5 minutes. Gradually add broth, cream and sherry. Heat thoroughly. Place spaghetti and wild rice in greased 5-quart casserole. Mix in 1 cup mozzarella cheese. Pour turkey mixture in casserole; lightly mix. Top with remaining 1 cup mozzarella cheese and parsley. Cover with foil. Bake 30 minutes. Remove foil; continue baking 10 minutes or until lightly browned.

Makes 8 to 10 servings

Favorite recipe from **Minnesota Cultivated Wild Rice Council**

Slow Cooker Pizza Casserole

        4 jars (14 ounces each) pizza sauce
1½ pounds ground beef, cooked and drained
        1 pound sausage, cooked and drained
        1 pound corkscrew pasta, cooked and drained
        2 cups (8 ounces) shredded mozzarella cheese
        2 cups freshly grated Parmesan cheese
        2 cans (4 ounces each) mushroom stems and pieces, drained
        2 packages (3 ounces each) sliced pepperoni
        ½ cup finely chopped onion
        ½ cup finely chopped green bell pepper
        1 clove garlic minced

Slow Cooker Directions

1. Combine all ingredients in slow cooker.

2. Cover; cook on LOW 4 hours or on HIGH 2 hours.

Makes 6 servings

Tip: This is a great dish for potlucks and large gatherings.

Classico® Two Sauce Lasagna

1 jar (26 ounces) CLASSICO® Tomato & Basil pasta sauce
1 jar (17 ounces) CLASSICO® Alfredo pasta sauce
1 box lasagna noodles (12 noodles), cooked and drained
1 container (15 ounces) Ricotta cheese
2 cups (16 ounces) shredded mozzarella cheese
¼ cup grated parmesan cheese
3 eggs

Optional
1 package (10 ounces) frozen chopped spinach, thawed and drained
1 pound Italian sausage browned and drained

Preheat oven to 350°F. In large bowl, combine ricotta, mozzarella, 2 tablespoons parmesan and eggs; mix well. In a 13×9 baking dish, spread 1 cup Classico® Tomato Basil sauce. Layer 4 lasagna noodles over sauce. Top noodles with half remaining cheese mixture, spinach, remaining Classico® Tomato Basil sauce and sausage. Repeat layers and spread remaining mixture. Top with 4 remaining lasagna noodles. Spread Classico® Alfredo sauce evenly on top, and sprinkle with remaining parmesan. Cover with aluminum foil and bake for about 40 minutes. Uncover; bake for 15 minutes longer or until bubbly. Let stand 10 minutes before serving. *Makes 10 to 12 servings*

Cook Time: 55 minutes

Slow Cooker Macaroni and Cheese

2 eggs
¾ cup milk
1 package (16 ounces) cooked elbow macaroni
4 cups (16 ounces) grated Cheddar cheese
1 can (12 ounces) evaporated milk
1 can (10¾ ounces) condensed Cheddar cheese soup, undiluted
½ cup (1 stick) margarine or butter, melted

Slow Cooker Directions

1. Combine eggs and milk in small bowl; whisk well.

2. Add egg mixture and remaining ingredients to slow cooker; mix well. Cover; cook on LOW 3 hours. *Makes 6 servings*

Triple Mushroom Kugel

  3 tablespoons Butter Flavor CRISCO® Shortening
  1 large onion, finely diced
12 ounces white mushrooms, quartered
  6 ounces portabella mushrooms, sliced
  6 ounces crimini mushrooms, quartered
  3 tablespoons chopped garlic
  2 teaspoons dried rosemary, crushed
  1 tablespoon dried thyme leaves
  4 eggs, beaten
  2 cups sour cream
  1 tablespoon cider vinegar
  1 tablespoon Worcestershire sauce
  1 (12 ounce) package wide egg noodles, cooked and well drained
  ½ cup bread crumbs

Preheat oven to 375°F.

In large sauté pan, melt CRISCO® until very hot. Add onion and sauté until transparent.

Add mushrooms and sauté for 5 minutes. Add garlic, rosemary and thyme; continue to cook for additional 3 minutes. Cool mushrooms in colander reserving juices.

Mix eggs, sour cream, vinegar and Worcestershire until well blended.

Toss mushrooms with noodles then fold in egg mixture.

Pour into well greased 13×9 glass pan and top with bread crumbs. Bake for 35 to 40 minutes. Let cool for 15 minutes before cutting into portions. *Makes 4 to 6 servings*

Hearty Noodle Casserole

1 pound Italian sausage, casings removed
1 jar (26½ ounces) spaghetti sauce
1 pint (16 ounces) ricotta or cottage cheese
1 package (12 ounces) extra-wide egg noodles, cooked
1 package (8 ounces) shredded mozzarella cheese, divided
1 can (4 ounces) sliced mushrooms
½ cup chopped green bell pepper

1. Preheat oven to 350°F. Cook sausage in large skillet over medium-high heat about 5 minutes or until no longer pink, stirring to separate.

2. Combine sausage, sauce, ricotta cheese, noodles, half the mozzarella cheese, mushrooms and bell pepper in large bowl. Spoon into 3-quart or 13×9-inch baking pan. Top with remaining mozzarella cheese.

3. Bake, uncovered, about 25 minutes or until heated through.   *Makes 4 to 6 servings*

Creamy Creole Turkey Bake

⅔ cup chopped onion
⅔ cup chopped celery
⅓ cup chopped green bell pepper
1 garlic clove, minced
1 tablespoon margarine
¼ pound mushrooms, sliced
4 ounces light cream cheese, softened
1 can (8 ounces) low-sodium stewed tomatoes, drained
1½ teaspoons creole seasoning
4 ounces uncooked fettuccini, cooked according to package directions
2 cups ½-inch cubed cooked turkey
Vegetable cooking spray
¼ cup grated Parmesan cheese

1. In medium non-stick skillet, over medium-high heat, sauté onion, celery, green pepper and garlic in margarine 4 to 5 minutes or until vegetables are crisp-tender. Add mushrooms and sauté 2 minutes. Remove from heat.

2. In medium bowl blend cream cheese, tomatoes and creole seasoning. Fold in vegetable mixture, fettuccini and turkey.

3. Pour mixture into 9-inch square dish, sprayed with vegetable cooking spray. Sprinkle cheese over top and bake at 325°F for 30 minutes or until bubbly. *Makes 4 servings*

*Favorite recipe from **National Turkey Federation***

Easy Chicken Alfredo

1½ pounds chicken breast, cut into ½-inch pieces
1 medium onion, chopped
1 tablespoon olive oil
1 tablespoon dried chives
1 tablespoon dried basil leaves
1 teaspoon lemon pepper
¼ teaspoon ground ginger
½ pound broccoli, coarsely chopped
1 red bell pepper, chopped
1 can (8 ounces) sliced water chestnuts, drained
1 cup baby carrots
3 cloves garlic, minced
1 jar (16 ounces) Alfredo sauce
1 package (8 ounces) wide egg noodles, cooked and drained

Slow Cooker Directions

1. Combine chicken, onion, olive oil, chives, basil, lemon pepper and ginger in slow cooker; stir thoroughly. Add broccoli, bell pepper, water chestnuts, carrots and garlic. Mix well.

2. Cover; cook on LOW 8 hours or on HIGH 3 hours.

3. Add Alfredo sauce and cook an additional 30 minutes or until heated through.

4. Serve over hot cooked egg noodles. *Makes 6 servings*

Hearty Soups & Stews

Pork Stew with Cactus

1½ pounds pork steaks or chops, trimmed of fat and cubed
2 tablespoons canola oil
2 medium onions, chopped
2 cloves garlic, minced
1 teaspoon ground cumin
1 teaspoon salt
1 can (7 ounces) mild diced green chilies
1 jar (16 to 20 ounces) water-packed nopalitos, drained (see tip)
8 medium potatoes, peeled and diced

1. Brown meat in oil in large, deep skillet over medium-high heat. Add onions, garlic, cumin and salt. Reduce heat to medium-low and cook until onion is soft but not browned, about 5 minutes.

2. Add nopalitos, potatoes and chilies. Cover and simmer 1 hour, adding water, as needed.
   Makes 8 servings

Tip: Nopales (noh-PAH-lays) are the fleshy, oval pads of the nopal, or prickly pear cactus. Long popular in Mexico, they are gaining popularity in the U.S. Nopales that have been diced or cut into strips are called nopalitos. They are available canned (pickled or packed in water) in many supermarkets. Nopalitos resemble green beans and have a delicate, slightly tart green-bean flavor.

Creamy Slow Cooker Seafood Chowder

1 quart (4 cups) half-and-half
2 cans (14½ ounces each) whole white potatoes, drained and cubed
2 cans (10¾ ounces) condensed cream of mushroom soup, undiluted
1 bag (16 ounces) frozen hash brown potatoes
1 onion, minced
½ cup (1 stick) butter, diced
1 teaspoon salt
1 teaspoon black pepper
5 cans (about 8 ounces each) whole oysters, drained and rinsed
2 cans (about 6 ounces each) minced clams
2 cans (about 4 ounces each) cocktail shrimp, drained and rinsed

Slow Cooker Directions

1. Combine half-and-half, canned potatoes, soup, frozen potatoes, onion, butter, salt and pepper in 5- or 6-quart slow cooker. Mix well.

2. Add oysters, clams and shrimp; stir gently.

3. Cover; cook on LOW for 4 to 5 hours.

Makes 8 to 10 servings

Tip: This chowder is great served with grilled cheese sandwiches!

Smoked Sausage Gumbo

1 can (14½ ounces) diced tomatoes, undrained
1 cup chicken broth
¼ cup all-purpose flour
2 tablespoons olive oil
¾ pound Polish sausage, cut into ½-inch pieces
1 medium onion, diced
1 green bell pepper, diced
2 ribs celery, chopped
1 carrot, peeled and chopped
2 teaspoons dried oregano leaves
2 teaspoons dried thyme leaves
⅛ teaspoon ground red pepper
1 cup uncooked rice
Chopped parsley (optional)

Slow Cooker Directions

1. Combine tomatoes with juice and broth in slow cooker. Sprinkle flour evenly over bottom of small skillet. Cook over high heat without stirring 3 to 4 minutes or until flour begins to brown. Reduce heat to medium; stir flour about 4 minutes. Stir in oil until smooth. Carefully whisk flour mixture into slow cooker.

2. Add sausage, onion, bell pepper, celery, carrot, oregano, thyme and red pepper to slow cooker. Stir well. Cover; cook on LOW 4½ to 5 hours or until juices are thickened.

3. About 30 minutes before gumbo is ready to serve, prepare rice. Cook rice according to package directions. Serve gumbo over rice. Sprinkle with parsley, if desired.

Makes 4 servings

Tip: If gumbo thickens upon standing, stir in additional broth.

Cajun Chili

1½ pounds ground beef
2 cans (15 ounces each) Cajun-style mixed vegetables, undrained
2 cans (10¾ ounces each) condensed tomato soup, undiluted
1 can (14½ ounces) diced tomatoes, undrained
3 sausages with Cheddar cheese (about 8 ounces), quartered and sliced into bite-size pieces
Shredded cheddar cheese (optional)

Slow Cooker Directions

1. Cook and stir ground beef in medium skillet over medium-high heat until no longer pink. Drain well.

2. Place ground beef, mixed vegetables, soup, tomatoes with juice and sausage in slow cooker. Cover; cook on HIGH 2 hours. Serve with shredded cheese, if desired.

Makes 10 servings

Rustic Vegetable Soup

1 jar (16 ounces) picante sauce
1 package (10 ounces) frozen mixed vegetables, thawed
1 package (10 ounces) frozen cut green beans, thawed
1 can (10 ounces) condensed beef broth, undiluted
1 to 2 baking potatoes, cut into ½-inch pieces
1 medium green bell pepper, chopped
½ teaspoon sugar
¼ cup finely chopped fresh parsley

Slow Cooker Directions

Combine all ingredients except parsley in slow cooker. Cover; cook on LOW 8 hours or on HIGH 4 hours. Stir in parsley; serve.

Makes 8 servings

Nancy's Chicken Noodle Soup

1 can (48 ounces) chicken broth
2 boneless skinless chicken breasts, cut into bite-size pieces
4 cups water
⅔ cup diced onion
⅔ cup diced celery
⅔ cup diced carrots
⅔ cup sliced mushrooms
½ cup frozen peas
4 chicken bouillon cubes
2 tablespoons margarine
1 tablespoon parsley flakes
1 teaspoon salt
1 teaspoon ground cumin
1 teaspoon dried marjoram leaves
1 teaspoon black pepper
2 cups cooked egg noodles

Slow Cooker Directions

1. Combine all ingredients except noodles in slow cooker.

2. Cover; cook on LOW 4 to 6 hours or on HIGH 3 to 4 hours. Add noodles 30 minutes before serving.

Makes 4 servings

Potato & Spinach Soup with Gouda

Soup

  9 medium Yukon Gold potatoes, peeled and cubed (about 6 cups)
  2 cans (14 ounces each) chicken broth
  ½ cup water
  1 small red onion, finely diced
  5 ounces baby spinach leaves
  ½ teaspoon salt
  ¼ teaspoon ground red pepper
  ¼ teaspoon black pepper
2½ cups shredded smoked Gouda cheese, divided
  1 can (12 ounces) evaporated milk

Garnish

  4 tablespoons olive oil
  4 cloves garlic, cut into thin slices
  5 to 7 sprigs parsley, finely chopped

Slow Cooker Directions

1. Combine potatoes, chicken broth, water, onion, spinach, salt, red and black pepper in slow cooker.

2. Cover; cook on LOW 10 hours or until potatoes are tender.

3. Slightly mash potatoes in slow cooker; add 2 cups Gouda and evaporated milk. Cover; cook on HIGH 15 to 20 minutes or until cheese is melted.

4. Heat oil in small saucepan over low heat. Cook and stir garlic until golden brown; set aside. Pour soup into bowls. Sprinkle 2 to 3 teaspoons remaining Gouda cheese in each bowl. Add spoonful of garlic to center of each bowl; sprinkle with parsley.

Makes 8 to 10 servings

Serving Suggestion: This soup goes well with simple fish dinners, or you can add ham and serve it as an entire meal. If you add ham, eliminate the salt in the recipe.

Clam Chowder

    5 cans (10¾ ounces each) condensed cream of potato soup, undiluted
    2 cans (12 ounces each) evaporated skimmed milk
    2 cans (10 ounces each) whole baby clams, rinsed and drained
    1 can (14¾ ounces) cream-style corn
    2 cans (4 ounces each) tiny shrimp, rinsed and drained
    ¾ cup crisp-cooked and crumbled bacon (about ½ pound) or imitation bacon bits
       Lemon pepper to taste
       Oyster crackers

Slow Cooker Directions

Combine all ingredients except crackers in slow cooker. Cover; cook on LOW 3 to 4 hours, stirring occasionally. Serve with oyster crackers. *Makes 10 servings*

Black and White Chili

       Nonstick cooking spray
    1 pound chicken tenders, cut into ¾-inch pieces
    1 cup coarsely chopped onion
    1 can (15½ ounces) Great Northern beans, drained
    1 can (15 ounces) black beans, drained
    1 can (14½ ounces) Mexican-style stewed tomatoes, undrained
    2 tablespoons Texas-style chili powder seasoning mix

Slow Cooker Directions

1. Spray large saucepan with cooking spray; heat over medium heat until hot. Add chicken and onion; cook and stir 5 minutes or until chicken is browned.

2. Combine cooked chicken, onion, beans, tomatoes with juice and chili seasoning in slow cooker. Cover; cook on LOW 4 to 4½ hours. *Makes 6 servings*

Chicken and Wild Rice Soup

3 cans (14½ ounces each) chicken broth
1 pound boneless skinless chicken breasts or thighs, cut into bite-size pieces
2 cups water
1 cup sliced celery
1 cup diced carrots
1 package (6 ounces) converted long grain and wild rice mix with seasoning packet
    (not quick-cooking or instant rice)
½ cup chopped onion
1 tablespoon dried parsley flakes
½ teaspoon black pepper

Slow Cooker Directions

Combine all ingredients in slow cooker; mix well. Cover; cook on LOW 6 to 7 hours or on HIGH 4 to 5 hours or until chicken is tender. *Makes 9 (1½-cup) servings*

Prep Time: 20 minutes
Cook Time: 6 to 7 hours

Veal Stew with Horseradish

1¼ pounds lean veal, cut into 1-inch cubes
2 medium sweet potatoes, peeled and cut into 1-inch pieces
1 can (14½ ounces) diced tomatoes, undrained
1 package (10 ounces) frozen corn
1 package (9 ounces) frozen lima beans
1 large onion, chopped
1 cup vegetable broth
1 tablespoon chili powder
1 tablespoon extra-hot horseradish
1 tablespoon honey

Slow Cooker Directions

1. Place all ingredients in slow cooker; mix well.

2. Cover; cook on LOW 7 to 8 hours or until veal is tender. *Makes 6 servings*

Roast Tomato-Basil Soup

2 cans (28 ounces each) peeled whole tomatoes, drained and liquid reserved
2½ tablespoons packed dark brown sugar
1 medium onion, finely chopped
3 cups chicken broth
3 tablespoons tomato paste
¼ teaspoon ground allspice
1 can (5 ounces) evaporated milk
¼ cup shredded fresh basil leaves (about 10 large)
Salt and black pepper

Slow Cooker Directions

1. Preheat oven to 450°F. Line cookie sheet with foil; spray with nonstick cooking spray. Arrange tomatoes on foil in single layer. Sprinkle with brown sugar and top with onion. Bake about 25 to 30 minutes or until tomatoes look dry and light brown. Let tomatoes cool slightly; finely chop.

2. Place tomato mixture, 3 cups reserved liquid from tomatoes, chicken broth, tomato paste and allspice in slow cooker. Mix well. Cover; cook on LOW 8 hours or on HIGH 4 hours.

3. Add evaporated milk and basil; season with salt and pepper. Cook 30 minutes or until hot.

Makes 6 servings

Campfire Sausage and Potato Soup

8 ounces kielbasa sausage
1 can (15½ ounces) dark kidney beans, rinsed and drained
1 can (14½ ounces) diced tomatoes, undrained
1 can (10½ ounces) condensed beef broth
1 large baking potato, cut into ½-inch cubes
1 medium onion, diced
1 medium green bell pepper, diced
1 teaspoon dried oregano leaves
½ teaspoon sugar
1 to 2 teaspoons ground cumin

Slow Cooker Directions
Cut sausage lengthwise in half, then crosswise into ½-inch pieces. Combine all ingredients except cumin in slow cooker. Cover; cook on LOW 8 hours or on HIGH 4 hours. Season to taste with cumin before serving. *Makes 6 to 7 servings*

Skillet Taco Chili

1 pound ground beef
1 can (14½ ounces) DEL MONTE® Diced Tomatoes with Zesty Mild Green Chilies*
1 can (8 ounces) DEL MONTE Tomato Sauce
1 package (1¼ ounces) dry chili seasoning
1 can (15¼ ounces) DEL MONTE Golden Sweet Whole Kernel Corn, drained
1 can (15 ounces) kidney or pinto beans, drained

You can substitute 1 can (14½ ounces) DEL MONTE Chunky Diced Tomatoes-Zesty Chili Style or 1 can (14½ ounces) DEL MONTE Stewed Tomatoes-Mexican Recipe.

I. Brown meat in large skillet; drain.

2. Add undrained tomatoes, tomato sauce and chili seasoning.

3. Simmer, uncovered, 5 minutes, stirring occasionally. Add corn and beans; heat through. Serve mixture with taco shells or warm tortillas, if desired. *Makes 4 servings*

Prep & Cook Time: 15 minutes

Beef Fajita Soup

  1 pound beef for stew
  1 can (15 ounces) pinto beans, rinsed and drained
  1 can (15 ounces) black beans, rinsed and drained
  1 can (14½ ounces) diced tomatoes with roasted garlic, undrained
  1 can (14 ounces) beef broth
  1 small green bell pepper, thinly sliced
  1 small red bell pepper, thinly sliced
  1 small onion, thinly sliced
1½ cups water
  2 teaspoons ground cumin
  1 teaspoon seasoned salt
  1 teaspoon black pepper
    Toppings: sour cream, shredded Monterey Jack or Cheddar cheese, chopped olives

Slow Cooker Directions

1. Combine all ingredients, except toppings, in slow cooker.

2. Cover; cook on LOW 8 hours or until beef is tender. Serve with suggested toppings.

Makes 8 servings

Serving Suggestion: Excellent served with a crusty loaf of brown bread.

Vegetable Medley Soup

3 cans (about 14 ounces each) chicken broth
3 sweet potatoes, peeled and chopped
3 zucchini, chopped
2 cups chopped broccoli
2 white potatoes, peeled and shredded
1 onion, chopped
1 rib celery, finely chopped
¼ cup (½ stick) butter, melted
1 tablespoon salt
1 teaspoon ground cumin
1 teaspoon black pepper
2 cups half-and-half or milk

Slow Cooker Directions
Combine chicken broth, sweet potatoes, zucchini, broccoli, white potatoes, onion, celery, butter, salt, cumin and pepper in slow cooker; stir. Cover; cook on LOW 8 to 10 hours or on HIGH 4 to 5 hours. Add half-and-half; cook additional 30 minutes to 1 hour or until heated through.
Makes 12 servings

Peppery Potato Soup

2 cans (14½ ounces each) chicken broth
4 small baking potatoes, halved and sliced
1 large onion, quartered and sliced
1 rib celery with leaves, sliced
¼ cup all-purpose flour
¾ teaspoon black pepper
½ teaspoon salt
1 cup half-and-half
1 tablespoon butter
   Celery leaves or fresh parsley

Slow Cooker Directions

1. Combine broth, potatoes, onion, celery, flour, pepper and salt in slow cooker; mix well. Cover; cook on LOW 6 to 7½ hours.

2. Stir in half-and-half; cover and continue to cook 1 hour.

3. Remove slow cooker lid. Slightly crush potato mixture with potato masher. Continue to cook, uncovered, an additional 30 minutes until slightly thickened. Just before serving, stir in butter. Garnish with celery leaves, if desired. *Makes 6 (1¼-cup) servings*

Prep Time: 15 minutes
Cook Time: 6 to 8 hours

Sausage, Butter Bean and Cabbage Soup

 2 tablespoons butter, divided
 1 large onion, chopped
12 ounces smoked sausage such as kielbasa or andouille, cut into ½-inch slices
 8 cups chicken broth
½ savoy cabbage, coarsely shredded
 3 tablespoons tomato paste
 1 bay leaf
 4 medium tomatoes, chopped
 2 cans (14 ounces each) butter beans, drained
   Salt and black pepper

Slow Cooker Directions

1. Melt 1 tablespoon butter in large skillet over medium heat. Add onion; cook and stir 3 to 4 minutes or until golden. Place in slow cooker.

2. Melt remaining 1 tablespoon butter in same skillet; cook sausage until brown on both sides. Add to slow cooker.

3. Place chicken broth, cabbage, tomato paste and bay leaf in slow cooker; stir until well blended. Cover; cook on LOW 4 hours or HIGH 2 hours.

4. Add tomatoes and beans; season with salt and pepper. Cover; cook 1 hour until heated through. Remove and discard bay leaf. *Makes 6 servings*

Tip: Savoy cabbage is an excellent cooking cabbage with a full head of crinkled leaves varying from dark to pale green. Green cabbage may be substituted.

Fix-It-Fast Chili

½ pound ground beef
¾ cup chopped onion
½ teaspoon finely chopped garlic
1 can (14½ ounces) whole peeled tomatoes, undrained and chopped
1 cup water
1 package LIPTON® Sides Rice & Sauce—Mexican
2 teaspoons chili powder
½ teaspoon ground cumin (optional)
1 cup red kidney beans, rinsed and drained

In 12-inch skillet, cook ground beef, onion and garlic over medium-high heat, stirring occasionally, 5 minutes or until browned; drain. Stir in tomatoes, water, Rice & Sauce—Mexican, chili powder and cumin and bring to a boil. Reduce heat and simmer, stirring occasionally, 10 minutes or until rice is tender. Stir in beans and heat through. Top, if desired, with shredded cheddar cheese and crumbled corn muffins.

Makes about 4 servings

Summer Squash Stew

2 pounds cooked Italian turkey sausage or diced cooked chicken
4 cans (14½ ounces each) diced seasoned tomatoes
5 medium yellow squash, thinly sliced
5 medium zucchini, thinly sliced
1 red onion, finely chopped
2 tablespoons dried Italian herb mixture
1 tablespoon dried tomato, basil and garlic salt-free spice mixture
4 cups (16 ounces) shredded Mexican cheese blend

Slow Cooker Directions

1. Combine all ingredients except cheese in slow cooker. Cover; cook on LOW 3 hours.

2. Top stew with cheese and cook additional 15 minutes or until cheese melts.

Makes 6 servings

Mediterranean Lentil Soup

   2 tablespoons olive oil
   1 large sweet onion, diced
   1 stalk celery, chopped
   2 large cloves garlic, finely minced
   1 can (28 ounces) peeled whole plum tomatoes, drained and chopped
1½ cups dried lentils, soaked in cold water 1 hour, drained and rinsed*
   1 tablespoon tomato paste
1½ teaspoons dried thyme
   6 cups beef broth
   2 bay leaves

Vinaigrette
   ¾ cup packed fresh basil leaves
   ⅓ cup olive oil
   2 tablespoons minced fresh parsley leaves
   2 tablespoons red wine vinegar
   Salt and pepper to taste

Add 1 to 2 hours to cooking time if you do not soak lentils before cooking.

Slow Cooker Directions
1. In large saucepan over medium heat, heat olive oil. Add onion, celery and garlic, cook and stir 5 minutes; do not brown.

2. Stir in tomatoes, lentils, tomato paste and thyme. Add lentil mixture to slow cooker along with beef broth and bay leaves. Cover; cook on LOW 8 hours or on HIGH 4 hours or until lentils are soft.

3. While soup is simmering, prepare vinaigrette. Combine basil, oil, parsley and vinegar in blender or food processor. Process on high speed until smooth; set aside.

4. Stir vinaigrette into soup just before serving. Season with salt and pepper.
Makes 4 to 6 servings

Variation: For even easier preparation, place all soup ingredients except the vinaigrette in the slow cooker. Stir to combine; cover and cook on LOW 8 hours or on HIGH 4 hours.

Chinese Chicken Stew

1 pound boneless skinless chicken thighs, cut into 1-inch pieces
1 teaspoon Chinese five-spice powder*
½ to ¾ teaspoon red pepper flakes
1 tablespoon peanut or vegetable oil
1 large onion, coarsely chopped
1 package (8 ounces) fresh mushrooms, sliced
2 cloves garlic, minced
1 can (about 14 ounces) chicken broth, divided
1 tablespoon cornstarch
1 large red bell pepper, cut into ¾-inch pieces
2 tablespoons soy sauce
2 large green onions, cut into ½-inch pieces
1 tablespoon sesame oil
3 cups hot cooked white rice (optional)
¼ cup coarsely chopped fresh cilantro (optional)

Chinese five-spice powder is a blend of cinnamon, cloves, fennel seed, anise and Szechuan peppercorns. It is available in most supermarkets and at Asian grocers.

Slow Cooker Directions

1. Toss chicken with five-spice powder and red pepper flakes in small bowl. Heat peanut oil in large skillet. Add onion and chicken; cook and stir about 5 minutes or until chicken is browned. Add mushrooms and garlic; cook and stir until chicken is no longer pink.

2. Combine ¼ cup broth and cornstarch in small bowl; set aside. Place cooked chicken mixture, remaining broth, bell pepper and soy sauce in slow cooker. Cover; cook on LOW 3½ hours or until peppers are tender.

3. Stir in cornstarch mixture, green onions and sesame oil. Cook 30 to 45 minutes or until juices have thickened. Ladle into soup bowls; scoop ½ cup rice into each bowl and sprinkle with cilantro, if desired.   *Makes 6 servings (about 5 cups)*

Hearty Mushroom and Barley Soup

9 cups chicken broth
1 pound fresh mushrooms, sliced
1 large onion, chopped
2 carrots, chopped
2 ribs celery, chopped
½ cup pearled barley
½ ounce dried porcini mushrooms
3 cloves garlic, minced
1 teaspoon salt
½ teaspoon dried thyme leaves
½ teaspoon black pepper

Slow Cooker Directions
Combine all ingredients in slow cooker; stir until well blended. Cover; cook on LOW 4 to 6 hours. *Makes 8 to 10 servings*

Variation: Add a beef or ham bone to slow cooker with the rest of the ingredients. It adds more flavor to the soup.

Navy Bean & Ham Soup

6 cups water
5 cups navy beans, soaked overnight and drained
1 pound ham, cubed
1 can (15 ounces) corn, drained
1 can (4 ounces) diced green chilies, drained
1 onion, diced (optional)
Salt and black pepper to taste
Biscuits (optional)

Slow Cooker Directions
Place all ingredients in slow cooker, except biscuits. Cover; cook on LOW 8 to 10 hours or until beans are done. Serve with biscuits, if desired. *Makes 6 servings*

Crockpot Beef Stew

　2 pounds lean beef for stew, cut into 1-inch pieces
⅓ cup all-purpose flour
　4 medium potatoes, peeled and cut into 1-inch pieces
　3 to 4 celery stalks cut into ½-inch slices
　3 to 4 carrots, peeled and cut into 1-inch slices
　1 large onion, cut into wedges
1½ tablespoons MRS. DASH® All-Purpose Original Blend
　1 can (8 ounces) tomato sauce
　1 can (16 ounces) whole tomatoes, chopped
　1 bay leaf

Slow Cooker Directions

Coat beef pieces with flour. Combine beef, vegetables and All-Purpose Original Blend in slow cooker; mix well. Add tomato sauce and chopped tomatoes; stir gently to mix. Add bay leaf. Cover and cook at HIGH for 5 to 6 hours or at LOW for 11 to 12 hours. Remove bay leaf. Stir and serve.

Makes 8 servings

Preparation Time: 20 minutes
Cooking Time: 6 hours

Potato and Leek Soup

    4 cups chicken broth
    3 potatoes, peeled and diced
 1½ cups chopped cabbage
    1 leek, diced
    1 onion, chopped
    2 carrots, diced
    ¼ cup chopped fresh parsley
    1 teaspoon salt
    ½ teaspoon caraway seeds
    ½ teaspoon black pepper
    1 bay leaf
    ½ cup sour cream
    1 pound bacon, cooked and crumbled

Slow Cooker Directions

Combine chicken broth, potatoes, cabbage, leek, onion, carrots and parsley in large bowl; pour mixture into slow cooker. Stir in salt, caraway seeds, pepper and bay leaf. Cover; cook on LOW 8 to 10 hours or on HIGH 4 to 5 hours. Remove and discard bay leaf. Combine some hot liquid from slow cooker with sour cream in small bowl. Add mixture to slow cooker; stir. Stir in bacon.

Makes 6 to 8 servings

Red Bean Soup with Andouille Sausage

2 tablespoons unsalted butter
1 large sweet onion, diced
2 large cloves garlic, chopped
3 stalks celery, diced
1 ham hock
1½ cups dried red kidney beans, soaked in cold water 1 hour, drained and rinsed
8 cups chicken stock
1 bay leaf
1 pound andouille smoked sausage or other pork sausage, cut into ½-inch pieces
1 sweet potato, diced
2 parsnips, diced
Salt and black pepper to taste

Slow Cooker Directions

1. Melt butter in large saucepan over medium heat. Add onion, garlic and celery. Cook and stir 5 minutes; add to slow cooker along with ham hock, kidney beans, chicken stock and bay leaf. Cover; cook on HIGH 2 hours.

2. Remove ham hock and discard. Cover; cook 2 hours more. Add sausage, potato and parsnips. Cover; cook 30 minutes more or until kidney beans are soft. Season with salt and pepper. *Makes 6 to 8 servings*

Note: Use a 6-quart slow cooker for this recipe. If using a smaller slow cooker, cut recipe ingredients in half.

Chili

3 pounds cooked ground beef
2 cans (14½ ounces each) diced tomatoes
2 cans (14½ ounces each) chili beans
2 cups sliced onions
1 can (12 ounces) corn, drained
1 cup chopped green bell pepper
1 can tomato sauce
3 tablespoons chili powder
1 teaspoon garlic powder
½ teaspoon *each* cumin and oregano

Slow Cooker Directions
Combine all ingredients in slow cooker. Cover; cook on LOW 4 hours. *Makes 6 servings*

Chicken & White Bean Stew

1 tablespoon olive oil
2 medium carrots, sliced (about 2 cups)
1 medium onion, thinly sliced
2 cloves garlic, finely chopped
1 tablespoon balsamic vinegar
1 pound boneless, skinless chicken breast halves or thighs, cut into chunks
1 jar (1 pound 10 ounces) RAGÚ® Old World Style® Pasta Sauce
2 cans (15 ounces each) cannellini or white kidney beans, rinsed and drained
   Pinch crushed red pepper flakes (optional)

In 12-inch skillet, heat olive oil over medium heat and cook carrots, onion and garlic, stirring occasionally, 5 minutes or until vegetables are tender. Stir in vinegar and cook 1 minute. Remove vegetables; set aside.

In same skillet, thoroughly brown chicken over medium-high heat. Return vegetables to skillet. Stir in Ragú Old World Style Pasta Sauce, beans and red pepper flakes. Bring to a boil over high heat. Reduce heat to medium and simmer covered, stirring occasionally, 15 minutes or until chicken is thoroughly cooked. *Makes 6 servings*

Savory Bean Stew

1 cup frozen vegetable blend (onions, celery, red and green bell peppers)
1 can (15½ ounces) chick-peas (garbanzo beans), rinsed and drained
1 can (15 ounces) pinto beans, rinsed and drained
1 can (15 ounces) black beans, rinsed and drained
1 can (14½ ounces) diced tomatoes with roasted garlic, undrained
¾ teaspoon dried thyme leaves
¾ teaspoon dried sage leaves
½ to ¾ teaspoon dried oregano leaves
1 tablespoon all-purpose flour
¾ cup vegetable or chicken broth, divided

Polenta
3 cups water
¾ cup yellow cornmeal
¾ teaspoon salt
Additional salt and black pepper

Slow Cooker Directions

1. Combine frozen vegetable blend, chick-peas, beans, tomatoes with juice and herbs in slow cooker. Stir flour into ½ cup vegetable broth; pour into bean mixture and stir well. Cover; cook on LOW 4 hours or until vegetables are tender and juice is thickened.

2. Meanwhile, prepare polenta. Bring 3 cups water to a boil in large saucepan. Reduce heat; gradually stir in cornmeal and salt. Cook 15 minutes or until cornmeal thickens. Season to taste with additional salt and pepper. Keep warm.

3. Stir remaining ¼ cup broth into slow cooker. Spread polenta on plate and top with stew.

Makes 6 (1-cup) servings

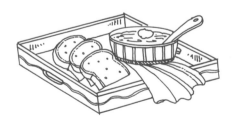

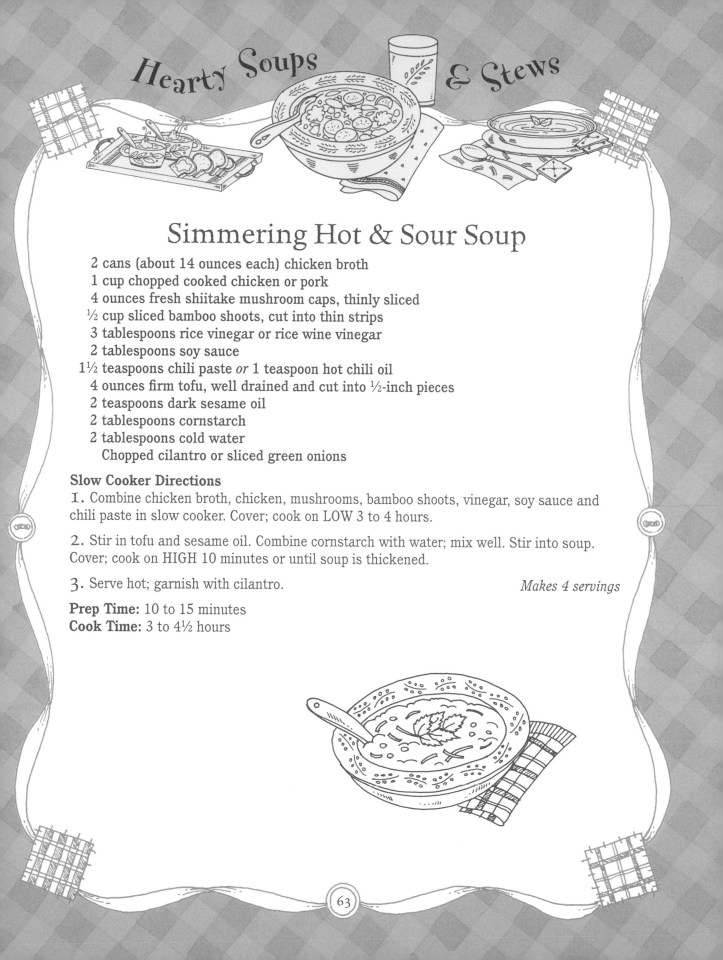

Simmering Hot & Sour Soup

2 cans (about 14 ounces each) chicken broth
1 cup chopped cooked chicken or pork
4 ounces fresh shiitake mushroom caps, thinly sliced
½ cup sliced bamboo shoots, cut into thin strips
3 tablespoons rice vinegar or rice wine vinegar
2 tablespoons soy sauce
1½ teaspoons chili paste *or* 1 teaspoon hot chili oil
4 ounces firm tofu, well drained and cut into ½-inch pieces
2 teaspoons dark sesame oil
2 tablespoons cornstarch
2 tablespoons cold water
Chopped cilantro or sliced green onions

Slow Cooker Directions

1. Combine chicken broth, chicken, mushrooms, bamboo shoots, vinegar, soy sauce and chili paste in slow cooker. Cover; cook on LOW 3 to 4 hours.

2. Stir in tofu and sesame oil. Combine cornstarch with water; mix well. Stir into soup. Cover; cook on HIGH 10 minutes or until soup is thickened.

3. Serve hot; garnish with cilantro. *Makes 4 servings*

Prep Time: 10 to 15 minutes
Cook Time: 3 to 4½ hours

Vegetarian Delights

Veggie Pie with Cucina Classica™ Parmesan Cheese

   2 tablespoons olive oil
   2 large carrots, thinly sliced
   4 shallots, sliced or 2 bunches (about 15) scallions,* cut into ½-inch pieces
 15 fresh green beans,* cut in half
   6 eggs, beaten or equivalent egg substitute
 ½ cup low fat milk
   1 tablespoon all-purpose flour
 ½ teaspoon salt
 ⅛ teaspoon pepper
 ½ cup CUCINA CLASSICA™ Grated Parmesan cheese

Medium yellow onion can be substituted for shallots; one-half cup peas can be substituted for green beans.

Preheat oven to 350°F. Grease 9-inch square baking dish or 9-inch quiche pan. Set aside.

In large skillet, heat olive oil over medium heat. Add carrots, shallots and beans. Cook 5 minutes or until shallots are glossy and carrots and beans are tender-crisp, stirring occasionally. Drain off any excess oil.

In large mixing bowl, mix eggs, milk, flour, salt, pepper and Cucina Classica™ Grated Parmesan cheese. Stir in vegetables. Pour into prepared baking dish. Bake 15 to 20 minutes or until set.

Makes 4 servings

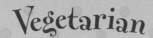 

Asparagus Pie

Crust
- 1 cup all-purpose flour
- ⅛ teaspoon salt
- 5 tablespoons butter, cut into small pieces
- 3 to 5 tablespoons cold water

Filling
- 1 pound asparagus, trimmed
- 2 tablespoons butter, melted
- 6 ounces BEL PAESE® semi-soft cheese, cut into small pieces
- 3 eggs
- 1¼ cups milk
- ⅛ teaspoon salt

For crust, combine flour and salt. Make well in center. Add butter pieces to well. Mix flour and butter. Add water, 1 tablespoon at a time; mix well. Shape into a ball. Cover and let dough rest for 30 minutes.

Meanwhile, cook asparagus in boiling salted water until tender-crisp, about 5 minutes. Drain and cut into 1-inch pieces. Toss with melted butter.

Preheat oven to 350°F. Grease 9-inch pie plate. Set aside. Roll out dough on floured board. Ease dough into pie plate. Trim and flute edge. Pierce bottom of crust several times with fork. Bake for 5 minutes.

Sprinkle asparagus in bottom of pie crust. Sprinkle cheese over asparagus. In medium mixing bowl, beat eggs, milk and salt. Pour into pie crust. Bake until set and golden brown, 40 to 50 minutes.

Makes 3 main-dish servings

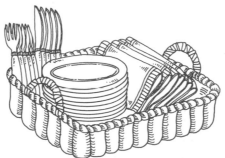

Vegetarian Sausage Rice

2 cups chopped green bell peppers
1 can (15½ ounces) dark kidney beans, drained and rinsed
1 can (14½ ounces) diced tomatoes with green bell peppers and onions, undrained
1 cup chopped onion
1 cup sliced celery
1 cup water, divided
¾ cup uncooked long-grain white rice
1¼ teaspoons salt
1 teaspoon hot pepper sauce
½ teaspoon dried thyme leaves
½ teaspoon red pepper flakes
3 bay leaves
1 package (8 ounces) vegetable protein breakfast patties, thawed
2 tablespoons olive oil
½ cup chopped fresh parsley
Additional hot pepper sauce (optional)

1. Combine bell peppers, beans, tomatoes with juice, onion, celery, ½ cup water, rice, salt, pepper sauce, thyme, red pepper flakes and bay leaves in slow cooker. Cover; cook on LOW 4 to 5 hours. Remove and discard bay leaves.

2. Dice breakfast patties. Heat oil in large nonstick skillet over medium-high heat. Add patties; cook 2 minutes or until lightly browned, scraping bottom of skillet occasionally.

3. Place patties in slow cooker. *Do not stir.* Add remaining ½ cup water to skillet; bring to a boil over high heat 1 minute, scraping up bits on bottom of skillet. Add liquid and parsley to slow cooker; stir gently to blend. Serve immediately with additional hot pepper sauce, if desired.

Makes 8 cups

Triple-Pepper Tomato Provolone Lasagna

1 red bell pepper, chopped
1 yellow bell pepper, chopped
1 green bell pepper, chopped
1 package (8 ounces) sliced fresh mushrooms
1 cup thinly sliced zucchini
½ cup chopped onion
4 cloves garlic, minced
1½ cups vegetable juice cocktail
1 can (16 ounces) diced tomatoes, undrained
1½ to 1¾ teaspoons dried Italian seasoning
1 tablespoon olive oil
9 uncooked lasagna noodles
1 cup cottage cheese
⅓ cup grated Parmesan cheese
4 ounces sliced provolone cheese

1. Preheat oven to 350°F. Combine peppers, mushrooms, zucchini, onion, garlic, vegetable juice cocktail, tomatoes and Italian seasoning in Dutch oven. Bring to a boil over high heat. Reduce heat to low; simmer, uncovered, 15 minutes. Remove from heat; stir in oil.

2. Spray 12×8-inch baking pan with nonstick cooking spray. Place 3 lasagna noodles on bottom of pan. Spread ⅓ sauce over noodles. Spread ½ cup cottage cheese evenly over sauce; sprinkle with 2 tablespoons Parmesan cheese. Repeat layers, ending with sauce.

3. Bake, uncovered, 1 hour or until bubbly. Tear provolone cheese in small pieces; place on top of lasagna. Sprinkle with remaining Parmesan cheese. Bake 5 minutes longer or until cheese is melted. Let stand 15 minutes before serving.   *Makes 6 servings*

Tip: For extra convenience, purchase 3 cups chopped red, green and yellow bell pepper mixture from the grocery store salad bar.

Chilaquiles

2 tablespoons vegetable oil
1 medium onion, chopped
1 package (1.0 ounce) LAWRY'S® Taco Spices & Seasonings
1 can (28 ounces) diced tomatoes, in juice
1 can (4 ounces) diced green chiles (optional)
6 ounces tortilla chips
4 cups (16 ounces) shredded Monterey Jack cheese
1 cup sour cream
½ cup (2 ounces) shredded cheddar cheese

In large skillet, heat oil over medium high heat. Add onion and cook until tender. Add Taco Spices & Seasonings, tomatoes and chiles; mix well. Bring to a boil; reduce heat to low and cook, uncovered, 10 minutes, stirring occasionally. Spray 2-quart casserole dish with nonstick cooking spray; arrange ½ of tortilla chips, sauce and Monterey Jack cheese. Repeat layers, top with sour cream. Bake in 350°F oven for 25 minutes. Sprinkle with cheddar cheese and bake 5 minutes longer. Let stand 10 minutes before serving.

Makes 6 to 8 servings

Serving Suggestion: Serve with a marinated vegetable salad and fresh fruit.

Prep Time: 12 to 15 minutes
Cook Time: 45 to 50 minutes

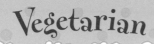

Southwest Spaghetti Squash

1 spaghetti squash (about 3 pounds)
1 can (about 14 ounces) Mexican-style diced tomatoes, undrained
1 can (about 14 ounces) black beans, rinsed and drained
¾ cup (3 ounces) shredded Monterey Jack cheese, divided
¼ cup finely chopped cilantro
1 teaspoon ground cumin
¼ teaspoon garlic salt
¼ teaspoon black pepper

1. Preheat oven to 350°F. Cut squash in half lengthwise. Remove and discard seeds. Place squash, cut side down, in greased baking pan. Bake 45 minutes to 1 hour or until just tender. Using fork, remove spaghetti-like strands from hot squash and place strands in large bowl. (Use oven mitts to protect hands.)

2. Add tomatoes with juice, beans, ½ cup cheese, cilantro, cumin, garlic salt and pepper; toss well.

3. Spray 1½-quart casserole with nonstick cooking spray. Spoon mixture into casserole. Sprinkle with remaining ¼ cup cheese.

4. Bake, uncovered, 30 to 35 minutes or until heated through. Serve immediately.

Makes 4 servings

Tip: This is a very simple dish you can throw together for those nights you want to go meatless! And, it's a "kid-friendly" meal too.

Vegetarian Paella

    1 tablespoon olive oil
    1 medium onion, chopped
    1 serrano pepper,* finely chopped
    1 red bell pepper, diced
    1 green bell pepper, diced
    3 cloves garlic, minced
    ½ teaspoon saffron threads, crushed
    ½ teaspoon paprika
    1 cup uncooked long-grain white rice
    3 cups water
    1 can (15 ounces) chick-peas (garbanzo beans), rinsed and drained
    1 can (14 ounces) artichoke hearts in water, drained and cut into halves
    1 cup frozen green peas
 1½ teaspoons grated lemon peel
       Fresh bay leaves (optional)
       Lemon slices (optional)

Serrano peppers can sting and irritate the skin; wear rubber gloves when handling peppers and do not touch eyes. Wash hands after handling.

1. Preheat oven to 375°F. Heat oil in heavy ovenproof skillet over medium-high heat. Add onion, serrano pepper and bell peppers; cook and stir about 7 minutes.

2. Add garlic, saffron and paprika; cook 3 minutes. Add rice; cook and stir 1 minute. Add water, chick-peas, artichoke hearts, green peas and lemon peel; mix well.

3. Cover; bake 25 minutes or until rice is tender. Garnish with fresh bay leaves and lemon slices, if desired.

Makes 6 servings

Pea and Spinach Frittata

   1 cup chopped onion
 ¼ cup water
   1 cup frozen peas
   1 cup torn stemmed washed spinach
   6 egg whites
   2 eggs
 ½ cup cooked brown rice
 ¼ cup fat-free (skim) milk
   2 tablespoons grated Romano or Parmesan cheese
   1 tablespoon chopped fresh mint *or* 1 teaspoon dried mint leaves, crushed
 ¼ teaspoon black pepper
 ⅛ teaspoon salt
    Additional grated Romano or Parmesan cheese for garnish

1. Combine onion and water in large skillet. Bring to a boil over high heat. Reduce heat to medium. Cover; cook 2 to 3 minutes or until onion is tender. Stir in peas. Cook until peas are heated through; drain. Stir in spinach. Cook and stir about 1 minute or until spinach just starts to wilt.

2. Meanwhile, combine egg whites, eggs, rice, milk, 2 tablespoons Romano cheese, mint, pepper and salt in medium bowl. Coat skillet with nonstick cooking spray. Add egg mixture to skillet. Cook, without stirring, 2 minutes until eggs begin to set. Run large spoon around edge of skillet, lifting eggs for even cooking. Remove skillet from heat when eggs are almost set but surface is still moist.

3. Cover; let stand 3 to 4 minutes or until surface is set. Garnish top with additional Romano cheese. Cut into 4 wedges.   *Makes 4 servings*

Gourmet Bean & Spinach Burritos

Avocado Relish (page 73)
1 pound spinach leaves, divided
2 teaspoons olive oil
1 cup finely chopped onion
2 cloves garlic, minced
2 cans (15 ounces each) black beans, drained
1 can (10 ounces) whole tomatoes with green chilies, undrained
2 teaspoons ground cumin
½ teaspoon ground oregano
8 flour tortillas (8-inch diameter)
2 cups (8 ounces) shredded Monterey Jack cheese
Sour cream (optional)

1. Prepare Avocado Relish.

2. Wash and dry spinach. Remove and discard stems from spinach leaves. Set aside 24 to 30 large leaves. Stack remaining leaves and cut crosswise into ¼-inch-wide pieces. Set aside.

3. Heat olive oil in large nonstick skillet over medium heat until hot. Add onion and garlic; cook and stir 5 minutes or until tender. Add beans, tomatoes, cumin and oregano. Simmer, uncovered, until mixture is dry. Remove from heat; mash bean mixture with potato masher.

4. Preheat oven to 350°F. Arrange 3 to 4 whole spinach leaves on each tortilla. Spoon bean mixture onto bottom half of tortillas; sprinkle cheese evenly over bean mixture. Roll up to enclose filling. Repeat with remaining tortillas, spinach and bean mixture. Arrange, seam side down, in 12×8-inch baking dish. Cover with foil. Bake 20 minutes or until heated through.

5. To serve, arrange about ½ cup spinach pieces on each serving plate; top with 2 burritos. Serve with Avocado Relish. Garnish with sour cream, if desired. *Makes 4 servings*

Avocado Relish

1 large, firm, ripe avocado, finely diced
2 tablespoons fresh lime juice
¾ cup finely chopped, seeded tomato
½ cup minced green onions
⅓ cup minced fresh cilantro
½ to 1 teaspoon hot pepper sauce

Combine avocado and lime juice in bowl; toss. Add tomato, onions, cilantro and hot sauce; toss gently. Cover and refrigerate 1 hour. Serve at room temperature.

Makes about 2¼ cups

Summer Squash Skillet

2 tablespoons butter
1 medium sweet or yellow onion, thinly sliced
2 medium zucchini or yellow squash *or* 1 of each, sliced
¾ teaspoon salt
¼ teaspoon freshly ground black pepper
1 large tomato, chopped
¼ cup julienned or chopped fresh basil leaves
2 tablespoons grated Parmesan cheese

1. Melt butter in large skillet over medium-high heat. Separate onion into rings; add to skillet and mix well with butter. Reduce heat to medium; uncover skillet. Cook about 3 minutes, stirring frequently, until onions are golden brown and caramelized.

2. Add squash, salt and pepper; cover and cook 5 minutes, stirring once. Add tomato; cook uncovered about 2 minutes or until squash is tender. Stir in basil and top with cheese.

Makes 4 servings

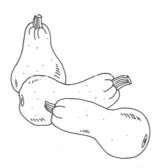

Eggplant Italiano

1¼ pounds eggplant
2 medium onions
2 ribs celery
½ cup pitted ripe olives
2 tablespoons olive oil, divided
1 can (16 ounces) diced tomatoes, drained
2 tablespoons balsamic vinegar
1 tablespoon sugar
1 tablespoon capers, drained
1 teaspoon dried oregano or basil leaves, crushed
Salt and black pepper to taste
Fresh basil leaves, leaf lettuce and red jalapeño pepper* for garnish

*Jalapeño peppers can sting and irritate the skin; wear rubber gloves when handling peppers and do not touch eyes. Wash hands after handling.

1. Cut eggplant into 1-inch cubes. Thinly slice onions. Cut celery into 1-inch pieces. Cut olives crosswise in half; set aside.

2. Heat wok or large skillet over medium-high heat 1 minute or until hot. Drizzle 1 tablespoon oil into wok and heat 30 seconds. Add onions and celery; stir-fry about 2 minutes or until tender. Move onions and celery up side of wok. Reduce heat to medium.

3. Add remaining 1 tablespoon oil to bottom of wok and heat 30 seconds. Add eggplant; stir-fry about 4 minutes or until tender. Add tomatoes; mix well. Cover and cook 10 minutes.

4. Stir olives, vinegar, sugar, capers and oregano into eggplant mixture. Season with salt and black pepper. Transfer to serving dish. Garnish, if desired. *Makes 6 servings*

Broccoli Lasagna

2 tablespoons olive oil
1 cup thinly sliced fresh mushrooms
3 cloves garlic, chopped
1 can (14½ ounces) diced tomatoes, undrained
1 can (8 ounces) tomato sauce
1 can (6 ounces) tomato paste
1 tablespoon red wine vinegar
1 teaspoon dried oregano *or* 2 teaspoons fresh oregano, chopped
1 teaspoon dried basil *or* 2 teaspoons fresh basil, chopped
   Pinch red pepper flakes
2 cups ricotta cheese
1 cup mozzarella cheese, divided
¼ cup chopped fresh parsley
9 lasagna noodles, cooked and well drained
3 cups chopped broccoli (about 1 large bunch), cooked and well drained
1 to 2 tablespoons grated Parmesan cheese

1. Preheat oven to 350°F. Spray 8×8-inch pan with cooking spray.

2. Heat oil in large saucepan over medium heat. Add mushrooms and garlic; cook and stir about 5 minutes or until mushrooms are browned and beginning to release liquid. Stir in tomatoes, tomato sauce, tomato paste, vinegar, oregano, basil and pepper flakes. Simmer over low heat, stirring occasionally.

3. Meanwhile, combine ricotta, mozzarella and parsley in medium bowl; set aside.

4. Place 3 lasagna noodles in bottom of prepared pan. (Trim to fit.) Spread half the ricotta mixture over noodles. Layer half of broccoli over ricotta mixture. Spoon about ⅓ tomato mixture over broccoli. Repeat layers. Place last 3 noodles over second layer; spread remaining tomato mixture over noodles. Cover with foil sprayed with nonstick cooking spray.

5. Bake 25 minutes. Uncover; sprinkle with remaining ¼ cup mozzarella and Parmesan cheeses. Bake, uncovered, 10 minutes or until cheese melts. Let stand at least 10 minutes before serving.

Makes 9 servings

My Mac & Cheese

¼ cup (½ stick) butter
¼ cup all-purpose flour
2 cups milk
½ pound sharp Cheddar cheese, cut into ½-inch cubes
8 slices (about 2 ounces) pepper-Jack cheese, cut into pieces (optional)
½ cup chopped onion
2 cups (about 16 ounces) broccoli florets, steamed until tender
2 cups macaroni, cooked and drained
2 English muffins, cut into ½-inch pieces

1. Preheat oven to 350°F.

2. Melt butter in large saucepan over medium heat. Stir in flour to make smooth paste; cook and stir 2 minutes. Gradually add milk, stirring constantly, until mixture is slightly thickened.

3. Add Cheddar cheese, pepper-Jack cheese, if desired, and onion to milk mixture. Cook, stirring constantly, until cheese melts. Add broccoli; stir well.

4. Place macaroni in 3-quart casserole. Add cheese mixture; mix well. Sprinkle English muffin pieces evenly over top. Bake 15 to 20 minutes or until muffin pieces are golden brown.

Makes 4 to 6 servings

Zucornchile Rajas Bake

2 cups tomato sauce
2 tablespoons chili powder
2 tablespoons tomato paste
1 tablespoon cider vinegar
1 teaspoon ground cumin
½ teaspoon salt
½ teaspoon garlic powder
¼ teaspoon ground red pepper
6 corn tortillas
   Vegetable oil for frying
1 pound zucchini, thinly sliced (about 3 cups)
1½ cups (6 ounces) shredded Monterey Jack or manchego cheese,* divided
1 cup corn kernels
1 can (4 ounces) diced green chilies, drained
½ to 1 cup sour cream
3 green onions, chopped

Manchego cheese is a popular Spanish cheese that melts easily. Look for it at specialty food markets.

1. Preheat oven to 350°F. Oil 13×9-inch baking dish.

2. Combine tomato sauce, chili powder, tomato paste, vinegar, cumin, salt, garlic powder and red pepper in medium saucepan. Bring to a boil over high heat; reduce heat to low and simmer 10 minutes, stirring occasionally.

3. Meanwhile, cut tortillas into ¼-inch-wide strips. Heat enough oil to cover bottom of medium skillet by ½ inch. Fry tortilla strips in batches until crisp; drain on paper towels.

4. Steam zucchini 5 minutes; drain. Transfer to large bowl. Add ¾ cup cheese, corn, chilies and tortilla strips. Toss lightly to combine; spoon into prepared baking dish. Spread tomato sauce mixture over zucchini mixture and top with remaining ¾ cup cheese. Bake 30 minutes or until heated through.

5. Spread sour cream over top and sprinkle with green onions. Serve immediately.

Makes 6 to 8 servings

Vegetarian Lasagna

1 small eggplant, sliced into ½-inch rounds
½ teaspoon salt
2 tablespoons olive oil, divided
1 tablespoon butter
8 ounces mushrooms, sliced
1 small onion, diced
1 can (26 ounces) pasta sauce
1 teaspoon dried basil
1 teaspoon dried oregano
2 cups part-skim ricotta cheese
1½ cups (6 ounces) shredded Monterey Jack cheese
1 cup grated Parmesan cheese, divided
1 package (8 ounces) whole wheat lasagna noodles, cooked and drained
1 medium zucchini, thinly sliced

Slow Cooker Directions

1. Sprinkle eggplant with salt; let sit 10 to 15 minutes. Rinse and pat dry; brush with 1 tablespoon olive oil. Brown on both sides in medium skillet over medium heat. Set aside.

2. Heat remaining 1 tablespoon olive oil and butter in same skillet over medium heat; cook and stir mushrooms and onion until softened. Stir in pasta sauce, basil and oregano. Set aside.

3. Combine ricotta cheese, Monterey Jack cheese and ½ cup Parmesan cheese in medium bowl. Set aside.

4. Spread ⅓ sauce mixture in bottom of slow cooker. Layer with ⅓ lasagna noodles, ½ eggplant, ½ cheese mixture. Repeat layers once. For last layer, use remaining ⅓ of lasagna noodles, zucchini, remaining ⅓ of sauce mixture and top with remaining ½ cup Parmesan.

5. Cover; cook on LOW 6 hours. Let sit 15 to 20 minutes before serving.

Makes 4 to 6 servings

Italian Vegetable Strata

   1 loaf (12 ounces) Italian bread, cut into 1-inch slices
   6 eggs, beaten
   3 cups RAGÚ® Chunky Gardenstyle Pasta Sauce
   1 cup water
1½ cups shredded mozzarella cheese (about 6 ounces)
  ¼ cup grated Parmesan cheese
   1 jar (7 ounces) roasted red peppers packed in oil, drained
   1 medium zucchini, thinly sliced

Preheat oven to 350°F. In greased 13×9-inch baking dish, arrange bread slices; set aside.

In large bowl, combine remaining ingredients; pour mixture over bread. Let stand 15 minutes. Bake covered 35 minutes or until vegetables are tender. *Makes 6 servings*

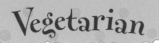 

Luscious Vegetarian Lasagna

8 ounces lasagna noodles
1 can (14½ ounces) whole peeled tomatoes, undrained and coarsely chopped
1 can (12 ounces) tomato sauce
1 teaspoon *each* dried oregano leaves and dried basil leaves
Dash black pepper
2 tablespoons olive oil
1 large onion, chopped
1½ teaspoons minced garlic
2 small zucchini, diced
1 large carrot, diced
1 green bell pepper, diced
8 ounces mushrooms, sliced
2 cups 1% milk-fat cottage cheese
1 cup (4 ounces) shredded mozzarella cheese
1 cup grated Parmesan or Romano cheese
Parsley sprigs for garnish

1. Cook lasagna according to package directions; drain.

2. Place tomatoes with juice, tomato sauce, oregano, basil and black pepper in medium saucepan. Bring to a boil over high heat. Reduce heat to low. Simmer, uncovered, 6 to 10 minutes.

3. Heat oil in large skillet over medium-high heat. Cook and stir onion and garlic until onion is golden. Add zucchini, carrot, bell pepper and mushrooms. Cook and stir 5 to 10 minutes or until vegetables are tender. Stir vegetables into tomato mixture; bring to a boil. Reduce heat to low. Simmer, uncovered, 15 minutes.

4. Preheat oven to 350°F. Combine cottage, mozzarella and Parmesan cheeses in large bowl; blend well. Spoon about 1 cup sauce in bottom of 12×8-inch baking pan. Place a layer of noodles over sauce, then half the cheese mixture and half the remaining sauce. Repeat layers of noodles, cheese mixture and sauce.

5. Bake lasagna 30 to 45 minutes or until bubbly. Let stand 10 minutes. Garnish with parsley.
Makes 6 to 8 servings

Stuffed Bell Peppers

1 package (8½ ounces) cornbread mix *plus* ingredients to prepare
6 green bell peppers
1 large onion, thinly sliced
1 teaspoon olive oil
1 can (16 ounces) no-salt-added diced tomatoes, drained
1 package (10 ounces) frozen corn, thawed and drained
1 can (2¼ ounces) sliced black olives, drained
⅓ cup raisins
1 tablespoon chili powder
1 teaspoon ground sage
1 cup (4 ounces) shredded Monterey Jack cheese, divided
  Cherry tomato halves and fresh herbs for garnish (optiona)

Prepare cornbread according to package directions. Cut into cubes. *Reduce oven temperature to 350°F.* Slice tops off bell peppers; discard stems and seeds. Finely chop tops to equal 1 cup; set aside. Rinse peppers. Bring 2 to 3 inches water to a boil over high heat in large saucepan. Add 1 or more peppers and boil 1 minute, turning peppers with tongs to blanch evenly. Rinse with cold water; drain. Repeat with remaining peppers.

Place onion and oil in Dutch oven. Cover and cook over medium-high heat, stirring occasionally, 8 to 10 minutes or until onion is tender and browned. Add 1 to 2 tablespoons water, if needed, to prevent sticking. Add chopped bell pepper; stir 1 minute more. Remove from heat. Add tomatoes, corn, olives, raisins, chili powder and sage; stir. Stir in corn bread (it will crumble) and ¾ cup cheese. Spoon filling into peppers. Top with remaining ¼ cup cheese. Place peppers in baking dish; bake 20 to 30 minutes or until heated through. Garnish, if desired.

Makes 6 servings

Vegetable Lasagna

2 cups low fat cottage cheese (1% milkfat)
1 (10-ounce) package frozen chopped spinach, thawed and well drained
1 cup shredded carrots
½ cup EGG BEATERS®
2 tablespoons minced onion
1 teaspoon dried Italian seasoning
2 cups no-salt-added spaghetti sauce, divided
9 lasagna noodles, cooked in unsalted water and drained
1 cup (4 ounces) shredded part-skim mozzarella cheese
2 tablespoons grated Parmesan cheese

In medium bowl, combine cottage cheese, spinach, carrots, Egg Beaters®, onion and Italian seasoning; set aside.

Spread ½ cup spaghetti sauce in bottom of greased 13×9×2-inch baking dish. Top with 3 noodles and ⅓ each spinach mixture and remaining sauce. Repeat layers 2 more times. Sprinkle with mozzarella and Parmesan cheese; cover. Bake at 375°F for 20 minutes. Uncover; bake for 25 minutes more or until set. Let stand 10 minutes before serving.

Makes 8 servings

Prep Time: 20 minutes
Cook Time: 45 minutes

Eggplant Parmigiana

2 eggs, beaten
¼ cup milk
   Dash of garlic powder
   Dash of onion powder
   Dash of salt
   Dash of black pepper
1 large eggplant, cut into ½-inch-thick slices
½ cup seasoned dry bread crumbs
   Vegetable oil for frying
1 jar (about 26 ounces) spaghetti sauce
4 cups (16 ounces) shredded mozzarella cheese
2½ cups (10 ounces) shredded Swiss cheese
¼ cup grated Parmesan cheese
¼ cup grated Romano cheese

1. Preheat oven to 350°F. Combine eggs, milk, garlic and onion powders, salt and pepper in shallow bowl. Dip eggplant into egg mixture; coat in bread crumbs.

2. Add enough oil to large skillet to cover bottom by ¼ inch. Heat over medium-high heat. Brown eggplant in batches on both sides; drain on paper towels. Cover bottom of 13×9-inch baking dish with 2 or 3 tablespoons spaghetti sauce. Layer ½ of eggplant, ½ of mozzarella cheese, ½ of Swiss cheese and ½ of remaining sauce in dish. Repeat layers. Sprinkle with Parmesan and Romano cheeses.

3. Bake 30 minutes or until heated through and cheeses are melted. *Makes 4 servings*

Seafood Favorites

Spanish Shrimp

  1 package UNCLE BEN'S NATURAL SELECT® Spanish Rice
  2 tablespoons olive oil
  ½ cup red bell pepper, sliced
  ½ cup red onion, sliced
1½ cups water
  1 pound shrimp, peeled, deveined
  1 tablespoon capers
  ½ cup artichokes, drained, quartered
  1 lemon wedge
  1 parsley sprig

1. In skillet with lid, heat oil and sauté peppers and onions for 1 minute.

2. Add rice and water; bring to a boil. Cover, reduce heat to medium low.

3. Simmer 5 minutes. Add shrimp, capers and artichokes. Recover, cook 5 to 7 minutes. Garnish with lemon wedge and parsley sprig.

Makes 4 servings

Preparation Time: 25 minutes

Louisiana Crawfish Pie

½ cup butter or margarine
¼ cup all-purpose flour
1 cup chopped white onion
½ cup thinly sliced green onion tops
⅓ cup chopped green bell pepper
3 tablespoons chopped celery
3 tablespoons finely minced fresh parsley
2 teaspoons finely minced garlic
¼ cup whipping cream
1 teaspoon salt
¾ teaspoon black pepper
2 pounds shelled crawfish tail meat*
1 (9-inch) Classic CRISCO® Double Crust (page 94)

Substitute shrimp for crawfish, if desired.

1. Melt butter in large skillet over low heat. Add flour gradually. Cook, stirring constantly, until smooth, slightly thickened and light golden brown. Add onions, bell pepper, celery, parsley and garlic. Cook, stirring, until vegetables are soft. Add cream, salt and black pepper. Mix gently but thoroughly. Cook 3 minutes on low heat. Add crawfish. Cook until tender. Remove from heat. Cool slightly.

2. Prepare crust. Divide dough in half. Roll and press bottom crust into deep dish pie plate. Spoon filling into unbaked pie shell. Moisten pastry edge with water.

3. Roll top crust same as bottom. Lift onto filled pie. Trim ½ inch beyond edge of pie plate. Fold top edge under bottom crust. Flute. Cut 6 slits in top crust.

4. Bake at 350°F 25 to 30 minutes or until crust is golden brown. Cut into wedges. Serve while still warm.

Makes one 9-inch pie

Ceviche Roll-Ups

1 pound firm, whitefish (such as cod, scrod, haddock), thawed and cut into
    bite-sized pieces

⅔ cup fresh lime juice

12 ounces JARLSBERG or JARLSBERG LITE™ Cheese, shredded (reserve
    1 cup for topping)

Zest of 2 limes

1 medium tomato, seeded and chopped

2 green onions, chopped

4 ounces finely chopped chili peppers, drained

½ cup fresh chopped cilantro leaves

1 teaspoon ground cumin

4 large radishes, sliced

12 oil-cured olives, seeded and chopped *or* ¼ cup chopped pimiento-stuffed olives
    (optional)

8 flour tortillas (7-inch)

In glass, stainless steel or crockery bowl, marinate fish in lime juice 1½ hours, stirring frequently. Drain. Combine with remaining ingredients except tortillas and reserved cup of cheese. Preheat oven to 375°F.

Place about 1 cup mixture on each tortilla. Roll up and place in glass or enamel baking pan sprayed with nonstick oil. Top with reserved cheese. Cover with foil. Bake 25 to 30 minutes, uncovering last 5 minutes.
Makes 4 servings

Note: Vegetables may be substituted with hot peppers, celery or diced jicama. Ceviche may be served as an appetizer or as a main dish with black beans and brown rice. Scallops also work well as a substitute for the fish pieces.

Poached Salmon & Asparagus

2 tablespoons butter
1 cup onion, sliced
2 stalks celery, sliced
1 cup asparagus stems, sliced
2 packages UNCLE BEN'S NATURAL SELECT® Garlic & Butter Flavor Rice
3 cups water
6 pieces salmon fillets
1 cup asparagus tips

1. In large skillet with tight-fitting lid, melt butter over medium heat and sauté onion, celery and asparagus stems for about 3 minutes.

2. Add rice and water; bring to a boil. Carefully place fillets on top of rice; reduce heat. Cover and simmer about 4 minutes.

3. Arrange asparagus tips around salmon fillets; cover and simmer 6 to 8 minutes longer.

Makes 6 servings

Preparation Time: 10 minutes

Cheesy Tuna Pie

2 cups cooked rice
2 cans (6 ounces each) tuna, drained and flaked
1 cup mayonnaise
1 cup (4 ounces) shredded Cheddar cheese
½ cup sour cream
½ cup thinly sliced celery
1 can (4 ounces) sliced black olives
2 tablespoons onion flakes
1 refrigerated pie crust

1. Preheat oven to 350°F. Spray 9-inch, deep-dish pie pan with nonstick cooking spray.

2. Combine all ingredients except pie crust in medium bowl; mix well. Spoon into prepared pie pan. Place pie crust over tuna mixture; press edge to pie pan to seal. Cut slits for steam to escape. Bake 20 minutes or until crust is browned and filling is bubbly.

Makes 6 servings

Festive Stuffed Fish

2 whole red snappers, about 2½ pounds each (or substitute any firm whitefish), cleaned

Lemon and lime wedges

2 cloves garlic, minced

2 tablespoons Lucini Premium Select extra virgin olive oil

2 medium onions, finely chopped

1 cup seeded and chopped medium-hot pepper* (such as poblano, serrano, Anaheim or green bell variety)

1 cup chopped red bell pepper

8 ounces JARLSBERG or JARLSBERG LITE™ Cheese, shredded

12 tomatillos, thinly sliced, then chopped (about 2 cups)

1 cup dry white wine or unsweetened apple juice

Additional lemon and lime wedges

Chili peppers can sting and irritate the skin; wear rubber gloves when handling peppers and do not touch eyes. Wash hands after handling.

Score flesh on each fish ¼-inch deep on the diagonal every 1½ inches. Insert lemon wedges, peel side out. Cook garlic in olive oil in medium skillet over medium-high heat. Add onions and cook until translucent. Add peppers; cook 2 minutes. Place in large bowl; stir in cheese and tomatillos. Stuff fish cavity with cheese mixture. Use kitchen string to tie each fish closed every 2 inches (3 or 4 ties). Set aside. Preheat oven to 375°F.

In same skillet, bring wine to a boil. Place fish in large glass or enamel baking dish. Pour hot wine over fish and cover tightly.

Bake 30 minutes or until fish is opaque. Transfer to serving platter and remove string. Garnish with additional lemon and lime wedges.

Makes 4 to 6 servings

Zesty Shrimp Primavera

8 ounces uncooked angel hair pasta
1 tablespoon olive oil
2 cups thin carrot sticks
2 cups thin strips red bell pepper
2 small zucchini, thinly sliced
3 cloves garlic, minced and divided
½ teaspoon crushed red pepper flakes
2 tablespoons butter
1½ pounds medium shrimp, shelled and deveined
¼ cup grated Parmesan cheese
1 tablespoon slivered fresh basil leaves *or* 1 teaspoon dried basil

1. Cook pasta according to package directions. Drain; place in large shallow pasta bowl and keep warm.

2. Heat oil in large nonstick skillet over medium-high heat. Stir in carrots, bell peppers, zucchini, 1 teaspoon garlic and red pepper flakes. Cook, stirring constantly, 5 minutes or until carrots are crisp-tender. Add to pasta.

3. Melt butter in same skillet over medium heat. Add shrimp and remaining garlic. Cook and stir 2 to 3 minutes until shrimp turn pink. Return pasta and vegetables to skillet. Add Parmesan cheese. Toss to thoroughly mix. Return to pasta bowl. Sprinkle with basil.

Makes 6 servings

Seafood Lasagna

4 ounces lasagna noodles
1 jar (28 ounces) spaghetti, pasta sauce or favorite homemade recipe
1 package (6 ounces) frozen cooked salad shrimp, thawed and drained
4 ounces Surimi Seafood, thawed and thinly sliced
½ cup low-fat ricotta cheese
¼ cup freshly grated Parmesan cheese
1 tablespoon minced fresh parsley
⅛ teaspoon black pepper
⅔ cup shredded low-fat mozzarella cheese

Heat oven to 375°F. Prepare lasagna according to package directions. Empty spaghetti sauce into saucepan and simmer for 10 minutes until thickened and reduced to about 3 cups; stir in shrimp and Surimi Seafood. Combine ricotta cheese, Parmesan cheese, parsley and pepper in small bowl.

To assemble lasagna, place half of noodles in 8×8-inch casserole. Top with half of seafood sauce and drop half of ricotta mixture by small teaspoonfuls on top. Sprinkle with half of mozzarella cheese. Repeat layers. Bake for 35 minutes or until bubbly. Let stand 10 minutes before cutting.

Makes 6 servings

Favorite recipe from **National Fisheries Institute**

Tuna Noodle Casserole

1 tablespoon CRISCO® Oil* plus additional for oiling baking dish
1 cup sliced celery
⅓ cup chopped onion
¼ cup chopped green bell pepper
1 can (6½ ounces) chunk white tuna packed in water, drained and flaked
6 ounces egg noodles (3½ cups dry), cooked and well drained
½ cup sour cream
1 jar (2 ounces) sliced pimientos, drained (optional)
½ teaspoon salt
1 can (10¾ ounces) condensed cream of celery soup
½ cup milk
4 slices (¾ ounce each) Cheddar or American cheese, chopped
2 tablespoons plain dry bread crumbs

Use your favorite Crisco Oil product.

1. Heat oven to 425°F. Oil 2-quart baking dish lightly.

2. Heat 1 tablespoon oil in large skillet on medium heat. Add celery, onion and green pepper. Cook and stir until tender. Add tuna, noodles, sour cream, pimientos and salt. Stir to blend. Remove from heat.

3. Combine soup and milk in small saucepan. Stir on medium heat until warmed. Add cheese. Stir until cheese melts. Stir into noodle mixture. Spoon into baking dish. Sprinkle with bread crumbs.

4. Bake at 425°F for 20 to 25 minutes or until hot and bubbly. *Do not overbake.*

Makes 6 servings

Salmon Vera Cruz

   1 package UNCLE BEN'S® Long Grain & Wild Rice Original Recipe
   3 tablespoons honey
   3 tablespoons pine nuts, chopped
   3 salmon fillets, 6 to 8 ounces, skinned
2⅓ cups water
   1 tablespoon margarine (optional)
   ¾ cup sun-dried tomatoes, whole
   ½ cup green olives, sliced lengthwise
   ½ cup carrots, julienned
   ½ cup red onion, diced
   1 medium jalapeño pepper*, seeded and minced
1½ cups fresh spinach, cleaned, stems removed

Jalapeño peppers can sting and irritate the skin; wear rubber gloves when handling peppers and do not touch eyes. Wash hands after handling.

1. Combine honey and pine nuts. Coat tops of salmon fillets.

2. In large skillet with cover, combine rice, seasoning, water and margarine. Bring to a boil, reduce heat, and simmer 10 minutes.

3. Place salmon on rice, recover, and simmer 8 minutes. Remove salmon, keep warm.

4. Stir in tomatoes, olives, carrots, onion and jalapeño pepper. Simmer 5 to 7 minutes. Remove from heat, stir in spinach.

5. Replace salmon on top of rice. Let stand 5 minutes. Garnish with chopped cilantro.

Makes 3 to 4 servings

Preparation Time: 25 minutes

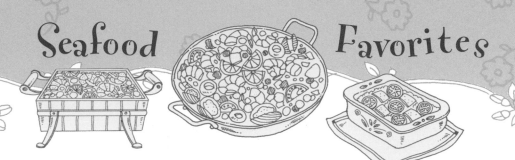
Easy Halibut Steaks
with Tomato and Broccoli Sauce

2 tablespoons olive oil
2 cups freshly chopped broccoli
2½ cups diced tomatoes
2 tablespoons lemon juice
1 tablespoon chopped garlic
1 tablespoon fresh tarragon *or* 1 teaspoon dried tarragon
½ teaspoon sugar
½ teaspoon *each* salt and black pepper
4 halibut steaks (4 ounces *each*)

Heat oil in large skillet over medium heat 1 minute. Add broccoli; cook about 5 minutes. Add all remaining ingredients except halibut; cook, stirring occasionally, 5 minutes more. Add steaks, cover and cook 5 minutes on each side. *Makes 4 servings*

Seafood Newburg Casserole

1 can (10¾ ounces) condensed cream of shrimp soup, undiluted
½ cup half-and-half
1 tablespoon dry sherry
¼ teaspoon ground red pepper
3 cups cooked rice
2 cans (6 ounces each) lump crabmeat, drained
¼ pound raw medium shrimp, peeled and deveined
¼ pound raw bay scallops
1 jar (4 ounces) pimientos, drained and chopped
¼ cup finely chopped fresh parsley

1. Preheat oven to 350°F. Spray 2½-quart casserole with nonstick cooking spray.

2. Whisk together soup, half-and-half, sherry and red pepper in large bowl until combined. Add rice, crabmeat, shrimp, scallops and pimientos; toss well.

3. Transfer mixture to prepared casserole; sprinkle with parsley. Cover; bake about 25 minutes or until shrimp and scallops are opaque. *Makes 6 servings*

Cajun-Style Corn with Crayfish

6 ears corn
1 tablespoon vegetable oil
1 medium onion, chopped
½ cup *each* chopped green and red bell peppers
1 cup water
1 teaspoon salt
⅛ teaspoon black pepper
⅛ teaspoon ground red pepper
¾ pound crayfish tail meat

1. Cut corn from cobs in two or three layers so that kernels are not left whole. Scrape cobs to remove remaining juice and pulp.

2. Heat oil in large skillet over medium heat. Add onion and bell peppers; cook 5 minutes, stirring occasionally. Add corn, water, salt, black pepper and ground red pepper; bring to a boil. Reduce heat to low; simmer 10 to 15 minutes.

3. Add crayfish; return mixture to a simmer. Cook 3 to 5 minutes or just until crayfish turn opaque. *Makes 6 servings*

9-inch Classic Crisco® Double Crust

2 cups all-purpose flour
1 teaspoon salt
¾ CRISCO® Stick or ¾ CRISCO® all-vegetable shortening
5 tablespoons cold water

1. Spoon flour into measuring cup and level. Combine flour and salt in medium bowl.

2. Cut in shortening using pastry blender or 2 knives until flour is blended to form pea-size chunks.

3. Sprinkle with water, 1 tablespoon at a time. Toss with fork until dough forms a ball.

4. Divide dough in half. Press half of dough between hands to form a 5- to 6-inch "pancake."

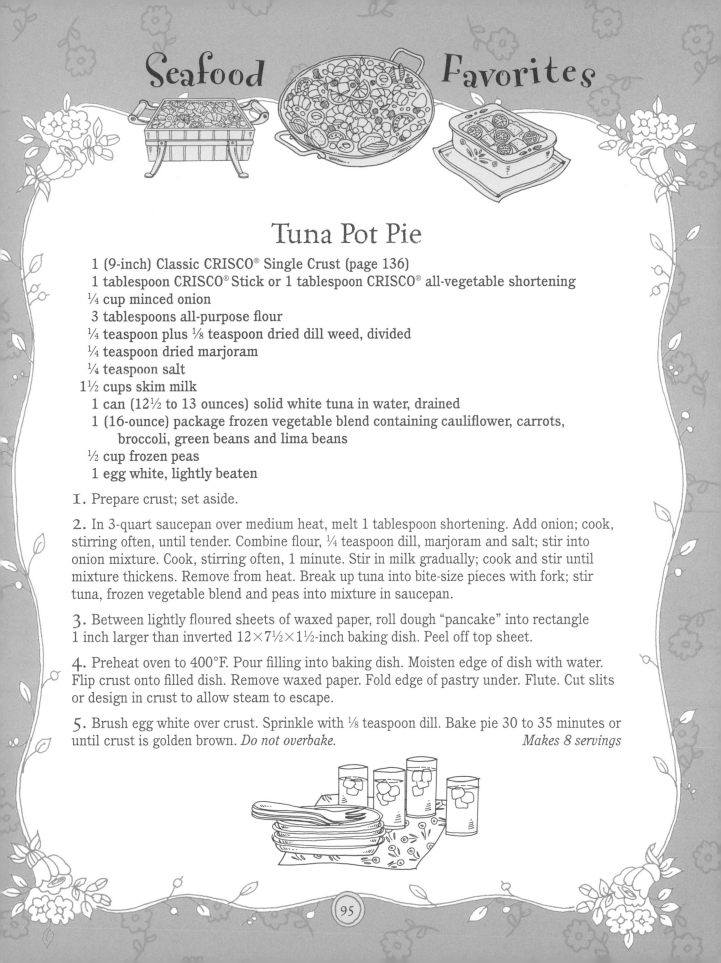

Tuna Pot Pie

1 (9-inch) Classic CRISCO® Single Crust (page 136)
1 tablespoon CRISCO® Stick or 1 tablespoon CRISCO® all-vegetable shortening
¼ cup minced onion
3 tablespoons all-purpose flour
¼ teaspoon plus ⅛ teaspoon dried dill weed, divided
¼ teaspoon dried marjoram
¼ teaspoon salt
1½ cups skim milk
1 can (12½ to 13 ounces) solid white tuna in water, drained
1 (16-ounce) package frozen vegetable blend containing cauliflower, carrots, broccoli, green beans and lima beans
½ cup frozen peas
1 egg white, lightly beaten

1. Prepare crust; set aside.

2. In 3-quart saucepan over medium heat, melt 1 tablespoon shortening. Add onion; cook, stirring often, until tender. Combine flour, ¼ teaspoon dill, marjoram and salt; stir into onion mixture. Cook, stirring often, 1 minute. Stir in milk gradually; cook and stir until mixture thickens. Remove from heat. Break up tuna into bite-size pieces with fork; stir tuna, frozen vegetable blend and peas into mixture in saucepan.

3. Between lightly floured sheets of waxed paper, roll dough "pancake" into rectangle 1 inch larger than inverted 12×7½×1½-inch baking dish. Peel off top sheet.

4. Preheat oven to 400°F. Pour filling into baking dish. Moisten edge of dish with water. Flip crust onto filled dish. Remove waxed paper. Fold edge of pastry under. Flute. Cut slits or design in crust to allow steam to escape.

5. Brush egg white over crust. Sprinkle with ⅛ teaspoon dill. Bake pie 30 to 35 minutes or until crust is golden brown. *Do not overbake.*   *Makes 8 servings*

Lemon Shrimp

    1 package (12 ounces) uncooked egg noodles
    ½ cup (1 stick) butter, softened
    2 pounds cooked shrimp
    3 tomatoes, chopped
    1 cup chicken broth
    1 cup shredded carrots
    1 can (4 ounces) sliced mushrooms, drained
    2 tablespoons fresh lemon juice
    2 cloves garlic, chopped
    ½ teaspoon celery seed
    ¼ teaspoon black pepper

1. Preheat oven to 350°F.

2. Cook noodles according to package directions. Drain and mix with butter in large bowl, stirring until butter is melted and noodles are evenly coated. Add remaining ingredients and mix again. Transfer to 3-quart casserole.

3. Bake 15 to 20 minutes or until heated through.   *Makes 8 servings*

Tuna Veg•All® Casserole

    3 cups cooked egg noodles
    1 can (15 ounces) VEG•ALL® Original Mixed Vegetables, with liquid
    1 can (10¾ ounces) cream of mushroom soup
    1 can (9 ounces) white tuna in water, drained
    1 cup shredded cheddar cheese

Preheat oven to 350°F. Combine all ingredients in 1½-quart casserole. Bake for 30 minutes or until heated through.   *Makes 6 servings*

Prep Time: 7 minutes

Salmon Casserole

  2 tablespoons margarine or butter
  2 cups mushroom slices
1½ cups chopped carrots
  1 cup frozen peas
  1 cup chopped celery
½ cup chopped onion
½ cup chopped red bell pepper
  1 tablespoon chopped fresh parsley
  1 clove garlic, minced
  1 teaspoon salt
½ teaspoon black pepper
½ teaspoon dried basil leaves
  4 cups cooked rice
  1 can (14 ounces) red salmon, drained and flaked
  1 can (10¾ ounces) condensed cream of mushroom soup, undiluted
  2 cups (8 ounces) grated Cheddar or American cheese
½ cup sliced black olives

1. Preheat oven to 350°F. Spray 2-quart casserole with nonstick cooking spray; set aside.

2. Melt margarine in large skillet or Dutch oven over medium heat. Add mushrooms, carrots, peas, celery, onion, bell pepper, parsley, garlic, salt, black pepper and basil; cook and stir 10 minutes or until vegetables are tender. Add rice, salmon, soup and cheese; mix well.

3. Transfer to prepared casserole. Sprinkle olives over top. Bake 30 minutes or until hot and bubbly.

Makes 8 servings

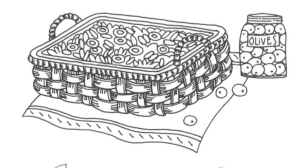

Halibut Provençale

Nonstick cooking spray
1 can (28 ounces) reduced-sodium diced tomatoes
2 cups fennel, stems and fronds removed, sliced thin and chopped
1 cup finely chopped onion
2 tablespoons minced orange zest
2 teaspoons dried herbes de Provence*
4 halibut steaks (4 ounces *each*)
1 tablespoon olive oil

Topping
¼ teaspoon salt
½ teaspoon black pepper
1 teaspoon paprika
2 cloves garlic, minced
¼ cup dry bread crumbs
1 tablespoon Parmesan cheese, grated
Minced basil (optional)

Herbes de Provence spice mixes usually contain dried basil, fennel seed, lavender, marjoram, rosemary, sage, summer savory and thyme.

1. Coat large ovenproof skillet with cooking spray; place over medium heat until hot. Add tomatoes, fennel, onion, orange zest and herbes de Provence. Cook 10 minutes, stirring often.

2. Place halibut over vegetables; sprinkle with oil. Mix salt, pepper, paprika, garlic, bread crumbs and cheese together. Sprinkle over fish. Cover skillet and cook until fish flakes easily.

3. Alternatively, heat broiler. Place skillet under broiler until bread crumbs are golden brown, 1 to 2 minutes. Sprinkle fish with minced basil, if desired.   *Makes 4 servings*

Chicken and Shrimp Jambalaya

1 pound fully cooked smoked sausage link, cut into ¼-inch slices
2 cups chopped onion
2 cups sliced celery
2 cups chopped green bell pepper
¼ cup chopped jalapeño peppers*
1 tablespoon minced garlic
1 (28-ounce) can whole tomatoes
3 cups water
2 cups cooked, cubed chicken
2 cups cubed ham
1 cup uncooked long-grain white rice
1 tablespoon HERB-OX® instant chicken bouillon or 3 bouillon cubes
1½ teaspoons paprika
½ teaspoon dried basil leaves
½ teaspoon coarsely ground black pepper
½ teaspoon dried thyme leaves
⅛ to ¼ teaspoon cayenne pepper
2 bay leaves
1 pound fresh or frozen raw shrimp, shelled and deveined**
Hot pepper sauce

*Jalapeño peppers can sting and irritate the skin; wear rubber gloves when handling peppers and do not touch eyes. Wash hands after handling.

**12 ounces frozen, cooked shrimp may be substituted for 1 pound fresh or frozen raw shrimp.

In Dutch oven over medium heat, cook sausage, onion, celery, peppers and garlic until tender. Add remaining ingredients except shrimp and hot pepper sauce. Bring to a boil. Cover; reduce heat and simmer 20 to 25 minutes or until rice is tender. Add shrimp. Cook 2 to 3 minutes or until shrimp turn pink. Remove and discard bay leaves. Serve with hot pepper sauce.   *Makes 12 servings*

Prep Time: 30 minutes
Total Time: 1¼ hours

Crab-Artichoke Casserole

8 ounces uncooked small shell pasta
2 tablespoons butter
6 green onions, chopped
2 tablespoons all-purpose flour
1 cup half-and-half
1 teaspoon dry mustard
½ teaspoon ground red pepper
    Salt and black pepper
½ cup (2 ounces) shredded Swiss cheese, divided
1 package (about 8 ounces) imitation crabmeat chunks
1 can (about 14 ounces) artichoke hearts, drained and cut into bite-size pieces

1. Preheat oven to 350°F. Grease 2-quart casserole. Cook pasta according to package directions; drain and set aside.

2. Heat butter in large saucepan over medium heat; add green onions. Cook and stir about 2 minutes. Add flour; cook and stir 2 minutes more. Gradually add half-and-half, whisking constantly until mixture begins to thicken. Whisk in mustard and red pepper; season to taste with salt and black pepper. Remove from heat and stir in ¼ cup cheese until melted.

3. Combine crabmeat, artichokes and pasta in casserole. Add sauce mixture and stir well. Top with remaining ¼ cup cheese. Bake about 40 minutes or until hot, bubbly and lightly browned.   *Makes 6 servings*

Tip: This can also be baked in individual ovenproof dishes. Reduce cooking time to about 20 minutes.

Tuna Tomato Casserole

2 cans (6 ounces each) tuna, drained
1 cup mayonnaise
1 small onion, finely chopped
¼ teaspoon salt
¼ teaspoon black pepper
1 package (12 ounces) uncooked wide egg noodles
8 to 10 plum tomatoes, sliced ¼ inch thick
1 cup (4 ounces) shredded Cheddar or mozzarella cheese

1. Preheat oven to 375°F.

2. Combine tuna, mayonnaise, onion, salt and pepper in medium bowl. Mix well and set aside.

3. Prepare noodles according to package directions, cooking just until tender. Drain noodles and return to pot.

4. Add tuna mixture to noodles; stir until well combined.

5. Layer half of noodle mixture, half of tomatoes and half of cheese in 13×9-inch baking dish. Press down slightly. Repeat layers with remaining ingredients.

6. Bake 20 minutes or until cheese is melted and casserole is heated through.

Makes 6 servings

Louisiana Shrimp Creole Pie

1 (9-inch) Classic CRISCO® Double Crust (page 94)
½ cup butter or margarine
¼ cup all-purpose flour
1 cup chopped white onion
½ cup thinly sliced green onion tops
⅓ cup chopped green bell pepper
3 tablespoons chopped celery
3 tablespoons finely minced fresh parsley
2 teaspoons finely minced garlic
¼ cup whipping cream
1 teaspoon salt
¾ teaspoon black pepper
2 pounds shelled and deveined small shrimp (crawfish tail meat can be substituted)

1. Heat oven to 350°F. Prepare crust.

2. Divide dough in half. Roll and press bottom crust into 9-inch deep dish pie plate. Trim edge even with pie plate. *Do not bake.*

3. Melt butter in 10-inch skillet over medium heat. Add flour; cook, stirring constantly, 3 minutes or until light golden brown. Add onions, bell pepper, celery, parsley and garlic. Cook, stirring constantly, until vegetables are very soft. Add cream, salt and black pepper. Mix gently; reduce heat to low and cook 3 minutes. Add shrimp; cook until tender. Remove from heat and allow filling to cool slightly.

4. Spoon filling into unbaked 9-inch pie shell. Roll top crust same as bottom. Lift top crust onto filled pie. Fold top edge under bottom crust; flute or make rope edge. Cut slits or design in top crust to allow steam to escape.

5. Bake pie for 25 to 30 minutes or until top is golden. *Do not overbake.*

Makes 8 servings

Seafood Favorites

Lickety-Split Paella Pronto

1 tablespoon olive oil
1 large onion, chopped
2 cloves garlic, minced
1 jar (16 ounces) salsa
1 can (14½ ounces) diced tomatoes, undrained
1 can (14 ounces) artichoke hearts, drained and quartered
1 can (14 ounces) chicken broth
1 package (about 8 ounces) uncooked yellow rice
1 can (12 ounces) solid white tuna, drained and flaked
1 package (9 to 10 ounces) frozen green peas
2 tablespoons finely chopped green onions (optional)
2 tablespoons finely chopped red bell pepper (optional)

1. Heat oil in large nonstick skillet over medium heat until hot. Add onion and garlic; cook and stir about 5 minutes or until onion is tender.

2. Stir in salsa, tomatoes with juice, artichokes, broth and rice. Bring to a boil. Cover; reduce heat to low and simmer 15 minutes.

3. Stir in tuna and peas. Cover; cook 5 to 10 minutes or until rice is tender and tuna and peas are heated through. Sprinkle each serving with green onions and red bell pepper, if desired.

Makes 4 to 6 servings

Shrimp Noodle Supreme

1 package (8 ounces) spinach noodles, cooked and drained
1 package (3 ounces) cream cheese, cubed and softened
1½ pounds medium shrimp, peeled and deveined
½ cup (1 stick) butter, softened
   Salt and black pepper
1 can (10¾ ounces) condensed cream of mushroom soup, undiluted
1 cup sour cream
½ cup half-and-half
½ cup mayonnaise
1 tablespoon snipped chives
1 tablespoon chopped fresh parsley
½ teaspoon Dijon mustard
¾ cup (6 ounces) shredded sharp Cheddar cheese

1. Preheat oven to 325°F. Combine noodles and cream cheese in medium bowl. Spread noodle mixture in bottom of greased 13×9-inch glass casserole. Cook shrimp in butter in large skillet over medium-high heat until pink and tender, about 5 minutes. Season to taste with salt and pepper. Spread shrimp over noodles.

2. Combine soup, sour cream, half-and-half, mayonnaise, chives, parsley and mustard in another medium bowl. Spread over shrimp. Sprinkle Cheddar cheese over top. Bake 25 minutes or until hot and cheese is melted. *Makes 6 servings*

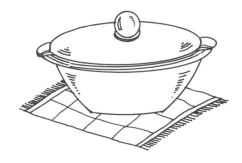

Slow-Simmered Jambalaya

2 cans (14½ ounces each) stewed tomatoes, undrained
2 cups diced boiled ham
2 medium onions, coarsely chopped
1 medium green bell pepper, diced
2 ribs celery, sliced
1 cup uncooked long-grain converted rice
2 tablespoons vegetable oil
2 tablespoons ketchup
3 cloves garlic, minced
½ teaspoon dried thyme leaves
½ teaspoon black pepper
⅛ teaspoon ground cloves
1 pound fresh or frozen shrimp, peeled and deveined

Slow Cooker Directions

1. Thoroughly mix all ingredients except shrimp in slow cooker. Cover; cook on LOW 8 to 10 hours.

2. One hour before serving, turn slow cooker to HIGH. Stir in uncooked shrimp. Cover; cook until shrimp are pink and tender.   *Makes 4 to 6 servings*

Brazilian Corn and Shrimp Moqueca Casserole

   2 tablespoons olive oil
½ cup chopped onion
¼ cup chopped green bell pepper
¼ cup tomato sauce
   2 tablespoons chopped parsley
½ teaspoon TABASCO® brand Pepper Sauce
   1 pound medium cooked shrimp
      Salt to taste
   2 tablespoons flour
   1 cup milk
   1 can (16 ounces) cream-style corn
      Grated Parmesan cheese

Preheat oven to 375°F. Heat oil in large oven-proof skillet over medium-high heat. Add onion, bell pepper, tomato sauce, parsley and TABASCO® Sauce; cook, stirring occasionally, for 5 minutes. Add shrimp and salt. Cover and reduce heat to low, and simmer for 2 to 3 minutes. Sprinkle flour over shrimp mixture; stir. Add milk gradually, stirring after each addition. Cook over medium heat until mixture thickens. Remove from heat. Pour corn over mixture; do not stir. Sprinkle with Parmesan cheese. Bake for 30 minutes or until browned.

Makes 4 servings

Surimi Seafood-Zucchini Frittata with Fresh Tomato Sauce

 2 tablespoons vegetable oil
 1 zucchini, thinly sliced
 ½ cup chopped onion
 ¼ cup chopped green bell pepper
 3 eggs
 6 egg whites
 2 teaspoons finely chopped fresh basil *or* ½ teaspoon dried basil
 ½ teaspoon salt, optional
 ¼ teaspoon black pepper
 6 ounces crab or lobster-flavored surimi seafood, chunk style
 2 tablespoons butter or margarine
 3 cups tomato sauce

Preheat oven to 375°F. Heat oil in 10-inch heavy metal skillet over medium heat. Add zucchini, onion and bell pepper; cook 5 minutes, stirring often. Place in medium bowl; set aside to cool slightly. In large bowl, beat eggs and egg whites with basil, salt and black pepper until well blended. Add zucchini mixture and surimi seafood; beat well. Meanwhile, melt butter in same skillet over medium heat, swirling skillet to coat evenly with butter. Pour in egg-surimi seafood mixture and place skillet on middle shelf of oven. Bake 12 to 15 minutes, or until eggs are set throughout. Loosen around edges with metal spatula; cut into wedges. Serve hot with ½ cup tomato sauce over each frittata slice.

Makes 6 servings

Favorite recipe from **National Fisheries Institute**

Shrimp Veg•All® Pot Pie
with Lemon Dill Crust

    2 tablespoons butter
    1 clove garlic, minced
    ⅓ cup white wine
    2 cans (15 ounces each) VEG•ALL® Original Mixed Vegetables, drained and liquid
        reserved from 1 can
    2 tablespoons cornstarch
    2 tablespoons cold water
    1 package (16 ounces) frozen cooked jumbo shrimp, peeled and deveined

Crust
    1 egg, beaten
    ½ cup milk
    1 cup biscuit mix
    1 teaspoon grated lemon peel
    1 teaspoon dill weed

Preheat oven to 400°F. In large skillet, melt butter. Add garlic and cook over medium-high heat. Stir in wine and reserved liquid from 1 can of Veg•All. In small bowl, blend cornstarch with water. Add to skillet and cook for 2 to 3 minutes, stirring constantly, until mixture bubbles and thickens. Remove from heat. Add Veg•All and shrimp to skillet; stir to combine. Pour into greased 2-quart casserole.

To make crust, in medium mixing bowl, combine egg and milk. Add biscuit mix, lemon peel, and dill; stir with fork until blended. Pour topping over vegetable mixture. Bake for 30 to 40 minutes or until heated through and crust is golden. *Makes 6 servings*

Shrimp Creole

     2 tablespoons olive oil
 1½ cups chopped green bell pepper
     1 medium onion, chopped
 ⅔ cup chopped celery
     2 cloves garlic, finely chopped
     1 cup uncooked long-grain rice
     1 can (about 14 ounces) diced tomatoes, drained and juice reserved
     1 teaspoon dried oregano leaves
 ¾ teaspoon salt
 ½ teaspoon dried thyme leaves
     2 teaspoons hot pepper sauce, or to taste
        Black pepper
     1 pound raw shrimp, peeled and deveined
     1 tablespoon chopped fresh parsley (optional)

1. Preheat oven to 325°F. Heat olive oil in large skillet over medium-high heat. Add bell pepper, onion, celery and garlic; cook and stir 5 minutes or until vegetables are soft.

2. Add rice; cook and stir 5 minutes over medium heat until rice is opaque. Add tomatoes, oregano, salt, thyme, hot sauce and black pepper to skillet; cook and stir to combine. Pour reserved tomato juice into measuring cup. Add enough water to measure 1¾ cups liquid; add to skillet. Cook and stir 2 minutes.

3. Transfer mixture to 2½-quart casserole. Stir in shrimp. Bake, covered, 55 minutes or until rice is tender and liquid is absorbed. Sprinkle with parsley, if desired.

Makes 4 to 6 servings

Beef's Up

Delicious Ground Beef Medley

 1 pound ground beef
 ½ cup chopped onion
 ¼ cup chopped celery
 2 cups uncooked elbow macaroni
 1 can (10¾ ounces) condensed cream of chicken soup
 1 can (10¾ ounces) condensed cream of mushroom soup
 ⅔ cup milk
 ½ teaspoon salt
  Dash of black pepper
 ½ cup chopped green bell pepper
 1 can (16 ounces) whole kernel corn, drained

1. Brown ground beef with onion and celery, stirring to break up meat. Drain.

2. Cook macaroni according to package directions. Drain.

3. In 2½-quart casserole dish, combine soups with milk, salt and black pepper. Add ground beef, macaroni, green pepper and corn. Bake at 350°F for 30 minutes.

Makes 8 servings

*Favorite recipe from **North Dakota Beef Commission***

Slow-Cooked Korean Beef Short Ribs

4 to 4½ pounds beef short ribs
¼ cup chopped green onions with tops
¼ cup tamari or soy sauce
¼ cup beef broth or water
1 tablespoon brown sugar
2 teaspoons minced fresh ginger
2 teaspoons minced garlic
½ teaspoon black pepper
2 teaspoons dark sesame oil
    Hot cooked rice or linguini pasta
2 teaspoons sesame seeds, toasted

Slow Cooker Directions

1. Place ribs in slow cooker. Combine green onions, tamari, broth, brown sugar, ginger, garlic and pepper in medium bowl; mix well and pour over ribs. Cover; cook on LOW 7 to 8 hours or until ribs are fork tender.

2. Remove ribs from cooking liquid, cool slightly. Trim excess fat. Cut rib meat into bite-size pieces discarding bones and fat.

3. Let cooking liquid stand 5 minutes to allow fat to rise. Skim off fat.

4. Stir sesame oil into liquid. Return beef to slow cooker. Cover; cook on LOW 15 to 30 minutes or until mixture is hot.

5. Serve with rice or pasta; garnish with sesame seeds.   *Makes 6 servings*

Variation: Three pounds boneless short ribs can be substituted for beef short ribs.

Prep Time: 10 to 15 minutes
Cook Time: 7 to 8½ hours

Wild Rice Beef and Curry Casserole

    1 pound lean ground beef
 ½ cup butter
    1 cup chopped onion
    1 cup chopped red bell pepper
 ¼ cup all-purpose flour
1½ teaspoons curry powder
 ½ teaspoon salt
 ½ teaspoon garlic powder
 ¼ teaspoon ground red pepper
    2 cups milk
    1 box (10 ounces) frozen mixed vegetables, thawed
    4 cups cooked wild rice
 ½ cup sunflower seeds

Preheat oven to 325°F. In large skillet, brown beef; drain and set aside. Melt butter; sauté onion and bell pepper. In small bowl, mix flour and seasonings; add to onion mixture. Cook, stirring constantly until bubbly. Gradually stir in milk until creamy. Mix in beef, vegetables, wild rice and sunflower seeds. Pour into 3-quart casserole. Bake uncovered 25 to 30 minutes.   *Makes 8 to 10 servings*

*Favorite recipe from **Minnesota Cultivated Wild Rice Council***

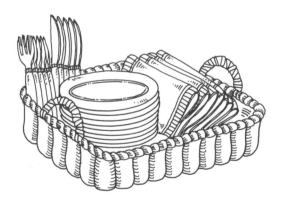

Thai Beef & Peanuts

1 pound beef full cut round steak, cut into 2×½×¼-inch strips
2 tablespoons vegetable oil, divided
2 medium onions, cut into half-rings
¼ to ½ teaspoon red pepper flakes
2 red bell peppers, cut into ¼-inch strips
2 medium yellow squash (about 4 ounces), julienned
½ cup Thai peanut sauce*
¼ cup dry roasted peanuts, coarsely chopped
   Hot cooked couscous or rice

Available in larger grocery stores or specialty markets.

1. In large skillet, heat 1 tablespoon oil over medium-high heat until hot. Add beef strips. Cook, stirring frequently, about 4 minutes or until outside surface is no longer pink. Remove beef from skillet.

2. Add remaining 1 tablespoon oil to skillet. Add onions and red pepper flakes, stirring constantly about 3 minutes or until onions begin to soften.

3. Add bell peppers, stirring constantly about 3 minutes or until bell peppers begin to soften.

4. Add squash; cook about 1 minute.

5. Add peanut sauce and return beef to skillet; cook about 3 to 5 minutes or until heated through.

6. Sprinkle peanuts over beef mixture. Serve over cooked couscous.   *Makes 4 servings*

Favorite recipe from **North Dakota Beef Commission**

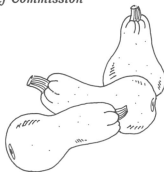

Wild Lasagna Casserole

    1 cup chopped onion
    ¾ cup chopped green bell pepper
    1 can (14½ ounces) clear beef broth, divided
    1 pound lean ground beef
    ½ teaspoon *each* salt, dried oregano leaves and garlic powder
    1 can (6 ounces) tomato paste
    4 cups cooked wild rice
    1 package (16 ounces) frozen vegetable medley with broccoli, carrots, water
        chestnuts & red bell peppers, thawed and drained
    1½ cups (6 ounces) shredded mozzarella cheese, divided
    1 cup light ricotta cheese

Preheat oven to 350°F. In large skillet, sauté onion and pepper in ⅓ cup broth until tender; remove and set aside. Brown beef and drain; stir in seasonings, remaining broth and tomato paste. Add onion mixture, wild rice, vegetables and 1 cup mozzarella cheese; toss to blend. Pour half of mixture into 3-quart casserole; dollop with ricotta cheese. Add remaining mixture. Top with remaining ½ cup mozzarella cheese. Cover and bake 40 minutes. Uncover; bake 10 minutes.   *Makes 8 to 10 servings*

Favorite recipe from **Minnesota Cultivated Wild Rice Council**

Lemon-Thyme Beef with Beans

1 beef chuck roast (about 3 pounds), trimmed and cut into 2-inch pieces
2 cans (15 ounces each) white or pinto beans, rinsed and drained
1 can (15 ounces) red kidney beans, rinsed and drained
1 cup beef broth
1 medium onion, chopped
2 cloves garlic, minced
1 teaspoon salt
1 teaspoon grated lemon peel
1 teaspoon dried thyme leaves
1 teaspoon black pepper
    Chopped fresh parsley

Slow Cooker Directions

1. Place ingredients in slow cooker, except parsley. Cover; cook on LOW 8 to 9 hours or until beef is tender.

2. Adjust seasonings before serving, if desired. Arrange beef on top of beans. Garnish with parsley.
Makes 6 to 8 servings

Prep Time: 20 minutes
Cook Time: 8 to 9 hours

Beefy Mac & Double Cheddar

½ pound ground beef
3½ cups water
  2 cups uncooked elbow macaroni
  1 jar (1 pound) RAGÚ® Cheese Creations!® Double Cheddar Sauce

In 12-inch skillet, brown ground beef; drain. Remove from skillet and set aside.

In same skillet, bring water to a boil over high heat. Stir in uncooked macaroni and cook 6 minutes or until tender; do not drain. Return ground beef to skillet. Stir in Ragú Cheese Creations! Double Cheddar Sauce; heat through. Season, if desired, with salt and ground black pepper.
Makes 4 servings

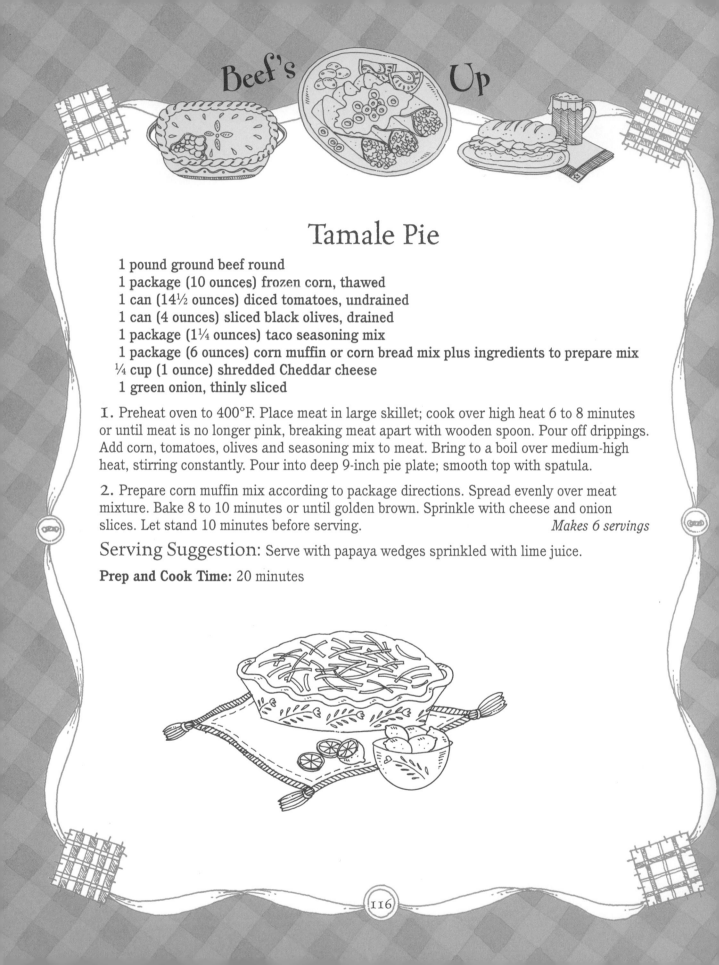

Tamale Pie

1 pound ground beef round
1 package (10 ounces) frozen corn, thawed
1 can (14½ ounces) diced tomatoes, undrained
1 can (4 ounces) sliced black olives, drained
1 package (1¼ ounces) taco seasoning mix
1 package (6 ounces) corn muffin or corn bread mix plus ingredients to prepare mix
¼ cup (1 ounce) shredded Cheddar cheese
1 green onion, thinly sliced

I. Preheat oven to 400°F. Place meat in large skillet; cook over high heat 6 to 8 minutes or until meat is no longer pink, breaking meat apart with wooden spoon. Pour off drippings. Add corn, tomatoes, olives and seasoning mix to meat. Bring to a boil over medium-high heat, stirring constantly. Pour into deep 9-inch pie plate; smooth top with spatula.

2. Prepare corn muffin mix according to package directions. Spread evenly over meat mixture. Bake 8 to 10 minutes or until golden brown. Sprinkle with cheese and onion slices. Let stand 10 minutes before serving. *Makes 6 servings*

Serving Suggestion: Serve with papaya wedges sprinkled with lime juice.

Prep and Cook Time: 20 minutes

Beef Bordelaise

1 cup red wine
2 teaspoons TABASCO® brand Pepper Sauce
2 whole cloves
1 bay leaf
2 cloves garlic, divided
6 whole black peppercorns
3 pounds lean stewing beef, cut into 2-inch cubes
4 slices bacon, cut into small pieces
2 cups beef stock or canned beef bouillon
1 teaspoon salt
½ teaspoon dried thyme leaves
4 carrots, cut into 1-inch slices
12 small white onions
1 pound mushrooms, quartered
1 (10-ounce) package frozen green peas, cooked
   Chopped parsley
   Hot cooked noodles

Combine wine, TABASCO® Sauce, cloves, bay leaf, 1 clove garlic and peppercorns in deep dish. Add beef cubes; toss to coat. Marinate in refrigerator 1 hour, stirring every 15 minutes.

Cook bacon in ovenproof casserole or Dutch oven over low heat 2 to 3 minutes. Remove bacon to small dish with slotted spoon. Heat bacon drippings in casserole until very hot.

Thinly slice remaining 1 clove garlic. Remove beef from marinade and pat dry with paper towel. Add beef and garlic to casserole; cook over high heat until beef is dark brown on all sides. Add bacon, marinade, beef stock, salt and thyme; bring to boil and cook 10 minutes. Reduce heat and simmer about 30 minutes.

Preheat oven to 350°F. Add carrots, onions and mushrooms to beef mixture; bake 1½ hours or until beef is tender. Stir in peas and adjust seasoning. Sprinkle with parsley; serve with noodles.

Makes 8 servings

Jackpot Casserole

2 tablespoons butter or olive oil
2 medium onions, chopped
2 ribs celery, chopped
1 package (8 ounces) mushrooms, sliced *or* 1 can (4 ounces) sliced mushrooms, drained
1 to 1½ pounds ground beef
1 can (4 ounces) sliced olives, drained
1½ cups cooked rice
1 can (8 ounces) tomato sauce
Salt and black pepper

I. Preheat oven to 350°F.

2. Melt butter in large skillet over medium heat. Add onions and celery; cook and stir until almost tender. Add mushrooms; cook and stir until vegetables are tender.

3. In separate medium skillet, cook beef over medium-high heat 10 minutes or until no longer pink, stirring to separate meat. Pour off fat.

4. Combine vegetable mixture, beef, olives and rice in 3- to 4-quart casserole. Add tomato sauce, salt and pepper; mix well.

5. Cover; bake 1 hour or until heated through.

Makes 4 to 6 servings

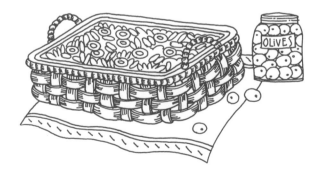

Shelby Slow Cooker Rouladen

12 slices top round beef, pounded thin (¼-inch thick)
   Salt and black pepper
   Garlic pepper
  4 tablespoons Dijon mustard
1½ cups chopped onion
1½ cups chopped dill pickle
  ¼ cup (½ stick) butter
  ¼ cup plus 2 tablespoons flour
  2 cans (14½ ounces each) beef broth
  1 pound peeled baby carrots
  4 stalks celery, cut into 1-inch pieces

Slow Cooker Directions

1. Place 1 slice of beef on clean cutting board, season with salt, black and garlic peppers. Spread with about 1 teaspoon of mustard and top with about ⅛ cup each onion and pickle. Starting at one short side of beef fold about ⅓ of slice over on itself, tuck in long sides, then roll tightly. Secure with toothpick. Repeat with remaining slices of beef.

2. Brown half of rolled beef slices in large skillet coated with nonstick cooking spray over medium-high heat until browned on all sides. Brown remaining rolls; remove from skillet.

3. In same skillet, melt butter. Sprinkle with flour, and stir to make a smooth paste. Add beef broth, stirring constantly. Cook and stir until mixture thickens.

4. Pour half of gravy in slow cooker. Add beef rolls and cover with remaining gravy. Top with carrots and celery.

5. Cover; cook on LOW 8 to 10 hours or on HIGH 4 to 5 hours. *Makes 6 to 8 servings*

Chipotle Taco Filling

        2 pounds ground beef chuck
        2 cups chopped yellow onion
        2 cans (15 ounces each) pinto beans, rinsed and drained
        1 can (14½ ounces) diced tomatoes with peppers and onions, drained
        4 chipotle peppers in adobo sauce, mashed*
        1 tablespoon beef bouillon granules
        1 tablespoon sugar
    1½ teaspoons ground cumin
        Taco shells or flour tortillas (optional)
        Additional toppings: shredded cheese, lettuce, salsa and sour cream (optional)

Chipotle peppers can sting and irritate the skin; wear rubber gloves when handling peppers and do not touch eyes. Wash hands after handling peppers.

Slow Cooker Directionss

1. Place medium skillet over medium-high heat until hot. Add beef and cook 6 minutes or until just beginning to brown, stirring frequently.

2. Place beef, accumulated juices and remaining ingredients into slow cooker. Cover; cook on LOW 4 hours or on HIGH 2 hours.

3. Serve with taco shells or flour tortillas, if desired. Top with shredded cheese, lettuce, salsa and sour cream, if desired.

Makes 8 cups, enough for 16 tacos

Best Beef Brisket Ever

1 to 2 beef briskets (about 5 pounds total)
2 cups apple cider, divided
1 head garlic, cloves separated, crushed and peeled
2 tablespoons whole peppercorns
2 tablespoons dried thyme leaves *or* 1 cup fresh thyme
1 tablespoon mustard seed
1 tablespoon Cajun seasoning
1 teaspoon ground cumin
1 teaspoon celery seed
1 teaspoon ground allspice
2 to 4 whole cloves
1 bottle (12 ounces) dark beer

Slow Cooker Directions

1. Place brisket, ⅓ cup cider, garlic, peppercorns, thyme, mustard seed, Cajun seasoning, allspice, cumin, celery seed and cloves in resealable plastic food storage bag; seal and marinate in refrigerator overnight.

2. Place brisket and marinade in slow cooker. Add remaining 1½ cups apple cider and beer.

3. Cover; cook on LOW 10 hours or until brisket is tender. Strain sauce and pour over meat.　　　　　　　　　　　　　　　　　　　　　　　　*Makes 12 servings*

Serving Suggestion: The beef from this recipe may also be sliced and served as corned beef sandwiches.

Rainbow Casserole

5 potatoes, peeled and cut into thin slices
1 pound ground beef
1 onion, peeled, halved and cut into thin slices
  Salt and black pepper
1 can (about 28 ounces) stewed tomatoes, drained, juice reserved
1 cup frozen peas *or* 1 can (about 6 ounces) peas

1. Preheat oven to 350°F. Spray 3-quart casserole with nonstick cooking spray.

2. Boil potatoes in salted water in large saucepan until almost tender. Drain and reserve. Meanwhile, cook and stir ground beef in medium skillet until no longer pink. Drain fat.

3. Layer ½ of ground beef, ½ of potatoes, ½ of onion, salt and pepper, ½ of tomatoes and ½ of peas. Repeat layers. Add reserved tomato juice.

4. Bake, covered, about 40 minutes or until most of liquid is absorbed.

Makes 4 to 6 servings

Slow Cooker Beef & Noodles

1 can (10¾ ounces) condensed French onion soup, undiluted
1 can (10¾ ounces) condensed cream of mushroom soup, undiluted
1 to 1½ pounds beef for stew
1 bag (12 ounces) extra-wide egg noodles, cooked according to package directions

Slow Cooker Directions
Combine soups and meat in slow cooker; stir. Cover; cook on LOW 8 to 10 hours or until beef is tender. Serve with hot cooked noodles.

Makes 4 to 6 servings

Mexican Meatloaf

    2 pounds ground beef
    2 cups crushed corn chips
    1 cup shredded Cheddar cheese
    ⅔ cup salsa
    2 eggs, beaten
    4 tablespoons taco seasoning
      Meat Glaze (recipe follows, optional)

Slow Cooker Directions

1. Combine all ingredients in large bowl; mix well.

2. Shape meat mixture into loaf and place in slow cooker. Cover; cook on LOW 8 to 10 hours. Prepare meat glaze, if desired. *Makes 4 to 6 servings*

Meat Glaze: For a glaze, mix together ½ cup ketchup, 2 tablespoons brown sugar and 1 teaspoon dry mustard. Spread over meatloaf. Cover; cook on HIGH 15 minutes.

Cheezy Bean Wrap

    ½ pound lean ground beef
    1 cup HEINZ® Tomato Ketchup
    1 cup bottled tomato salsa
    1 can (15½ ounces) pinto or kidney beans, drained
    8 (8-inch) flour tortillas, warmed
    1 cup shredded Cheddar cheese
      Shredded lettuce

Brown beef; drain fat. Add ketchup, salsa and beans; heat. Spoon about ½ cup beef mixture down center of each tortilla; sprinkle with 2 tablespoons cheese. Fold tortilla around filling. Line serving plates with lettuce. Place tortillas seam-side down on lettuce. Top with additional cheese and salsa, if desired. *Makes 4 servings*

Spicy Beefy Noodles

1½ pounds ground beef
1 small onion, minced
1 small clove garlic, minced
1 tablespoon chili powder
1 teaspoon paprika
⅛ teaspoon *each* dried basil leaves, dill weed, dried thyme leaves and dried marjoram
    leaves
Salt
Black pepper
1 can (10 ounces) diced tomatoes with green chilies, undrained
1 can (8 ounces) tomato sauce
1 cup water
3 tablespoons Worcestershire sauce
1 package (about 10 ounces) egg noodles, cooked according to package directions
½ cup (2 ounces) *each* shredded Cheddar, mozzarella, pepper-Jack and provolone
    cheeses

1. Cook and stir ground beef, onion and garlic in large skillet over medium heat until meat is no longer pink, stirring to separate meat. Pour off drippings. Add chili powder, paprika, basil, dill, thyme and marjoram. Season with salt and pepper. Cook and stir 2 minutes.

2. Add tomatoes with juice, tomato sauce, water and Worcestershire sauce; mix well. Simmer, covered, 20 minutes.

3. In 2-quart microwavable casserole, combine meat mixture and noodles. Mix shredded cheeses and sprinkle evenly over top.

4. Microwave at HIGH (100% power) 3 minutes. Let stand 5 minutes. Microwave at HIGH 3 minutes longer or until cheeses melt.

Makes 6 servings

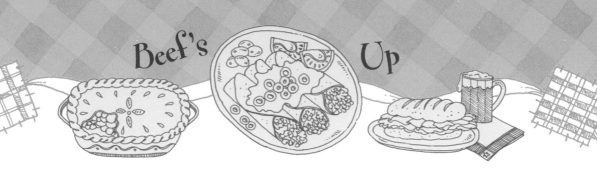

It's a Keeper Casserole

1 tablespoon vegetable oil
½ cup chopped onion
¼ cup chopped green bell pepper
1 clove garlic, minced
2 tablespoons all-purpose flour
1 teaspoon sugar
½ teaspoon salt
½ teaspoon dried basil leaves
½ teaspoon black pepper
1 can (about 16 ounces) whole tomatoes, cut up and drained
1 package (about 16 ounces) frozen fully-cooked meatballs, cooked*
1½ cups cooked vegetables (any combination)
1 teaspoon beef bouillon granules
1 teaspoon Worcestershire sauce
1 can refrigerated buttermilk biscuits

Cooked ground beef or sliced hot dogs can be substituted for the meatballs.

1. Preheat oven to 400°F. Heat oil in large saucepan. Cook and stir onion, bell pepper and garlic over medium heat until vegetables are tender.

2. Stir in flour, sugar, salt, basil and black pepper. Slowly blend in tomatoes, meatballs, vegetables, bouillon and Worcestershire sauce. Cook and stir until slightly thickened and bubbling; pour into 2-quart casserole.

3. Unroll biscuits; place on top of casserole. Bake, uncovered, 15 minutes or until biscuits are golden.

Makes 4 servings

Beef Enchiladas

Red Chili Sauce (page 127)
1½ pounds boneless beef chuck shoulder, cut into 1-inch cubes
½ teaspoon salt
2 tablespoons vegetable oil
½ cup finely chopped white onion
¾ cup beef broth
¼ cup raisins
1 clove garlic, minced
½ teaspoon ground cloves
¼ teaspoon anise seeds, crushed
12 (6-inch) corn tortillas
1 cup (4 ounces) shredded mild Cheddar cheese
¾ cup sour cream
⅓ cup sliced pitted black olives
Basil sprig and tomato wedge for garnish

1. Prepare Red Chili Sauce.

2. Sprinkle beef with salt. Brown beef in batches in hot oil in large skillet over medium-high heat 10 to 12 minutes. Remove to plate.

3. Reduce heat to medium. Add onion; cook and stir 4 minutes or until onion is soft. Return beef to skillet. Stir in broth, raisins, garlic, cloves, anise seeds and ¼ cup Red Chili Sauce. Bring to a boil over medium-high heat. Reduce heat to low. Cover and simmer 1½ to 2 hours until beef is very tender. Remove from heat. Using 2 forks, pull beef into coarse shreds in skillet.

4. Preheat oven to 375°F. Heat remaining Red Chili Sauce in medium skillet over medium heat until hot; remove from heat.

5. Dip 1 tortilla in sauce with tongs a few seconds until limp. Drain off excess sauce. Spread about 3 tablespoons meat filling down center of tortilla. Roll up; place in 13×9-inch baking dish. Repeat with remaining tortillas, sauce and meat filling. Pour remaining sauce over enchiladas. Sprinkle cheese over top.

6. Bake 25 minutes or until bubbly and cheese is melted. To serve, spoon sour cream down center of enchiladas. Sprinkle with olives. Garnish, if desired. *Makes 4 to 6 servings*

Red Chili Sauce

   3 ounces dried ancho chilies* (about 5), seeded, deveined and rinsed
2½ cups boiling water
   2 tablespoons vegetable oil
   2 tablespoons tomato paste
   1 clove garlic, minced
  ½ teaspoon salt
  ½ teaspoon dried oregano leaves
  ¼ teaspoon ground cumin
  ¼ teaspoon ground coriander

Ancho chilies can sting and irritate the skin; wear rubber gloves when handling peppers and do not touch eyes. Wash hands after handling peppers.

1. Place chilies in medium bowl; cover with boiling water. Let stand 1 hour.

2. Place chilies along with soaking water in blender; blend until smooth.

3. Whisk together chili mixture and remaining ingredients in medium saucepan. Bring to a boil. Reduce heat. Cover and simmer 10 minutes, stirring occasionally.

Makes about 2½ cups

Tip: Sauce can be covered and refrigerated up to 3 days or frozen up to 1 month.

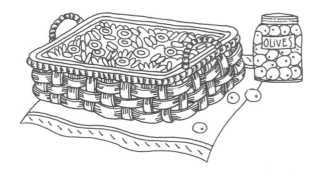

Meat and Potato Pie

¼ CRISCO® Stick or ¼ cup CRISCO® all-vegetable shortening
1 pound sirloin steak, trimmed and cut into ½-inch cubes
½ cup ½-inch diced onion
½ cup ½-inch diced carrots
¼ cup tomato paste
½ teaspoon dried basil leaves
½ teaspoon dried thyme leaves
½ teaspoon garlic powder
1 can (10½ ounces) condensed double strength beef broth
4½ cups peeled, ¾-inch cubed Idaho (russet) potatoes
1 tablespoon cornstarch
2 tablespoons cold water
½ cup frozen green peas, thawed
1 (9-inch) Classic CRISCO® Double Crust (page 94)

1. Melt ¼ cup shortening in large saucepan. Add steak. Brown on medium-high heat. Add onion and carrots. Cook until onion starts to brown, stirring often. Add tomato paste, basil, thyme and garlic powder. Cook 2 to 3 minutes, stirring constantly. Add broth and potatoes. Reduce heat to low; cover and simmer until potatoes are cooked through but still firm.

2. Dissolve cornstarch in water. Add to saucepan. Cook and stir until thickened. Remove from heat. Stir in peas. Cool to room temperature.

3. Prepare crust. Heat oven to 375°F. Divide dough in half. Roll and press bottom crust into 9-inch deep-dish pie plate or casserole. Spoon in filling. Moisten pastry edge with water. Roll out top crust. Lift onto filled pie. Cut slits in top crust to allow steam to escape. Bake 30 to 35 minutes or until browned. *Do not overbake.* Serve hot.

Makes one 9-inch pie

Beef & Wild Rice Casserole

1 pound ground beef
2 cups sliced fresh mushrooms
1 cup sliced celery
1 cup chopped onion
2 teaspoons minced garlic
2 (10½-ounce) cans cream of mushroom soup
2 cups water
1 (6-ounce) package long grain and wild rice blend
2 tablespoons Worcestershire sauce
1 tablespoon HERB-OX® instant beef bouillon granules
1½ teaspoons paprika
¼ teaspoon coarsely ground black pepper
½ cup cashews

Heat oven to 375°F. In large skillet, brown ground beef; drain. Add mushrooms, celery, onion and garlic. Cook 10 to 12 minutes or until vegetables are tender. In large bowl, combine meat mixture with remaining ingredients except seasoning packet from rice and cashews. Pour mixture into 2-quart casserole. Cover and bake for 30 minutes. Remove from oven and top with cashews. Return casserole to oven and bake, uncovered, 30 additional minutes or until rice is tender. *Makes 8 servings*

Prep Time: 20 minutes
Total Time: 1 hour, 20 minutes

Quick Tamale Casserole

1½ pounds ground beef
¾ cup sliced green onions
1 can (4 ounces) chopped green chilies, drained and divided
1 can (16 ounces) whole kernel corn, drained
1 can (10¾ ounces) condensed tomato soup, undiluted
¾ cup salsa
1 can (2¼ ounces) chopped pitted ripe olives (optional)
1 tablespoon Worcestershire sauce
1 teaspoon chili powder
¼ teaspoon garlic powder
4 slices (¾ ounce each) American cheese, halved
4 corn muffins, cut into ½-inch cubes
Mexican Sour Cream Topping (recipe follows, optional)

Preheat oven to 350°F. Cook ground beef and onions in medium skillet over medium-high heat until beef is brown. Reserve 2 tablespoons chilies for Mexican Sour Cream Topping, if desired. Stir remaining chilies, corn, tomato soup, salsa, olives, Worcestershire sauce, chili and garlic powders into skillet until well blended. Place in 2-quart casserole. Top with cheese, then evenly spread muffin cubes over cheese. Bake 5 to 10 minutes or until cheese is melted. Meanwhile, prepare Mexican Sour Cream Topping, if desired. Serve casserole with topping, if desired.

Makes 6 servings

Mexican Sour Cream Topping

1 cup sour cream
2 tablespoons chopped green chilies, reserved from above
2 teaspoons chopped jalapeño peppers* (optional)
2 teaspoons lime juice

Jalapeño peppers can sting and irritate the skin; wear rubber gloves when handling peppers and do not touch eyes. Wash hands after handling.

Combine all ingredients in small bowl; mix until well blended.

Makes about 1 cup

Slow Cooker Steak Fajitas

1 beef flank steak (about 1 pound)
1 medium onion, cut into strips
½ cup medium salsa
2 tablespoons fresh lime juice
2 tablespoons chopped fresh cilantro
2 cloves garlic, minced
1 tablespoon chili powder
1 teaspoon ground cumin
½ teaspoon salt
1 small green bell pepper, cut into strips
1 small red bell pepper, cut into strips
Flour tortillas, warmed
Additional salsa (optional)

Slow Cooker Directions

1. Cut flank steak lengthwise in half, then crosswise into thin strips. Combine all ingredients except bell peppers, tortillas and additional salsa in slow cooker. Cover; cook on LOW 5 to 6 hours. Add bell peppers. Cover; cook on LOW 1 hour.

2. Serve with tortillas and additional salsa, if desired.

Makes 4 servings

Prep Time: 20 minutes
Cook Time: 6 to 7 hours

Vegetable Beef Pot Pie

⅓ cup all-purpose flour
1 teaspoon salt
¼ teaspoon black pepper
2 pounds lean stewing beef, cut into cubes
¼ Butter Flavor CRISCO® Stick or ¼ cup Butter Flavor CRISCO® all-vegetable
     shortening plus additional for greasing, divided
1 medium onion, finely chopped
2 cups beef broth
½ cup red cooking wine
2 tablespoons tomato paste or ketchup
2 tablespoons finely chopped parsley
1 teaspoon minced garlic
¼ teaspoon dried thyme leaves
1 package (32 ounces) or 1½ packages (20 ounces each) frozen vegetables for stew
1 (9-inch) Classic CRISCO® Single Crust (page 136)
1 egg, lightly beaten

1. Combine flour, salt and pepper in paper or plastic bag. Add beef, shake until well coated.

2. Melt 3 tablespoons shortening in Dutch oven. Brown beef on all sides in batches. Remove beef with slotted spoon to separate container. Melt remaining 1 tablespoon shortening in Dutch oven. Sauté onion until soft. Add broth, wine, tomato paste, parsley, garlic and thyme. Stir to combine.

3. Return meat to Dutch oven. Bring to a boil. Reduce heat. Simmer, uncovered, 2 to 2½ hours or until meat is tender, stirring occasionally. Add frozen vegetables. Mix to combine. Keep warm.

4. Heat oven to 375°F. Grease 13×9×2-inch pan with shortening.

5. Prepare crust. Press dough between hands to form 5-inch square. Roll dough into 13×9-inch rectangle between sheets of waxed paper. Peel off top sheet. Spoon beef mixture into pan. Flip pastry carefully over filling. Remove other sheet of waxed paper. Tuck in pastry or flute edge. Cut slits in crust for escape of steam. Brush crust with beaten egg.

6. Bake 30 to 45 minutes or until lightly browned. *Do not overbake.* Serve hot.

Makes 8 servings

Santa Fe Wild 'n Corny Casserole

1 pound lean ground beef
1 cup chopped onion
1 package (16 ounces) frozen corn, broccoli and sweet red peppers vegetable mixture
1 can (14½ ounces) clear beef broth
1 teaspoon salt
1 teaspoon ground cumin
½ teaspoon pepper
3 cups cooked wild rice
1 can (16 ounces) whole peeled tomatoes, chopped
1 can (6 ounces) tomato paste
1½ cups (6 ounces) shredded colby-jack cheese, divided

Preheat oven to 350°F. In large saucepan, brown beef and onion; drain. Add vegetables, broth and seasonings. Bring to a boil; cook 5 minutes. Stir in wild rice, tomatoes, tomato paste and 1 cup cheese. Place in greased 12×8-inch casserole. Top with remaining ½ cup cheese. Cover; bake 30 minutes. Uncover; bake 10 minutes. *Makes 8 to 10 servings*

Favorite recipe from **Minnesota Cultivated Wild Rice Council**

Emily's Goulash

½ cup all-purpose flour
3 teaspoons salt, divided
2 teaspoons black pepper, divided
¼ cup plus 2 tablespoons vegetable oil, divided
2 pounds boneless beef chuck shoulder, cut into bite-size pieces
2 shallots, finely chopped
3 cloves garlic, finely chopped
1 can (about 28 ounces) diced tomatoes, undrained
1 tablespoon paprika
3½ cups water
1 teaspoon dried parsley leaves
1 teaspoon dried thyme leaves
2 bay leaves
3 tablespoons sour cream
Hot cooked egg noodles

I. Combine flour, 2 teaspoons salt and 1 teaspoon pepper in shallow bowl. Heat large ovenproof Dutch oven over medium-high heat. Add ¼ cup vegetable oil. Dip pieces of beef into flour mixture; shake off excess and brown thoroughly in batches in Dutch oven. Do not crowd pan. Transfer beef to plate and set aside. Drain fat and wipe out pan.

2. Preheat oven to 325°F. Add 2 tablespoons oil to Dutch oven; cook and stir shallots and garlic over medium heat about 2 minutes. Add tomatoes with juice and paprika; simmer 2 minutes. Add reserved beef, any accumulated juices, water, parsley, thyme and bay leaves. Cover; bake about 1½ hours or until beef is tender.

3. Remove from oven; simmer over medium heat 20 minutes, stirring occasionally. Reduce heat to low and stir in sour cream. Cook and stir until liquid has reduced to sauce-like consistency, about 20 minutes. Stir in remaining 1 teaspoon salt and 1 teaspoon pepper. Remove and discard bay leaves. Serve over noodles. *Makes 4 to 6 servings*

Beef & Zucchini Quiche

    1 unbaked 9-inch pie shell
 ½ pound lean ground beef
    1 medium zucchini, shredded
    3 green onions, sliced
 ¼ cup sliced mushrooms
    1 tablespoon all-purpose flour
    1 cup milk
    3 eggs, beaten
 ¾ cup (3 ounces) shredded Swiss cheese
1½ teaspoons chopped fresh thyme *or* ½ teaspoon dried thyme leaves
 ½ teaspoon salt
    Dash black pepper
    Dash ground red pepper

1. Preheat oven to 475°F.

2. Line pie shell with foil; fill with dried beans or rice. Bake 8 minutes. Remove from oven; carefully remove foil and beans. Return pie shell to oven. Continue baking 4 minutes; set aside. *Reduce oven temperature to 375°F.*

3. Brown ground beef in medium skillet, stirring to break up meat; drain. Add zucchini, onions and mushrooms; cook, stirring occasionally, until vegetables are tender. Stir in flour; cook 2 minutes, stirring constantly. Remove from heat.

4. Combine milk, eggs, cheese and seasonings in medium bowl. Stir into ground beef mixture; pour into crust. Bake 35 minutes or until knife inserted near center comes out clean.

Makes 6 servings

Classic Crisco® Single Crust

1⅓ cups all-purpose flour
½ teaspoon salt
½ CRISCO® Stick or ½ cup CRISCO® all-vegetable shortening
3 tablespoons cold water

1. Spoon flour into measuring cup and level. Combine flour and salt in medium bowl.

2. Cut in ½ cup shortening using pastry blender or 2 knives until all flour is blended to form pea-size chunks.

3. Sprinkle with water, 1 tablespoon at a time. Toss lightly with fork until dough forms a ball.

4. Press dough between hands to form 5- to 6-inch "pancake." Flour rolling surface and rolling pin lightly. Roll dough into circle. Trim circle 1 inch larger than upside-down pie plate. Carefully remove trimmed dough. Set aside to reroll and use for pastry cutout garnish, if desired.

5. Fold dough into quarters. Unfold and press into pie plate. Fold edge under. Flute.

6. **For recipes using a baked pie crust,** heat oven to 425°F. Prick bottom and side thoroughly with fork (50 times) to prevent shrinkage. Bake at 425°F for 10 to 15 minutes or until lightly browned.

7. **For recipes using an unbaked pie crust,** follow directions given for that recipe.

Makes 1 (9-inch) single crust

Santa Fe Corn Bake

1 pound ground beef
1 medium onion, chopped
1 clove garlic, minced
½ teaspoon dried oregano
2 cans (14½ ounces each) DEL MONTE® Diced Tomatoes with Zesty Mild Green Chilies
1 can (15¼ ounces) DEL MONTE Whole Kernel Golden Sweet Corn, drained
1 package (8½ ounces) corn muffin mix, plus ingredients to prepare mix

1. Brown meat with onion, garlic and oregano in large skillet over medium-high heat; drain. Season with salt and pepper, if desired.

2. Add tomatoes and corn. Pour into 2-quart baking dish. Prepare muffin mix according to package directions. Spread evenly over meat mixture.

3. Bake at 400°F, 25 to 30 minutes or until golden.

Makes 8 servings

Prep Time: 5 minutes
Cook Time: 35 minutes

Pleasing Poultry

Chicken and Sweet Potato Ragoût

2 tablespoons vegetable oil, divided
1 (3-pound) chicken, cut into 8 pieces
1 large onion, chopped
1 (14½-ounce) can chicken broth
3 small sweet potatoes, peeled and cut into ¼-inch slices
2 cups shredded green cabbage
1 tablespoon TABASCO® brand Pepper Sauce
1 teaspoon salt
¼ cup water
1 tablespoon flour
¼ cup peanut butter

Heat 1 tablespoon oil in 12-inch skillet over medium heat. Add chicken; cook until well browned. Remove to plate. Add remaining 1 tablespoon oil and onion to skillet; cook 5 minutes. Return chicken to skillet; add broth, potatoes, cabbage, TABASCO® Sauce and salt. Heat to boiling over high heat. Reduce heat to low; cover and simmer 30 minutes or until tender, stirring occasionally.

Combine water and flour in small cup. Gradually stir into skillet with peanut butter. Cook over high heat until mixture thickens.   *Makes 4 servings*

Mexican Turkey Lasagna

1 pound ground turkey
1 cup onion, chopped
½ cup green bell pepper, chopped
2 cloves garlic, minced
1 can (15 ounces) tomato sauce
1 jar (12 ounces) salsa
1 teaspoon ground cumin
6 flour tortillas
1 cup sliced green onions
1 can (4 ounces) ripe olives, sliced
2 cups (8 ounces) shredded reduced-fat Monterey Jack cheese with jalapeño peppers

I. In large skillet over medium-high heat, sauté turkey, onion, green pepper and garlic 5 minutes or until turkey is no longer pink. Add tomato sauce, salsa and cumin. Bring to boil. Reduce heat to low; cover and simmer 10 minutes.

2. Spray 13×9-inch baking dish with vegetable cooking spray. Spoon 1 cup sauce onto bottom of prepared dish; top with 2 tortillas. Cut 2 tortillas into quarters; place in corners of dish. Cover with ½ of remaining sauce; sprinkle with ½ of the green onions, olives and cheese. Top with remaining tortillas, sauce, onions and olives. Cover with foil.

3. Bake at 350°F 30 minutes. Remove foil. Sprinkle lasagna with remaining 1 cup cheese. Continue baking 15 minutes or until lasagna is bubbly and cheese is melted.

Makes 8 servings

*Favorite recipe from **National Turkey Federation***

Chicken Athena

1 pound boneless chicken,* skinned and cut into cubes
1 tablespoon olive oil
1 medium onion, cut into chunks
1 can (14½ ounces) DEL MONTE® Stewed Tomatoes - Original Recipe
1 jar (6 ounces) marinated artichoke hearts
¼ teaspoon dried rosemary, crushed
⅓ cup crumbled feta cheese (optional)

*Substitute fresh turkey for chicken, if desired.

1. Brown chicken in oil in large skillet over medium-high heat; add onion and cook 2 minutes.

2. Stir in tomatoes, marinade from artichokes and rosemary; cook over medium heat 10 to 15 minutes or until thickened, stirring frequently.

3. Stir in artichoke hearts; heat through. Top with feta cheese. Garnish with chopped parsley, if desired.

Makes 4 to 6 servings

Prep Time: 5 minutes
Cook Time: 22 minutes

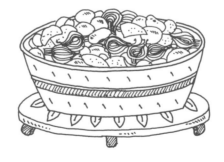

Spicy Chicken Burritos

   1 medium onion, halved and sliced
   1 small green bell pepper, diced
   1 tablespoon FLEISCHMANN'S® Original Margarine
  ½ pound shredded cooked chicken (1¼ cups)
   1 medium tomato, diced
1½ cups EGG BEATERS®
  ½ teaspoon seasoned pepper
  ¼ teaspoon garlic powder
  ½ cup (2 ounces) shredded reduced-fat Cheddar cheese
   6 (10-inch) flour tortillas, warmed
  ½ cup thick and chunky salsa
     Additional thick and chunky salsa, optional

In large nonstick skillet, over medium heat, sauté onion and bell pepper in margarine until tender. Add chicken and tomato; stir until heated through. Remove from skillet; keep warm.

In same skillet, over medium heat, cook Egg Beaters®, seasoned pepper and garlic powder, stirring occasionally until mixture is set. Stir in chicken mixture; sprinkle with cheese. Evenly divide and spoon mixture onto warm tortillas; top each with salsa. Fold two opposite ends of each tortilla over filling, then fold in sides like an envelope. Serve with additional salsa if desired. *Makes 6 servings*

Prep Time: 20 minutes
Cook Time: 20 minutes

Moroccan Chicken Tagine

3 pounds chicken pieces, skin removed
2 cups chicken broth
1 can (14½ ounces) diced tomatoes, undrained
2 onions, chopped
1 cup dried apricots, chopped
4 cloves garlic, minced
2 teaspoons ground cumin
1 teaspoon ground cinnamon
1 teaspoon ground ginger
½ teaspoon ground coriander
½ teaspoon ground red pepper
6 sprigs fresh cilantro
1 tablespoon cornstarch
1 tablespoon water
1 can (15 ounces) chick-peas (garbanzo beans), drained and rinsed
2 tablespoons chopped fresh cilantro
¼ cup slivered almonds, toasted*
  Hot cooked couscous or rice

To toast almonds, heat small nonstick skillet over medium-high heat. Add almonds; cook and stir about 3 minutes or until golden brown. Remove from pan at once. Let cool before adding to other ingredients.

Slow Cooker Directions
1. Place chicken in slow cooker. Combine broth, tomatoes with juice, onions, apricots, garlic, cumin, cinnamon, ginger, coriander, red pepper and cilantro in medium bowl; pour over chicken. Cover; cook on LOW 4 to 5 hours or until chicken is no longer pink in center. Transfer chicken to serving platter; cover to keep warm.

2. Combine cornstarch and water in small bowl; mix until smooth. Stir cornstarch mixture and chick-peas into slow cooker. Cover; cook on HIGH 15 minutes or until sauce is thickened. Pour sauce over chicken. Sprinkle with cilantro and toasted almonds and serve with couscous.   *Makes 4 to 6 servings*

Green Chili-Chicken Casserole

    4 cups shredded cooked chicken
1½ cups green enchilada sauce
    1 can (10¾ ounces) condensed cream of chicken soup, undiluted
    1 container (8 ounces) sour cream
    1 can (4 ounces) diced green chilies
    ½ cup vegetable oil
  12 (6-inch) corn tortillas
1½ cups (6 ounces) shredded Colby-Jack cheese, divided

1. Preheat oven to 325°F. Grease 13×9-inch casserole.

2. Combine chicken, enchilada sauce, soup, sour cream and chilies in large skillet. Cook and stir over medium-high heat until warm.

3. Heat oil in separate deep skillet. Fry tortillas just until soft; drain on paper towels. Place 4 tortillas on bottom of prepared casserole. Layer with ⅓ of chicken mixture and ½ cup cheese. Repeat layers twice.

4. Bake 15 to 20 minutes or until cheese is melted and casserole is heated through.

Makes 6 servings

Variation: Shredded Mexican cheese blend can be substituted for Colby-Jack cheese.

Kentucky Burgoo Pie

Burgoo Filling
  1½ pounds chicken, skinned
  ½ pound beef stew meat
  ½ pound pork shoulder roast
  ½ pound veal shoulder roast
  1½ cups water
  2 carrots, peeled and sliced
  2 potatoes, peeled and cubed
  2 tomatoes, peeled and chopped
  1 rib celery, chopped
  1 medium onion, chopped
  1 small green bell pepper, chopped
  1 cup fresh or drained canned butter beans or lima beans
  1 cup fresh or frozen whole kernel corn
  ½ cup tomato juice
  1 can (10½ ounces) tomato purée
  1 tablespoon salt
  1½ teaspoons hot pepper sauce
  1½ teaspoons Worcestershire sauce
  1 teaspoon black pepper
  ½ teaspoon ground red pepper

Crust
  1 (10-inch) Classic CRISCO® Double Crust (page 171)

Sauce
  ⅓ cup butter or margarine
  ⅓ cup all-purpose flour
  ½ teaspoon salt
  ¼ teaspoon black pepper
  ⅔ cup milk

Decorations
  1 (9-inch) Classic CRISCO® Single Crust (page 136)

1. For filling, combine chicken, beef, pork, veal and water in 5-quart Dutch oven. Cover and simmer, turning meat frequently, until tender, about 1½ to 2 hours. Add additional water, if necessary. Drain, reserving liquid; cool. Debone meat; cut into ¼-inch cubes. Place meat and reserved liquid in large container. Refrigerate several hours or overnight. Skim off and discard fat from surface.

2. Place meat and liquid in Dutch oven. Add carrots, potatoes, tomatoes, celery, onion, green pepper, butter beans, corn, tomato juice, tomato purée, 1 tablespoon salt, pepper sauce, Worcestershire sauce, 1 teaspoon black pepper and red pepper to Dutch oven. Simmer, covered, 1 hour. Uncover; simmer 2 hours. Remove from heat.

3. Prepare 10-inch crust. Divide dough in half. Roll and press bottom crust into 10-inch pie plate or 1½-quart casserole. *Do not bake.* Heat oven to 425°F.

4. For sauce, melt butter in medium saucepan. Stir in flour, ½ teaspoon salt and ¼ teaspoon black pepper. Cook and stir until bubbly. Remove from heat. Stir in milk. Return to heat; cook and stir 1 minute. Remove from heat. Stir in small amount of filling. Continue adding small amounts of filling until mixture in saucepan measures about 2 cups. Return to Dutch oven. Stir to blend. Spoon 3½ cups filling into unbaked pie crust. (Refrigerate or freeze remaining thickened filling for additional pie.) Moisten pastry edge with water.

5. Roll out top crust. Lift onto filled pie. Trim ½ inch beyond edge of pie plate. Fold top edge under bottom crust. *Do not flute.*

6. For decorations, prepare 9-inch crust. Roll dough into 10×8-inch rectangle. Cut 12 (⅜-inch) strips and 4 leaf shapes from crust. Braid strips. Moisten edge of top crust with water. Place braids on edge of pie. Moisten underside of leaves. Arrange on top of crust. Cut slits or shapes into top to allow steam to escape.

7. Bake at 425°F for 30 to 35 minutes. *Do not overbake.* Serve warm. Refrigerate leftover pie.

Makes one 10-inch pie

Chicken Divan

¾ pound fresh broccoli, cut into flowerets or 1 package (10 ounces) frozen broccoli
   flowerets
2 cups shredded cooked chicken
1 cup prepared HIDDEN VALLEY® The Original Ranch® Dressing
1 tablespoon grated Parmesan cheese
   Cherry tomatoes

Preheat oven to 350°F. In medium saucepan, cook broccoli in boiling water to cover until tender, about 4 minutes. Drain thoroughly; place in shallow baking dish. Top with chicken and salad dressing. Sprinkle with Parmesan cheese. Cover loosely with foil; bake until heated through, about 15 minutes. Garnish with cherry tomatoes.   *Makes 4 servings*

Cheesy Slow Cooker Chicken

6 boneless skinless chicken breasts (about 1½ pounds)
   Salt
   Black pepper
   Garlic powder
2 cans (10¾ ounces each) condensed cream of chicken soup, undiluted
1 can (10¾ ounces) condensed Cheddar cheese soup, undiluted
   Chopped fresh parsley (optional)

Slow Cooker Directions
1. Place 3 chicken breasts in slow cooker. Sprinkle with salt, pepper and garlic powder. Repeat with remaining 3 breasts and seasonings.

2. Combine soups in medium bowl; pour over chicken. Cover; cook on LOW 6 to 8 hours or until chicken is no longer pink in center. Garnish with parsley before serving, if desired.
      Makes 6 servings

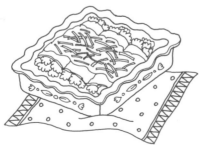

Chicken Rice Casserole

2 tablespoons MRS. DASH® Minced Onion Medley
2 cups 2% milk
¼ cup butter
2 tablespoons flour
¼ cup chopped fresh parsley
1 can (7 ounces) sliced mushrooms, drained *or* 1 cup sliced fresh mushrooms
3 cups cooked rice
2 cups cubed cooked chicken or turkey
½ cup diced cooked ham
2 cups coarsely chopped cooked broccoli

Preheat oven to 350°F. Combine Mrs. Dash Minced Onion Medley and milk in a small saucepan or 2-cup glass microwaveable measuring cup. Heat just until warm. Melt butter in a large nonstick skillet over medium heat. Whisk in flour. Gradually whisk in milk mixture and heat until thickened; whisk constantly. Remove from heat and stir in parsley and mushrooms. Spray a square glass 2-quart baking dish with nonstick coating spray. Layer rice, chicken, ham and broccoli in prepared dish. Pour sauce evenly over layered ingredients. Bake at 350°F for 25 to 30 minutes or until heated thoroughly.

Makes 8 servings

Preparation Time: 10 minutes
Cooking Time: 30 minutes

Easy Chicken Chalupas

1 roasted chicken (about 2 pounds)
8 flour tortillas
2 cups shredded Cheddar cheese
1 cup mild green chili salsa
1 cup mild red salsa

1. Preheat oven to 350°F. Spray 13×9-inch ovenproof dish with cooking spray.

2. Remove skin and bones from chicken; discard. Shred chicken meat.

3. Place 2 tortillas in bottom of prepared dish, overlapping slightly. Layer tortillas with 1 cup chicken, ½ cup cheese and ¼ cup of each salsa. Repeat layers, ending with cheese and salsas.

4. Bake casserole 25 minutes or until bubbly and hot.   *Makes 6 servings*

Tip: Serve this easy main dish with some custom toppings on the side such as sour cream, chopped cilantro, sliced black olives (pre-sliced from a can, of course!), sliced green onions (from the salad bar) and sliced avocado.

Spicy Shredded Chicken

6 boneless skinless chicken breasts (about 1½ pounds)
1 jar (16 ounces) prepared salsa

Slow Cooker Directions
Place chicken in slow cooker. Cover with salsa. Cover; cook on LOW 6 to 8 hours or until chicken is tender and no longer pink in center. Shred chicken with two forks before serving.   *Makes 6 servings*

Serving Suggestion: Serve on warm flour tortillas with taco fixings.

Spanish Braised Chicken with Green Olives and Rice

2 pounds bone-in skinless chicken thighs
1 teaspoon paprika
   Nonstick cooking spray
¾ cup dry sherry
1 can (14½ ounces) chicken broth plus water to measure 2¼ cups
¾ cup sliced pimiento-stuffed green olives
1½ teaspoons dried sage leaves
1½ cups uncooked long-grain white rice

1. Sprinkle chicken thighs with paprika. Spray large nonstick skillet with cooking spray; heat over medium-high heat. Add thighs; cook, without stirring, 3 to 4 minutes or until golden. Turn chicken; cook 3 to 4 minutes longer.

2. Add sherry to skillet. Slide metal spatula under chicken and scrape cooked bits from bottom of skillet. Add chicken broth, olives and sage; bring to a boil. Reduce heat to low; cover and simmer 10 minutes. Pour rice into liquid around chicken; gently stir to distribute evenly in skillet. Return to a boil; cover and simmer 18 minutes or until liquid is absorbed and rice is tender.

Makes 6 servings

Chicken with Italian Sausage

10 ounces bulk mild or hot Italian sausage
6 boneless skinless chicken thighs
1 can (about 15 ounces) white beans, rinsed and drained
1 can (about 15 ounces) red beans, rinsed and drained
1 cup chicken broth
1 medium onion, chopped
1 teaspoon black pepper
½ teaspoon salt
Chopped fresh parsley (optional)

Slow Cooker Directions

1. Brown sausage in large skillet over medium-high heat, stirring to separate; drain fat. Spoon into slow cooker.

2. Trim fat from chicken. Place chicken, beans, broth, onion, pepper and salt in slow cooker. Cover; cook on LOW 5 to 6 hours.

3. Adjust seasonings, if desired. Slice each chicken thigh on the diagonal. Serve with sausage and beans. Garnish with parsley, if desired. *Makes 6 servings*

Prep Time: 15 minutes
Cook Time: 5 to 6 hours

Mexican Style Skillet

1¾ cups water
1 (16-ounce) jar salsa
2 teaspoons HERB-OX® chicken flavored instant bouillon & seasoning
1½ cups instant rice, uncooked
1 (11-ounce) can whole kernel corn with diced bell peppers
1 (4.25-ounce) jar diced green chilies
1 (10-ounce) can HORMEL® chunk breast of chicken
1 cup shredded Monterey Jack & Cheddar cheese blend
   Tortilla chips, for garnish
   Additional toppings such as salsa, sour cream and guacamole

In large nonstick skillet, combine water, salsa and bouillon. Bring mixture to a boil. Stir in rice, corn and green chilies. Top with chicken and cheese. Cover and remove from heat; let stand for 5 minutes. If desired, garnish with tortilla chips and serve with additional salsa, sour cream and guacamole. *Makes 6 to 8 servings*

Prep Time: 5 minutes
Total Time: 15 minutes

Chicken Enchiladas

2 tablespoons vegetable oil
1 medium onion, chopped
3 to 4 cups cooked, shredded chicken or turkey
1 can (14½ ounces) diced tomatoes, in juice
1 can (8 ounces) tomato sauce
1 can (4 ounces) diced green chiles
1 package (1.0 ounce) LAWRY'S® Taco Spices & Seasonings
½ teaspoon LAWRY'S® Seasoned Salt
¼ teaspoon LAWRY'S® Garlic Powder With Parsley
1 dozen corn tortillas
2 cans (2¼ ounces each) sliced black olives, drained
5 cups (20 ounces) shredded Monterey Jack cheese

In large skillet, heat oil. Add onion and cook over medium-high heat until tender. Add chicken, tomatoes, tomato sauce, chiles, Taco Spices & Seasonings, Seasoned Salt and Garlic Powder With Parsley; mix well. Bring to a boil; reduce heat to low, cover and cook for 15 to 20 minutes. In greased 13×9×2-inch baking dish, place 4 corn tortillas. Pour ⅓ of chicken mixture over tortillas, spreading evenly. Layer with ⅓ of olives and ⅓ of cheese. Repeat layers 2 times ending with cheese. Bake, uncovered, in 350°F oven for 30 to 40 minutes; until chicken is thoroughly cooked. *Makes 6 to 8 servings*

Meal Idea: Serve with Mexican rice and a tossed green salad.

Prep Time: 15 minutes
Cook Time: 60 to 70 minutes

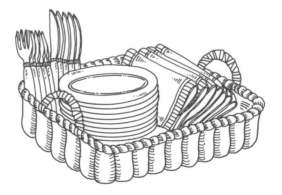

Cajun Chicken

2½ pounds chicken pieces, skinned (breasts, thighs, legs)
1 tablespoon vegetable oil
2 cloves garlic, crushed
½ teaspoon dried thyme
1 can (14½ ounces) DEL MONTE® Stewed Tomatoes - Original Recipe
1 red or green bell pepper, cut into strips
1 stalk celery, sliced
1 carrot, thinly sliced

1. Brown chicken in oil in large skillet over medium-high heat, 10 to 15 minutes; drain. Season with salt and black pepper, if desired.

2. Stir garlic and thyme into tomatoes; pour over chicken. Add pepper strips, celery and carrot.

3. Bring to boil; cover and simmer 15 minutes or until chicken is no longer pink. Garnish with sliced green onions and serve with hot pepper sauce, if desired.

Makes 4 to 6 servings

Prep Time: 8 minutes
Cook Time: 30 minutes

Chicken Breasts Florentine

    2 pounds boneless, skinless chicken breasts
    ¼ cup all-purpose flour
    2 eggs, well beaten
    ⅔ cup seasoned dry bread crumbs
    ¼ cup BERTOLLI® Olive Oil
    1 medium clove garlic, finely chopped
    ½ cup dry white wine
    1 envelope LIPTON® RECIPE SECRETS® Golden Onion Soup Mix
    1½ cups water
    2 tablespoons finely chopped fresh parsley
    ⅛ teaspoon ground black pepper
        Hot cooked rice pilaf or white rice
        Hot cooked spinach

Dip chicken in flour, then eggs, then bread crumbs.

In 12-inch skillet, heat oil over medium heat and cook chicken until almost done. Remove chicken. Reserve 1 tablespoon drippings. Add garlic and wine to reserved drippings and cook over medium heat 5 minutes. Stir in soup mix thoroughly blended with water; bring to a boil. Return chicken to skillet and simmer covered 10 minutes or until chicken is thoroughly cooked and sauce is slightly thickened. Stir in parsley and pepper. To serve, arrange chicken over hot rice and spinach; garnish as desired.   *Makes about 6 servings*

Hearty Cassoulet

1 tablespoon olive oil
1 large onion, finely chopped
4 boneless skinless chicken thighs (about 1 pound), chopped
¼ pound smoked turkey sausage, finely chopped
3 cloves garlic, minced
1 teaspoon dried thyme leaves
½ teaspoon black pepper
¼ cup tomato paste
2 tablespoons water
3 cans (about 15 ounces each) Great Northern beans, rinsed and drained
½ cup dry bread crumbs
3 tablespoons minced fresh parsley

Slow Cooker Directions

1. Heat oil in large skillet over medium heat until hot. Add onion, cook and stir 5 minutes or until onion is tender. Stir in chicken, sausage, garlic, thyme and pepper. Cook 5 minutes or until chicken and sausage are browned.

2. Remove skillet from heat; stir in tomato paste and water until blended. Place beans and chicken mixture in slow cooker. Cover; cook on LOW 4 to 4½ hours. Just before serving, combine bread crumbs and parsley in small bowl. Sprinkle over top of cassoulet.

Makes 6 servings

Spicy Chicken Casserole with Corn Bread

2 tablespoons olive oil
4 boneless skinless chicken breasts, cut into bite-size pieces
1 envelope (about 1 ounce) taco seasoning
1 can (about 15 ounces) black beans, rinsed and drained
1 can (14½ ounces) diced tomatoes, drained
1 can (about 10 ounces) Mexican-style corn, drained
1 can (about 4 ounces) diced green chilies, drained
½ cup mild salsa
1 box (about 8½ ounces) corn bread mix, plus ingredients to prepare
½ cup (2 ounces) shredded Cheddar cheese
¼ cup chopped red bell pepper

1. Preheat oven to 350°F. Spray 2-quart casserole with nonstick cooking spray. Set aside. Heat oil in large skillet over medium heat. Cook chicken until no longer pink.

2. Sprinkle taco seasoning over chicken. Add black beans, tomatoes, corn, chilies and salsa; stir until well blended. Transfer to prepared dish.

3. Prepare corn bread mix according to package directions, adding cheese and bell pepper. Spread batter over chicken mixture.

4. Bake 30 minutes or until corn bread is golden brown.   *Makes 4 to 6 servings*

Chicken, Asparagus & Mushroom Bake

1 tablespoon butter
1 tablespoon olive oil
2 boneless skinless chicken breasts (about ½ pound), cut into bite-size pieces
2 cloves garlic, minced
1 cup sliced mushrooms
2 cups sliced asparagus
　Black pepper
1 package (about 6 ounces) corn bread stuffing mix
¼ cup dry white wine (optional)
1 can (14½ ounces) chicken broth
1 can (10½ ounces) condensed cream of asparagus or cream of chicken soup, undiluted

I. Preheat oven to 350°F. Heat butter and oil in large skillet. Cook and stir chicken and garlic about 3 minutes over medium-high heat until chicken is no longer pink. Add mushrooms; cook and stir 2 minutes. Add asparagus; cook and stir about five minutes or until vegetables soften slightly. Season with pepper.

2. Transfer mixture to 2½-quart casserole or 6 small casseroles. Top with stuffing mix.

3. Add wine to skillet, if desired; cook and stir 1 minute over medium-high heat, scraping up any browned bits from bottom of skillet. Add broth and soup; cook and stir until well blended.

4. Pour broth mixture into casserole; mix well. Bake, uncovered, about 35 minutes (30 minutes for small casseroles) or until heated through and lightly browned.

Makes 6 servings

Deep Dish Chicken Pot Pie

1 (15-ounce) package refrigerated pie crusts
1 (10-ounce) package frozen mixed vegetables, thawed
½ cup chopped onion
¼ cup (½ stick) butter or margarine
⅓ cup all-purpose flour
1 tablespoon HERB-OX® chicken flavored bouillon granules, divided
¼ teaspoon dried thyme leaves
⅛ teaspoon ground black pepper
2 cups water
¾ cup milk
2½ cups diced, cooked chicken
1 (2-ounce) jar diced pimento
2 tablespoons chopped fresh parsley

Heat oven to 400°F. Place one pastry into 10-inch deep pie plate. In large saucepan, cook onion in butter until tender. Stir in flour, bouillon, thyme and pepper. Add water and milk all at once. Cook and stir until thickened and bubbly. Stir in mixed vegetables, chicken, pimento and parsley. Pour mixture into pie plate. Place top crust over chicken mixture. Flute edges of pastry and cut slits in top to allow steam to escape. Bake for 25 to 30 minutes or until pastry is golden brown and filling is hot. *Makes 6 to 8 servings*

Prep Time: 20 minutes
Total Time: 50 minutes

Quick Chicken Jambalaya

  8 boneless, skinless chicken thighs, cut in bite-size pieces
  ¼ teaspoon garlic salt
  1 tablespoon vegetable oil
2½ cups 8-vegetable juice
  1 bag (16 ounces) frozen pepper stir-fry mix
  ½ cup diced cooked ham
  1 teaspoon hot pepper sauce
1¾ cups quick cooking rice, uncooked

Sprinkle garlic salt over chicken. In large nonstick skillet, place oil and heat to medium-high temperature. Add chicken and cook, stirring occasionally, 8 minutes or until chicken is lightly browned. Add vegetable juice, pepper stir-fry mix, ham and hot pepper sauce. Heat to boiling; cover and cook over medium heat 4 minutes. Stir in rice; heat to boiling. Cover, remove pan from heat and let stand 5 minutes or until rice and vegetables are tender and liquid is absorbed.

Makes 4 servings

Favorite recipe from **Delmarva Poultry Industry, Inc.**

Mediterranean Chicken and Rice Skillet

2 tablespoons olive oil
1 pound boneless skinless chicken breasts, thinly sliced
1 cup green onions, sliced
¼ cup green bell pepper, chopped
¼ cup red bell pepper, chopped
2 to 3 cloves garlic, minced
1 teaspoon dried oregano leaves, crushed
1 can (10 ounces) diced tomatoes with green chilies, undrained
1 can (14½ ounces) chicken broth
¼ teaspoon ground black pepper
1 cup long grain white rice
½ cup small pitted ripe olives
½ cup grated Parmesan cheese
⅓ cup frozen peas, thawed
2 tablespoons chopped fresh basil *or* 2 teaspoons dried basil leaves
2 tablespoons chopped fresh parsley *or* 2 teaspoons parsley flakes

Heat oil in large skillet over medium-high heat. Add chicken; cook until no longer pink in center. Add green onions, bell peppers, garlic and oregano; stir to coat. Add tomatoes, chicken broth and black pepper; bring to a boil. Stir in rice. Cover; reduce heat and cook 20 minutes or until most of the liquid is absorbed. Stir in olives, cheese, peas, basil and parsley.

Makes 4 servings

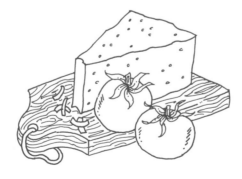

Coq au Vin

½ cup all-purpose flour
1¼ teaspoons salt
¾ teaspoon black pepper
3½ pounds chicken pieces
2 tablespoons butter or margarine
8 ounces mushrooms, cut in half if large
4 cloves garlic, minced
¾ cup chicken broth
¾ cup dry red wine
2 teaspoons dried thyme leaves
1½ pounds red potatoes, quartered
2 cups frozen pearl onions (about 8 ounces)
Chopped fresh parsley (optional)

1. Preheat oven to 350°F.

2. Combine flour, salt and pepper in large resealable plastic food storage bag. Add chicken, two pieces at a time; seal bag. Shake to coat chicken; remove chicken and set aside. Repeat with remaining pieces. Reserve remaining flour mixture.

3. Melt butter in ovenproof Dutch oven over medium-high heat. Arrange chicken in single layer in Dutch oven and cook 3 minutes per side or until browned. Transfer to plate; set aside. Repeat with remaining pieces.

4. Add mushrooms and garlic to Dutch oven; cook and stir 2 minutes. Sprinkle reserved flour mixture over mushroom mixture; cook and stir 1 minute. Add broth, wine and thyme; bring to a boil over high heat, stirring to scrape up browned bits on bottom of Dutch oven. Add potatoes and onions; return to a boil. Remove from heat and place chicken in Dutch oven, partially covering chicken with broth mixture.

5. Bake, covered, about 45 minutes or until chicken is no longer pink in centers, potatoes are tender and sauce is slightly thickened. Transfer chicken and vegetables to shallow bowls. Spoon sauce over chicken and vegetables. Sprinkle with parsley, if desired.

Makes 4 to 6 servings

Individual Chicken Rice Casseroles

1 bag SUCCESS® Rice
4 tablespoons reduced-calorie margarine, divided
½ pound fresh mushrooms, sliced
1 cup pasteurized process cheese cubes
1 cup evaporated skim milk
1 teaspoon white wine Worcestershire sauce
½ teaspoon salt
½ teaspoon white pepper
1½ cups chopped cooked chicken
1 package (10 ounces) frozen peas, thawed and drained
½ cup fresh bread crumbs

Prepare rice according to package directions.

Preheat oven to 350°F.

Add 2 tablespoons margarine to hot rice; mix lightly until margarine is melted. Melt remaining 2 tablespoons margarine in medium skillet. Add mushrooms; cook and stir until tender. Set aside. Combine cheese, milk, Worcestershire sauce, salt and pepper in medium saucepan. Cook, stirring constantly, over medium heat until cheese is melted. Remove from heat.

Layer half of rice in bottoms of six individual casseroles; cover with layers of chicken, mushrooms and peas. Top with remaining rice and cheese sauce; sprinkle with bread crumbs. Bake until hot and bubbly, 15 to 20 minutes. *Makes 6 servings*

Chicken Divan Casserole

1 cup uncooked rice
1 cup coarsely shredded carrots*
  Nonstick cooking spray
4 boneless skinless chicken breasts
2 tablespoons butter or margarine
3 tablespoons all-purpose flour
¼ teaspoon salt
  Black pepper
1 cup chicken broth
½ cup milk or half-and-half
¼ cup dry white wine
⅓ cup plus 2 tablespoons grated Parmesan cheese, divided
1 pound frozen broccoli florets

Coarsely shredded carrots are available in the produce sections of many large supermarkets or you can use a hand-held grater.

1. Preheat oven to 350°F. Lightly grease 12×8-inch baking dish.

2. Prepare rice according to package directions. Stir in carrots. Spread mixture into prepared baking dish.

3. Spray large skillet with cooking spray. Heat over medium-high heat. Brown chicken breasts about 2 minutes on each side. Arrange over rice.

4. To prepare sauce, melt butter in 2-quart saucepan over medium heat. Whisk in flour, salt and pepper to taste; cook and stir 1 minute. Gradually whisk in broth and milk. Cook and stir until mixture comes to a boil. Reduce heat; simmer 2 minutes. Stir in wine. Remove from heat. Stir in ⅓ cup cheese.

5. Arrange broccoli around chicken. Pour sauce over chicken and broccoli. Sprinkle remaining 2 tablespoons cheese over chicken.

6. Cover with foil; bake 30 minutes. Remove foil; bake 10 to 15 minutes or until chicken is no longer pink in center and broccoli is hot.   *Makes 6 servings*

Cranberry-Barbecue Chicken Wings

3 pounds chicken wings
Salt and black pepper
1 container (12 ounces) cranberry-orange relish
½ cup barbecue sauce
2 tablespoons quick-cooking tapioca
1 tablespoon prepared mustard
Hot cooked rice (optional)

Slow Cooker Directions

1. Preheat broiler. Rinse chicken and pat dry. Cut off and discard wing tips. Cut each wing in half at joint. Place chicken on rack in broiler pan; season with salt and pepper. Broil 4 to 5 inches from heat for 10 to 12 minutes or until browned, turning once. Transfer chicken to slow cooker.

2. Stir together relish, barbecue sauce, tapioca and mustard in small bowl. Pour over chicken. Cover; cook on LOW 4 to 5 hours. Serve with rice, if desired.

Makes 4 main-dish servings

Prep Time: 20 minutes
Cook Time: 4 to 5 hours

South-of-the-Border Cumin Chicken

1 package (16 ounces) frozen bell pepper stir-fry mixture *or* 3 bell peppers,
    sliced thin*
4 chicken drumsticks
4 chicken thighs
1 can (14½ ounces) stewed tomatoes
1 tablespoon mild pepper sauce
2 teaspoons sugar
1¾ teaspoons ground cumin, divided
1¼ teaspoons salt
1 teaspoon dried oregano leaves
¼ cup chopped fresh cilantro leaves
1 to 2 medium limes, cut in wedges

*If using fresh bell peppers, add 1 small onion, chopped.

Slow Cooker Directions

1. Place bell pepper mixture in slow cooker; place chicken on top.

2. Combine stewed tomatoes, pepper sauce, sugar, 1 teaspoon of cumin, salt and oregano in large bowl. Pour over chicken mixture. Cover; cook on LOW 8 hours or on HIGH 4 hours or until meat is just beginning to fall off bone.

3. Place chicken in shallow serving bowl. Stir remaining ¾ teaspoon cumin into tomato mixture and pour over chicken. Sprinkle with cilantro and serve with lime wedges. Serve over cooked rice or with toasted corn tortillas, if desired. *Makes 4 servings*

Chicken Pot Pie

1½ pounds chicken pieces, skinned
1 cup chicken broth
½ teaspoon salt
¼ teaspoon black pepper
1 to 1½ cups reduced-fat (2%) milk
3 tablespoons butter
1 medium onion, chopped
1 cup sliced celery
⅓ cup all-purpose flour
2 cups frozen mixed vegetables (broccoli, carrots and cauliflower combination),
    thawed
1 tablespoon chopped fresh parsley *or* 1 teaspoon dried parsley
½ teaspoon dried thyme leaves
1 (9-inch) refrigerated pastry crust
1 egg, lightly beaten

1. Combine chicken, chicken broth, salt and pepper in large saucepan over medium-high heat. Bring to a boil. Reduce heat to low. Cover; simmer 30 minutes or until juices run clear.

2. Remove chicken and let cool. Pour remaining chicken broth mixture into glass measure. Let stand; spoon off fat. Add enough milk to broth mixture to equal 2½ cups. Remove chicken from bones and cut into ½-inch pieces.

3. Melt butter in same saucepan over medium heat. Add onion and celery. Cook and stir 3 minutes. Stir in flour until well blended. Gradually stir in broth mixture. Cook, stirring constantly, until sauce thickens and boils. Add chicken, vegetables, parsley and thyme. Pour into 1½-quart deep casserole.

4. Preheat oven to 400°F. Roll out pastry 1 inch larger than diameter of casserole on lightly floured surface. Cut slits in pastry to vent; place on top of casserole. Roll edges and cut away extra pastry; flute edges. Reroll scraps to cut into decorative designs. Place on top of pastry. Brush pastry with beaten egg. Bake about 30 minutes until crust is golden brown and filling is bubbly.

Makes about 6 cups or 4 servings

Tomatillo Chicken

1 pound tomatillos
1 teaspoon ground cumin
1 pound boneless, skinless chicken breast halves
2 teaspoons olive oil
½ cup chicken broth
1 can (4 ounces) diced green chili peppers
¼ cup cilantro leaves
1 cup shredded Monterey Jack cheese

1. Remove papery husks from tomatillos; rinse under cold water. Cut into quarters and set aside.

2. Sprinkle cumin on both sides of chicken breasts. Heat large nonstick skillet over medium-high heat. Add oil and chicken; cook for 3 minutes on each side until chicken is browned (the chicken will not be cooked through at this point).

3. Add reserved tomatillos, broth, chilies and cilantro; bring to a simmer. Cover and simmer 25 to 30 minutes, stirring occasionally, or until chicken is no longer pink in center and tomatillos are tender. Transfer chicken and tomatillo sauce to serving plates; garnish with cheese. *Makes 4 servings*

Variation: In Step 3, transfer cooked chicken to serving plates. Carefully transfer tomatillo mixture to blender; purée. Pour puréed mixture over cooked chicken; garnish with cheese.

Chicken Cassoulet

   4 slices bacon
   ¼ cup all-purpose flour
     Salt and black pepper
1¾ pounds chicken pieces
   2 cooked chicken sausages, cut into ¼-inch pieces
   1 onion, chopped
1½ cups diced red and green bell pepper (2 small bell peppers)
   2 cloves garlic, finely chopped
   1 teaspoon dried thyme leaves
     Salt and black pepper
     Olive oil
   2 cans (about 15 ounces each) white beans, such as Great Northern, rinsed and
     drained
   ½ cup dry white wine (optional)

1. Preheat oven to 350°F. Cook bacon in large skillet over medium-high heat until crisp.
Remove and drain on paper towels. Cut into 1-inch pieces.

2. Pour off all but 2 tablespoons fat from skillet. Place flour in shallow bowl; season with
salt and black pepper. Dip chicken pieces in flour; shake off excess and brown in batches
over medium-high heat in skillet. Remove and set aside. Lightly brown sausages in same
skillet. Remove and set aside.

3. Add onion, bell peppers, garlic, thyme, salt and black pepper to skillet. Cook and stir
over medium heat about 5 minutes or until softened. Add olive oil as needed to prevent
sticking. Transfer to 13×9-inch baking dish. Add beans; mix well. Top with chicken,
sausages and bacon. If desired, add wine to skillet; cook and stir over medium heat,
scraping up brown bits. Pour over casserole.

4. Cover; bake 40 minutes. Uncover and bake 15 minutes more or until chicken is no
longer pink in center.

Makes 6 servings

Caribbean Brunch Strata

    6 BAYS® English Muffins, halved, split
    1 tablespoon Caribbean jerk seasoning (sweet and spicy)
    1 whole boneless, skinless chicken breast (about 8 ounces), cut into ½-inch pieces
    1 tablespoon oil
    ¼ cup sliced green onions with tops
    3 tablespoons flaked or shredded coconut
    4 ounces mild goat cheese, crumbled
    6 eggs
3¾ cups milk
    ¼ to ½ teaspoon liquid red pepper seasoning
    ½ teaspoon salt
      Mango Salsa (recipe follows)

Preheat oven to 325°F. Arrange half of English muffin pieces on bottom of buttered 2-quart glass casserole. Sprinkle jerk seasoning on chicken; coating evenly. In large skillet, heat oil over medium heat; add chicken. Cook and stir until firm, 3 to 5 minutes. Spoon over muffins. Sprinkle with green onions, coconut and goat cheese. Top with remaining muffin pieces. Beat eggs, milk, pepper seasoning and salt until blended. Ladle mixture over muffins. Cover and refrigerate several hours or overnight. When ready to bake, remove cover. Bake 50 to 60 minutes, until puffy and brown. (To prevent over browning, cover with foil during last 10 minutes of baking.) Serve with Mango Salsa.   *Makes 4 servings*

Mango Salsa

    1 medium mango, peeled, pitted and finely chopped (1 cup)
    1 red onion, peeled, thinly sliced
    1 tablespoon snipped parsley or cilantro
    1 teaspoon minced hot chili pepper*, seeded and deveined
    ¼ teaspoon grated lime rind
    1 to 2 tablespoons lime juice, to taste

Chili peppers can sting and irritate the skin; wear rubber gloves when handling peppers and do not touch eyes. Wash hands after handling.

Combine all ingredients. Cover and refrigerate to blend flavors.   *Makes 1 cup*

Cherry Chicken

1 package (about 1½ pounds) PERDUE® Fresh Skinless Split Chicken Breast
   Salt and black pepper
2 tablespoons canola oil
1 small onion, chopped (½ cup)
1 can (21 ounces) cherry pie filling
1½ cups water
¼ cup golden raisins
2 tablespoons Cognac or brandy
1 tablespoon dry sherry
1½ teaspoons Worcestershire sauce
1 tablespoon chopped parsley

Season chicken lightly with salt and pepper. In large nonstick skillet, over medium-high heat, heat oil. Add chicken; cook 4 to 5 minutes on each side or until browned. Remove chicken and set aside. Add onion to skillet; sauté about 2 minutes or until slightly softened. Stir in cherry pie filling, water, raisins, Cognac, sherry and Worcestershire; bring to a boil. Return chicken to skillet; reduce heat to medium-low. Cover and simmer 15 to 20 minutes or until chicken is cooked through.

To serve, spoon cherries over chicken and sprinkle with parsley. *Makes 4 servings*

10-inch Classic Crisco® Double Crust

2⅔ cups all-purpose flour
1 teaspoon salt
¾ CRISCO® Stick or ¾ cup CRISCO® all-vegetable shortening
7 to 8 tablespoons cold water

1. Spoon flour into measuring cup and level. Combine flour and salt in medium bowl.

2. Cut in ¾ cup shortening using pastry blender or 2 knives until all flour is blended to form pea-size chunks.

3. Sprinkle with water, 1 tablespoon at a time. Toss lightly with fork until dough forms a ball. Divide dough in half.

4. Press dough between hands to form 5- to 6-inch "pancake." Flour rolling surface and rolling pin lightly. Roll both halves of dough into circles. Trim one circle of dough 1 inch larger than upside-down pie plate. Carefully remove trimmed dough. Set aside to reroll and use for pastry cutout garnish, if desired.

5. Fold dough into quarters. Unfold and press into pie plate. Trim edge even with plate. Add desired filling to unbaked crust. Moisten pastry edge with water. Lift top crust onto filled pie. Trim ½ inch beyond edge of pie plate. Fold top edge under bottom crust. Flute. Cut slits in top crust to allow steam to escape. Follow baking directions given for that recipe.

Makes 1 double crust

Chicken Casserole Supreme

Stuffing
2 cups unseasoned dry bread crumbs
1 cup chopped green onions
⅓ cup margarine or butter, melted
2 tablespoons chopped fresh parsley

Chicken
¼ cup all-purpose flour
¼ cup cornmeal
¼ teaspoon pepper
6 boneless chicken breast halves (about 1½ pounds)
1 egg, beaten
⅓ cup margarine or butter

Sauce
¼ cup margarine or butter
3 cups sliced fresh mushrooms
1 can (14½ ounces) chicken broth, divided
⅓ cup all-purpose flour
¾ cup HOLLAND HOUSE® Vermouth Cooking Wine
½ cup whipping cream

In medium bowl, combine all stuffing ingredients; mix well. Place stuffing in 6 mounds in ungreased 13×9-inch baking dish. In shallow dish, combine ¼ cup flour, cornmeal and pepper. Dip chicken in beaten egg, then coat with flour mixture. Melt ⅓ cup margarine in large skillet. Cook chicken 7 to 8 minutes on each side or until browned. Remove chicken; place on top of stuffing.

Heat oven to 375°F. Melt ¼ cup margarine in large saucepan. Add mushrooms; cook until tender. Remove from pan. Stir in 1 cup chicken broth and ⅓ cup flour; mix well. Add remaining chicken broth, cooking wine and whipping cream. Cook until slightly thickened, stirring constantly. Stir in mushrooms. Pour over chicken; cover. Bake at 375°F for 1 to 1¼ hours or until chicken is tender and no longer pink. *Makes 6 servings*

Saffron Chicken & Vegetables

2 tablespoons vegetable oil
6 bone-in chicken thighs, skinned
1 bag (16 ounces) frozen mixed vegetables, such as broccoli, red peppers,
    mushrooms and onions, thawed
1 can (14½ ounces) roasted garlic-flavor chicken broth
1 can (10¾ ounces) condensed cream of chicken soup, undiluted
1 can (10¾ ounces) condensed cream of mushroom soup, undiluted
1 package (about 8 ounces) uncooked saffron yellow rice mix with seasonings
½ cup water
½ teaspoon salt
1 teaspoon paprika (optional)

1. Preheat oven to 350°F. Spray 3-quart casserole with nonstick cooking spray; set aside.

2. Heat oil in large skillet over medium heat. Brown chicken on both sides; drain fat.

3. Meanwhile, combine vegetables, chicken broth, soups, rice mix with seasonings, water and salt in large bowl. Place mixture in prepared casserole. Top with chicken. Sprinkle with paprika, if desired. Cover; bake 1½ hours or until chicken is no longer pink in center.

Makes 6 servings

Chicken Florentine

    1 bag SUCCESS® Rice
       Vegetable cooking spray
    1 package (10 ounces) frozen chopped spinach,* thawed and drained
    1 teaspoon garlic powder
    2 tablespoons margarine
    3 tablespoons flour
    1 teaspoon pepper
    1 teaspoon chopped fresh parsley
    ¼ teaspoon ground nutmeg
    ¼ teaspoon Worcestershire sauce
 1½ cups milk
    ½ cup plain nonfat yogurt
    2 cups chopped cooked chicken
    ½ cup (2 ounces) grated Parmesan cheese, divided

Or, use 1 package (10 ounces) frozen chopped broccoli.

Prepare rice according to package directions.

Preheat oven to 350°F.

Spray 1-quart casserole with cooking spray; set aside. Combine spinach and garlic powder in large bowl. Add rice; mix lightly. Spoon rice mixture into prepared casserole; set aside. Melt margarine in medium saucepan. Blend in flour, pepper, parsley, nutmeg and Worcestershire sauce. Gradually stir in milk and yogurt; cook until smooth. Add chicken and ¼ cup cheese; cook until cheese melts. Spoon over spinach mixture; sprinkle with remaining ¼ cup cheese. Bake until thoroughly heated, about 10 minutes.

Makes 4 servings

Italian BLT Chicken Strata

   8 slices bacon
   2 (16-ounce packages) PERDUE® Fit 'N Easy® Skinless & Boneless Chicken Breasts
 12 ounces focaccia bread, sliced into ½-inch-thick pieces
   2 large tomatoes, cored and sliced
   8 eggs or 2 cups egg substitute
1½ cups heavy cream, light cream or milk
   1 teaspoon salt
      Pepper, to taste
   2 cups grated Cheddar cheese

Preheat oven to 350°F.

In a large skillet, cook bacon over medium heat. Drain on paper towels. Keeping a little bacon fat in pan, add chicken and cook until cooked through. Set aside.

Cover the bottom of a 13×9-inch baking dish with focaccia slices. Cover bread with tomato slices, then bacon. Cut chicken into thin slices and lay over bacon. Top with more focaccia.

In large bowl, whisk together eggs, cream, salt and pepper. Pour mixture over strata and sprinkle top with cheese.

Bake 35 to 45 minutes, until cheese has melted and strata feels firm to the touch. Cut into 8 squares and serve hot.

Makes 8 servings

Prep Time: 25 minutes
Cook Time: 35 to 45 minutes

Chicken Hot Dish

   1 package (8 ounces) thin noodles or spaghetti
   3 tablespoons CRISCO® Oil*
  ½ cup chopped onion
   3 tablespoons all-purpose flour
   1 tablespoon chopped fresh parsley
  ¼ teaspoon salt
  ¼ teaspoon pepper
1½ cups chicken broth
   1 package (8 ounces) shredded Cheddar or Colby cheese, divided
   1 bag (16 ounces) frozen vegetables
   3 cups cubed cooked chicken

*Use your favorite Crisco Oil product.

1. Cook noodles according to package directions. Drain.

2. Heat oven to 350°F. Grease 3- to 4-quart baking dish.

3. Heat oil in medium saucepan on medium-high heat. Add onion. Cook until soft. Blend in flour, parsley, salt and pepper. Cook and stir for 1 minute. Add chicken broth. Cook and stir for 3 to 4 minutes or until mixture comes to a simmer. Reduce heat to low. Add 1½ cups cheese. Stir until just melted. Remove from heat.

4. Combine noodles, vegetables, chicken and cheese sauce in large bowl. Transfer to baking dish. Top with remaining ½ cup cheese.

5. Bake 30 minutes or until hot and bubbly. *Do not overbake.* Season with additional salt and pepper, if desired.   *Makes 12 servings*

Note: May be prepared a day ahead and refrigerated. Adjust baking time accordingly.

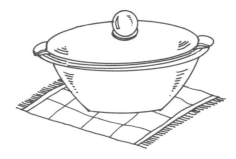

Creamy Chicken Success

1 bag SUCCESS® Rice
   Vegetable cooking spray
1½ cups fat-free sour cream
 1 can (4 ounces) chopped green chilies, drained
 1 cup (4 ounces) shredded Monterey Jack cheese
 1 cup (4 ounces) shredded low-fat Cheddar cheese
 1 tablespoon olive oil
 4 skinless, boneless chicken breasts, cut into strips
 1 tablespoon Worcestershire sauce

Prepare rice according to package directions. Cool.

Preheat oven to 375°F.

Spray 1½-quart casserole dish with cooking spray; set aside. Combine sour cream and chilies in small bowl; set aside. Combine cheeses in separate small bowl. Heat oil in large skillet over medium heat. Add chicken; cook and stir until no longer pink in center. Stir in Worcestershire sauce. Place chicken breasts in prepared casserole; cover with layers of rice, sour cream mixture and cheese mixture. Bake until cheese is melted, about 15 minutes.

Makes 4 servings

Wild Rice Chicken Casserole

6 cups cooked wild rice (1½ cups uncooked)
1 can (10¾ ounces) cream of chicken soup
1 can (10¾ ounces) cream of celery soup
1 can (about 14 ounces) chicken broth
1 can (4 ounces) mushrooms, drained
3 cups diced, cooked chicken
¼ cup chopped green bell pepper
¼ cup chopped red bell pepper
¼ teaspoon garlic powder
½ cup slivered almonds

Preheat oven to 350°F. Grease 13×9-inch casserole.

Mix rice, soups, broth, mushrooms, chicken, bell peppers and garlic powder in large bowl. Spread into prepared dish. Sprinkle with almonds. Bake, covered, 45 minutes. Uncover and continue baking 15 minutes or until heated through. *Makes 10 to 12 servings*

Favorite recipe from **Minnesota Cultivated Wild Rice Council**

Acknowledgments

The publisher would like to thank the companies and organizations listed below for the use of their recipes and photographs in this publication.

Bays English Muffin Corporation

Cucina Classica Italiana, Inc.

Delmarva Poultry Industry, Inc.

Del Monte Corporation

Egg Beaters®

Heinz North America

The Hidden Valley® Food Products Company

Holland House® is a registered trademark of Mott's, LLP

Hormel Foods, LLC

Lawry's® Foods

MASTERFOODS USA

McIlhenny Company (TABASCO® brand Pepper Sauce)

Minnesota Cultivated Wild Rice Council

Mrs. Dash®

National Fisheries Institute

National Turkey Federation

Norseland, Inc. Lucini Italia Co.

North Dakota Beef Commission

North Dakota Wheat Commission

Perdue Farms Incorporated

Reckitt Benckiser Inc.

Riviana Foods Inc.

The J.M. Smucker Company

Unilever Bestfoods North America

Veg•All®

Index

Index

Index

Index

Index

Index

Index

Index

Index

Index

Notes

Notes

METRIC CONVERSION CHART

VOLUME MEASUREMENTS (dry)

$^1/_8$ teaspoon = 0.5 mL
$^1/_4$ teaspoon = 1 mL
$^1/_2$ teaspoon = 2 mL
$^3/_4$ teaspoon = 4 mL
1 teaspoon = 5 mL
1 tablespoon = 15 mL
2 tablespoons = 30 mL
$^1/_4$ cup = 60 mL
$^1/_3$ cup = 75 mL
$^1/_2$ cup = 125 mL
$^2/_3$ cup = 150 mL
$^3/_4$ cup = 175 mL
1 cup = 250 mL
2 cups = 1 pint = 500 mL
3 cups = 750 mL
4 cups = 1 quart = 1 L

VOLUME MEASUREMENTS (fluid)

1 fluid ounce (2 tablespoons) = 30 mL
4 fluid ounces ($^1/_2$ cup) = 125 mL
8 fluid ounces (1 cup) = 250 mL
12 fluid ounces (1$^1/_2$ cups) = 375 mL
16 fluid ounces (2 cups) = 500 mL

WEIGHTS (mass)

$^1/_2$ ounce = 15 g
1 ounce = 30 g
3 ounces = 90 g
4 ounces = 120 g
8 ounces = 225 g
10 ounces = 285 g
12 ounces = 360 g
16 ounces = 1 pound = 450 g

DIMENSIONS

$^1/_{16}$ inch = 2 mm
$^1/_8$ inch = 3 mm
$^1/_4$ inch = 6 mm
$^1/_2$ inch = 1.5 cm
$^3/_4$ inch = 2 cm
1 inch = 2.5 cm

OVEN TEMPERATURES

250°F = 120°C
275°F = 140°C
300°F = 150°C
325°F = 160°C
350°F = 180°C
375°F = 190°C
400°F = 200°C
425°F = 220°C
450°F = 230°C

BAKING PAN SIZES

Utensil	Size in Inches/Quarts	Metric Volume	Size in Centimeters
Baking or Cake Pan (square or rectangular)	8×8×2	2 L	20×20×5
	9×9×2	2.5 L	23×23×5
	12×8×2	3 L	30×20×5
	13×9×2	3.5 L	33×23×5
Loaf Pan	8×4×3	1.5 L	20×10×7
	9×5×3	2 L	23×13×7
Round Layer Cake Pan	8×1½	1.2 L	20×4
	9×1½	1.5 L	23×4
Pie Plate	8×1¼	750 mL	20×3
	9×1¼	1 L	23×3
Baking Dish or Casserole	1 quart	1 L	—
	1½ quart	1.5 L	—
	2 quart	2 L	—